Sherlock
Holmes

The Unauthorized Biography

NICK RENNISON

ATLANTIC BOOKS

LONDON

First published in hardback in Great Britain in 2005 by Atlantic Books,
an imprint of Grove Atlantic Ltd.

1 3 5 7 9 8 6 4 2

A CIP catalogue record for this book is available from the British Library.

ISBN 1 84354 274 9

Designed by Nicky Barneby
Set in 11/13.5pt Monotype Baskerville by Barneby Ltd, London
Printed in Great Britain by MPG Books, Bodmin, Cornwall

Atlantic Books
An imprint of Grove Atlantic Ltd
Ormond House
26–27 Boswell Street
London WC1N 3JZ

THIS BOOK IS DEDICATED TO
EVE, WITH LOVE AND THANKS,
AND TO THE MEMORY OF
NORAH ALLENBY (1916–2005)

CONTENTS

ACKNOWLEDGEMENTS

Fɪʀsᴛ ᴀɴᴅ ꜰᴏʀᴇᴍᴏsᴛ ᴍʏ ᴛʜᴀɴᴋs must go to my editor at Atlantic, Angus MacKinnon, who had the original idea for this book and who approached me to see if I would be interested in writing it. His suggestion launched me on a very enjoyable investigation into the detective's life and career. Over the last two years, friends and family have been very tolerant of my growing obsession with Holmes and many have been kind enough to offer their own ideas and thoughts on the great man. Travis Elborough drew my attention to several books and newspaper articles about Holmes that I had not seen and introduced me to a study of Moriarty that had escaped my notice. Hugh Pemberton was one of the first people to provide a sympathetic audience for my thoughts about Holmes's role in the events of late Victorian England and his enthusiastic response was much appreciated. Allan Dodd bought me drinks at the Sherlock Holmes pub in central London and listened patiently as I described, in unnecessarily lengthy detail, my difficulties in sorting fact from legend in Holmes's life. Paul Skinner sent me information about Charles Augustus Howell which I would not otherwise have seen. Susan Osborne, Dawn Pomroy, Richard Shephard, Andrew Holgate, Gordon Kerr and Kathy Crocker have all shown a consistent interest in the project and have, possibly without realizing it, provided me with encouragement to finish it.

At Atlantic, Bonnie Chiang, Clara Farmer and Toby Mundy have all been extraordinarily encouraging and supportive and I could not have wished for a better publisher. My thanks also go to Celia Levett whose sympathetic copy-editing has added much to the text and to Mike Levett whose indexing skills are much appreciated.

Back in the 1960s my parents owned Penguin editions of several of the volumes of Holmes short stories and it was through these books that I was first introduced to the delights of Dr Watson's narratives. I would like to thank my parents for this introduction and also for the support they provided, forty years later, during the writing of this book. My greatest thanks go to my partner, Eve Gorton, who has spent more time in the company of Sherlock Holmes than she ever expected that she would. She has often been a greater believer in this book than its author and it is dedicated to her.

INTRODUCTION

THE YEAR IS 1895. London is swathed in dense yellow fog. As the greasy clouds swirl up the streets and condense in oily drops on windowpanes, two men peer out from rented rooms at 221B Baker Street. One is tall and gaunt with a narrow face, hawklike nose and high, intellectual brow. The other, shorter and stockier, is square-jawed and moustachioed. Outside, the smog envelops a vast city that holds a thousand sinister secrets but inside is a haven of comfort and bachelor domesticity. Suddenly, out of the surrounding gloom, a hansom cab emerges. A young woman descends from it, and looks up briefly at the two men at the window before ringing the doorbell of 221B. Another client, with a tale of mystery and potential danger, has come to consult Sherlock Holmes. The game is once again afoot, and Holmes and Dr Watson will soon be in pursuit of the truth about another dark story from the hidden metropolis.

Few individuals in English history are as well known as Sherlock Holmes. From the moment in 1887 when, in a narrative published in *Beeton's Christmas Annual* for that year, his colleague and friend Dr John Watson revealed the detective's extraordinary powers of analysis and deduction, he captured the imagination of the public. As Watson continued to act as Holmes's Boswell, recording more of his exploits and adventures in magazine articles and books, his fame spread. Watson's accounts have been translated into dozens of languages, from Afrikaans to Yiddish, from Armenian to Vietnamese. Students of Swahili can read *Mbwa wa Familia ya Baskerville*. Those fluent in Slovak can turn the pages of *Pes Baskervillský*. There are versions of the stories in Esperanto, in Pitman's shorthand and, of course, in Braille. There is even a translation of 'The Dancing Men' into the code that plays such a central role in that story.

Dramatized versions of Holmes's life began to appear in the 1890s and have continued to be performed to the present day. On any given day in 2005 an amateur dramatic society somewhere in England or America will be staging a play in which Sherlock Holmes makes an appearance. He has been the subject of hundreds of films from the early silent era to the present day. *Sherlock Holmes – The Musical* by Leslie Bricusse, screenwriter of the Dr Dolittle movie, opened in London in 1989. (Admittedly, it closed almost immediately and has rarely been seen on the stage since.) There has been a ballet called *The Great Detective*, produced at Sadler's Wells in 1953, and at least one opera has required a tenor Holmes and a bass Watson to sing feelingly of their mutually rewarding partnership and the joys of detective work.

Although Holmes has been dead for more than seventy years, people still write from around the world to ask for his help. Until recently Abbey House, the headquarters of the Abbey National Building Society, which stands on the site of his one-time lodgings in Baker Street, employed a secretary to answer the letters that were delivered to the address. Since his death in 1929, a growing army of Holmes scholars has produced a library of theses and dissertations on his life and work. In half the countries of the world there are Sherlock Holmes societies, their members dedicated to the minute examination of his life and work: the Singular Society of the Baker Street Dozen in Calgary, Canada; the Copenhagen Speckled Gang; Le Cercle Littéraire de l'Escarboucle Bleue in Toulouse; the Tokyo Nonpareil Club; the Ural Holmesian Society in Ekaterinburg; the Illustrious Clients of Indianapolis; the Friends of Irene Adler in Cambridge, Massachussetts; the Six Napoleons of Baltimore. All these and many more are devoted exclusively to the study of Sherlock Holmes. Even writers of fiction have taken the basic facts of his life and expanded them into novels and short stories of varying degrees of credibility.

Like other emblematic figures from the nation's past – Henry VIII, Robin Hood, Winston Churchill – he has been seized upon by the heritage industry. Pubs and hotels are named after him. Tours of Sherlock Holmes's London wind daily through the streets of the capital. Holmes memorabilia crowd the shelves of gift shops and tourist boutiques. Should you feel so inclined, it is possible to buy silver statuettes of Holmes and Watson, Sherlock Holmes fridge magnets, Hound of the Baskervilles coffee mugs, a 221B Baker Street board game and a Sherlock Holmes plastic pipe designed to provide the authentic Holmes aura without actually encouraging smoking. There is even a Sherlock Holmes teddy bear dressed in an Inverness cape and deerstalker hat.

Yet Holmes himself remains a curiously elusive figure. Apart from a few monographs on arcane subjects (types of tobacco ash; the polyphonic motets of the Renaissance composer Orlande de Lassus; ciphers and secret writings) as well as a manual on beekeeping, he published nothing under his own name. In one

narrative ('The Adventure of the Cardboard Box') Holmes claims
to have published two short monographs on ears in the *Journal of the
Anthropological Institute* but a trawl through nineteenth-century back
numbers of that periodical suggests that he was referring to works
that he had merely planned rather than completed. Two narratives
of his work, which he wrote in the first person, were published in
The Strand Magazine in 1926, three years before his death. Otherwise
the record is blank. His preferred means of communication was the
telegram, more impermanent in his time than the e-mail is today,
and no irrefutably authentic letters written by him survive.

For any students of Holmes's life and work, the alpha and the
omega of their research remain the texts written by his colleague
and friend Dr John H. Watson. There are fifty-six short narratives
and four longer ones, which all scholars and Holmesians agree are
the work of Watson or (in two instances) Holmes. There are a few
texts ('The Case of the Man Who Was Wanted', 'The Story of the
Lost Special') that some commentators wish to claim for the canon
but their status remains disputed. There are also those unidentified
papers, which once, almost certainly, existed but which seem to
have disappeared. 'Somewhere in the vaults of the bank of Cox &
Company at Charing Cross,' Watson wrote in 'The Problem of
Thor Bridge', 'there is a travel-worn and battered tin dispatchbox
with my name upon the lid. It is crammed with papers, nearly all
of which are records of cases to illustrate the curious problems
which Mr Sherlock Holmes had at various times to examine.' Cox
& Company's building in Charing Cross was destroyed in the
London Blitz and, if there were still papers in the vault, a decade
after Watson's death, they were lost in the conflagration.

It is always worth remembering just what a small proportion of
Holmes's cases is recorded in Watson's surviving narratives. In *The
Hound of the Baskervilles* Holmes refers in passing to the 'five

hundred cases of capital importance which I have handled'. The events in the Baskerville case took place more than a decade before Holmes's supposed retirement and, as we shall see, more than thirty years before his actual and final retirement from all involvement in criminal investigation. Those thirty years saw well over a thousand further cases. From a total of approximately 1,800, Watson gave us accounts of sixty. In other words, only between 3 and 4 per cent of the extant cases are recorded by the doctor.

Yet the primary source for Holmes's life remains the work of Watson and, as Holmes scholars have long known, Watson's narratives, for a variety of reasons, have to be interpreted with care. Often Holmes himself muddied the waters by misleading Watson, providing him with false information and spurious facts that merely sent the doctor off in pursuit of red herrings. Often Watson deliberately obscures the truth, hiding real characters under pseudonyms or disguising towns and cities beneath invented names. Sometimes he is quite simply wrong. It is easy to forget the circumstances in which Watson wrote his narratives. Although, as he points out in 'The Adventure of the Solitary Cyclist', 'I have preserved very full notes of these cases,' and clearly he must have had his notes beside him as he wrote, the full stories that he handed over to Arthur Conan Doyle for publication were not produced until years, sometimes decades, after the events they describe. 'The Adventure of the Devil's Foot', for instance, shows Holmes investigating the macabre deaths in the Tregennis family whilst he was holidaying in Cornwall with Watson in the spring of 1897 but it was not written up in full until 1910. In the case of the investigation known as 'The Adventure of the Creeping Man', Watson is recalling events from 1903 but the story was not published for another twenty years, appearing in *The Strand Magazine* for March 1923. In these circumstances it is not surprising that Watson occasionally slipped up. Even the most egregious errors – setting one of the stories at a time when Holmes was assumed to be dead, for example – become understandable to a degree.

Despite the difficulties imposed by the shortage of authentic records, few Victorian lives deserve study as much as does that of Sherlock Holmes. And a Victorian he undoubtedly was. Although he was only in his late forties when Victoria died, he remained rooted in the world into which he was born and in which he grew up. We think we know the Victorians. In contrast to our contradictory selves, grappling with the complexities of modernity and post-modernity, they seem the products of a simpler era. Frozen in the clichéd poses we have imagined for them, the Victorians appear immune to the fears and anxieties that trouble us. Staring at us from sepia-tinted photographs, they look certain of the world and their own place in it in a way that we cannot hope to match. Nothing, however, could be further from the truth. Anyone born, like Holmes, in the 1850s and growing up in the late Victorian era, lived through a period of intellectual and social upheaval just as dramatic and threatening as any the twentieth century was to offer. Religious beliefs were crumbling under the assault of new theories of man and his place in the world. The British Empire, on which the sun was supposed never to set, may have appeared to be everlasting but the seeds of its ultimate collapse had already been sown. Germany and America had emerged as its competitors on the world stage. New ideologies – socialism, communism, feminism – began to shake the foundations of state and family on which Victorian confidence and security were built. Scratching the surface of Victorian complacency soon reveals the underlying angst about a world that was changing rapidly and unpredictably.

The ambiguities of Holmes's character mirror those of the age in which he came to maturity. Highly rational and committed to the idea of progress, he was haunted by darker dreams and more troubling emotions. Drawn into the service of an empire that he knew, intellectually at least, had already passed its zenith, he remained steadfast in his commitment to it. Yet, even as he fought to preserve stability and the solid values of the age, he himself was driven by a lifelong search for change, stimulation and excitement. His own innermost beliefs – social, aesthetic, scientific – often clashed with those that he outwardly professed. To follow Holmes through the twists and turns of his career in the 1880s and 1890s is to watch the Victorian era battling with its own demons.

CHAPTER ONE

'MY ANCESTORS WERE COUNTRY SQUIRES'

THE VILLAGE OF HUTTON LE MOORS lies on the edge of the Yorkshire Moors, a dozen miles from the small town of Pickering. Despite the onslaught of the traffic passing along what is now the A170 to Scarborough, the heart of the village has changed surprisingly little in the past century and a half. Thirty or forty slate-roofed cottages, many of them dating back to the seventeenth century, straggle along both sides of the road. A pub, the Green Man, and the village church of St Chad still provide the central focuses for village life. Half a mile beyond the older cottages, on the edge of the village, stands a small estate of 1950s council houses. They were built on land that the council bought after the Second World War from a Bradford mill-owning family by the name of Binns. Until the mid-1920s, Hutton Hall, a sixteenth-century manor house, stood on the site. Photographs of the house, which appeared in *Country Life* in May 1922, show a half-timbered frontage studded with mullioned windows and surmounted by the elaborate chimneys so typical of the period. Shots of the interior reveal impressive oak panelling and a large fireplace, adorned with the initials RH and dating back to the time of Elizabeth I, all of which were still in existence when the Binns family lived there. Here, on 17 June 1854, William Sherlock Holmes was born.

Holmes, as recorded by Watson, makes very few remarks about his family and upbringing but those few are clear and unequivocal enough. 'My ancestors,' he tells Watson in 'The Adventure of the Greek Interpreter', 'were country squires, who seem to have led much the same life as is natural to their class.' He tells us nothing more. In fact Holmes's father, William Scott Holmes, inherited the remains of a substantial estate in north Yorkshire.

There had been Holmeses living in that part of Yorkshire for centuries. As far back as 1219 an Urkell de Holmes is mentioned in the records of York Assizes and, by the late Middle Ages, the Holmes family had risen from the ranks of yeomen farmers to the lesser gentry. The Walter Holmes from Kirkbymoorside, eight miles from Pickering, who is recorded as fighting with the Yorkist forces of Edward IV at the Battle of Towton in 1461, is almost certainly a direct antecedent of Sherlock and Mycroft. Walter had chosen the right side in the Wars of the Roses and he prospered as a consequence. Several years after the battle he was knighted by Edward and the family went up another rung on the social ladder. Walter survived the transition from a Yorkist monarchy to the reign of the Tudors with his status intact (he seems to have been one of the few Yorkshire baronets to have supported Henry VII before the Battle of Bosworth).

His grandson, Ralph, was to raise the Holmes profile even higher. In the mid-1530s, Sir Ralph, one of the century's more opportunist converts to Protestantism, was in a position to benefit substantially from the dissolution of the monasteries. As the great landholdings of monastic establishments such as Fountains Abbey and Rievaulx Abbey came under the hammer, Sir Ralph and people like him were poised to pounce. Much of the property owned by Fountains Abbey was sold, at a knockdown price, to entrepreneur Sir Richard Gresham. However, Sir Ralph Holmes, an associate of Gresham, received his share of the spoils in the form of an estate at Hutton le Moors as well as other landholdings dotted around the Vale of York and the fringes of the moors. It was Sir Ralph, made prosperous by his part in the despoliation of monastic property, who built Hutton Hall, the house in which, 300 years later, his most famous descendant was to be born.

Under the later Tudors and Stuarts the family made a point of avoiding the religious and political controversies of the time. Sir Stamford Holmes was a member of successive Elizabethan and Jacobean parliaments but an undistinguished one. There are records of only two contributions by him to their proceedings. In one he intervened in a debate on shipping convicts to Barbados to suggest that the colonies in New England might also be a good destination for lawbreakers. He was reminded by a fellow MP that, since felons were being sent there as indentured labourers, they were already being used for this purpose. In the other he asked the Speaker whether the doors of St Stephen's Chapel, Westminster, where Parliament met at the time, could be closed since he and other members were feeling the draught.

By the time of the confrontation between king and Parliament in the 1630s and 1640s, however, even the most lackadaisical of MPs and landowners were forced to choose sides. Although Sherlock Holmes, ascetic and intellectual, would probably be classified as one of life's Roundheads, his ancestors chose the king's cause and remained firm Royalists throughout the Civil War. Sir Symonds Holmes, grandson of Sir Stamford and great-great-grandson of Sir

Ralph, fought with Prince Rupert's cavalry at the Battle of Marston Moor in 1644. The family suffered for its loyalty although the Holmeses were not forced, like so many others, into exile during Cromwell's rule.

At the Restoration, monarchists such as the Holmes who had kept the faith stood to prosper. Sir Richmond Holmes, son of Sir Symonds, moved south to London in the 1670s after his father's death and thereafter spent more time on the fringes of Charles II's court than he did on his Yorkshire properties. In attempting to carve out a career there, he began the slow slide into indebtedness that plagued the family for generations to come. Friendship with the likes of the dissolute Earl of Rochester, poet and philanderer, was an expensive indulgence and, by the time of his death in 1687, Sir Richmond owed large sums to half the moneylenders in the capital.

The eighteenth century saw a continuous decline in the fortunes of the family. As one scapegrace spendthrift succeeded another, the estate was sold bit by bit until only the old manor house at Hutton le Moors, first built in the 1550s, was left. Sir Selwyn Holmes, reputed to be an associate of Sir Francis Dashwood and a member of the infamous Hell-Fire Club, was the most notorious of a succession of Holmes ancestors who more resembled Sir Hugo Baskerville than they did their intellectual descendant, Sherlock. Sir Seymour Holmes, Sherlock's great-grandfather, the last of these roistering Georgian roués who squandered most of the family inheritance, died of an apoplexy in 1810. He was succeeded in the baronetcy by his fourteen-year-old son. Sherlock Holmes's grandfather, Sheridan Holmes, inherited little but debts and the family name. Then at Harrow, the school that the Holmes males had attended for generations, the young Sheridan was in no position to improve the family fortunes but sufficient funds were eventually found to see him through Christ Church, Oxford, and to allow him later to travel abroad. (He seems to have departed Oxford without a degree.) It was on foreign shores, if nothing else, that he was to meet his future wife.

The only exotic influence in his family tree claimed by Holmes is his grandmother, the woman Sir Sheridan Holmes married, who was 'the sister of Vernet, the French artist'. 'Art in the blood,' he goes on to say, 'is liable to take the strangest forms.' The Vernets were a tribe of French painters, who produced distinguished artists in several generations. The patriarch of the family was Antoine Vernet (1689–1753), several of whose more than twenty children became artists. One, Claude-Joseph Vernet (1714–89), was so committed to his art that he arranged to be lashed to a ship's mast during a storm at sea so that he could observe the effects of light and turbulent water at close hand. The most famous of the Vernets, whose youngest sister married Holmes's paternal grandfather, was the grandson of Claude-Joseph, one Emile-Jean-Horace Vernet (1789–1863), known to his familt as Horace. Best known as a painter of scenes of military valour and derring-do, Horace was at the heart of the Parisian art establishment, serving as president of the French Academy from 1828 to 1834. His sister, Marie-Claude, was born in Paris in 1798. She was just nineteen when she met the Englishman who was to take her across the Channel to a life she could not have imagined as she was growing up in Napoleonic France.

We do not know the circumstances in which Sheridan Holmes, Sherlock's paternal grandfather, first encountered his wife to be. He was certainly in Paris for several months in the spring and summer of 1818 – a few surviving letters confirm this. It may well be that Sheridan harboured artistic ambitions and, in order to pursue them, travelled to Paris where he was introduced to one of the extensive Vernet clan. The marriage took place in London at

St George's, Hanover Square, in the early summer of the following year. The entry in the church's marriage register, with the bride's name misspelled as Verner, still exists. Holmes owed more to his French ancestry than he ever admitted. It is worth noting that the composer Mendelssohn, who knew the Vernet family well, said of Horace that his mind was so orderly that it was like a well-stocked bureau in which he had but to open a drawer to find what he needed. He added that Horace's powers of observation were so great that a single glance at a model was sufficient to fix the details of his or her appearance in his memory.

Sherlock's father, William Scott Holmes, the eldest of three children, was born in Hutton le Moors on 26 November 1819. Comparison of his date of birth and the date of his parents' marriage immediately reveals that Marie-Claude must have been pregnant with him as she walked down the aisle at St George's. Two further children followed in rapid succession, Maria in 1821, and Emily in 1822, whereupon Sir Sheridan, who had probably suffered from ill health most of his life, went into a decline and died of consumption in the autumn of 1823 at the age of only twenty-seven. He was succeeded by his four-year-old-son, Sherlock Holmes's father. Marie-Claude, still only in her mid-twenties and far from her Parisian birthplace, had to cope with her abrupt widowhood, living in an ancient and draughty house on the edge of the Yorkshire Moors with three young children to bring up alone. The new young baronet was educated, like so many of his forebears, at Harrow and Christ Church, Oxford, but he went one better than his father and graduated with a second-class degree in Classics in the spring of 1841. We do not know how he passed the next four years of his life. Perhaps, like his father, he travelled on the Continent but, if he did, he found no bride waiting for him in Paris. His own choice for a wife was made much nearer home.

On 12 July 1845, William Scott Holmes married Violet Mycroft at Hutton le Moors in the parish church of St Chad. The Mycrofts were another family of impoverished Yorkshire gentry who had lived at Marton Hall near the village of Nun Marton for centuries. There was little to distinguish them from dozens of other families of their class. The branch from which Violet descended had been clergymen for generations. Her father, Robert Mycroft, who married the couple, was rector of St Chad's and we can assume that William and Violet had known one another since childhood. Robert's grandfather, George Riley Mycroft, who was rector of Lastingham in the North Riding of Yorkshire for more than fifty years, gained some small renown as the author of *The Beauties of Creation: or a New Moral System of Natural History, Displayed in the Most Curious Quadrupeds, Birds, Insects and Flowers of Northern England*, published in York in 1727. George Mycroft, despite a desire to corral the natural world into his own moral view of the universe, was a scrupulous observer of the creatures he saw in his moorland parish and as a result his book was still being read at the end of the century. Erasmus Darwin, grandfather of Charles, makes a brief reference to 'Mycroft's remarkable acuity of observation' in a letter of 1791. Violet herself had been born at Skelton, just outside York, where her father was then curate, on 11 May 1823.

Sherlock Holmes once remarked, 'I have a theory that the individual represents in his development the whole procession of his ancestors, and that such a sudden turn to good or evil stands for some strong influence which came into the line of his pedigree. The person becomes, as it were, the epitome of the history of his own family.' It is difficult to believe that, if he looked back at his own pedigree, he could gain much support for his theory. The life of Sir Symonds Holmes, the seventeenth-century ancestor who fought for the king in the Civil War, conducted experiments in microscopy (he was one of the first subscribers to Robert Hooke's ground-breaking work *Micrographia* in 1665) and, in the 1660s, became an early member of the Royal Society, provides some evidence for an ancestral interest in the sciences. This link is strengthened by the fact that his mother's great-grandfather found such fascination in the natural history of the North of England. It would later be reflected in his own scientific bent. Otherwise the centuries-long procession of Holmes's ancestors differed little from many other families from the lower echelons of the English gentry.

Sherlock Holmes was the second child of his parents, arriving seven years after his brother Mycroft, born in 1847. Where did the name Sherlock originate? Conan Doyle, when in the mood to fuel the fantasy that he had invented Holmes, would claim that he had borrowed the name from a cricketer of the 1870s and 1880s, but the truth is more mundane. Sherlock, like Mycroft, was a family name. One of his great-uncles on his mother's side had been Joseph Sherlock, an eighteenth-century lawyer in the town of Pickering, and the name had already been used for several children over two generations. The practice of using these family surnames as first names was a common one. There is an exact parallel in the naming of Holmes's friend and agent, Arthur Conan Doyle, who took his middle name from his great-uncle, Michael Conan, a well-known editor and journalist.

In the seven years that separated the births of the two Holmes brothers, Violet Holmes – if the veiled hints that survive in a handful of letters are to be trusted – had twice been pregnant and twice lost the child through a miscarriage. In such matters, Victorians of her class used euphemisms more often than direct language but the references to her 'most delicate state of health' and her 'two sad losses' seem fairly clear. If we assume that Sherlock Holmes was born after his mother had lost two previous babies, it would explain much about his early childhood. We have little evidence on which to base speculation about his first years of life but what there is does suggest that he proved an anxiety to his family from the first. That anxiety can only have been increased by Violet's past history. A fragment of a letter that survives in the Vernet family archives in France, dated 21 November 1854, is almost certainly from Marie-Claude Holmes, in her Yorkshire exile, to her brother Horace, and the 'petit enfant' who is described as 'faible' is probably the five-month-old Sherlock. If Sherlock was 'faible' in his first year of life, he soon became stronger. There is no evidence that, physically, he was anything other than robust but from his early childhood onwards his parents worried about the mental and emotional development of their younger son.

In the 1880s, Watson described his room-mate's sudden swings of mood. 'Nothing could exceed his energy,' Watson says, 'when the working fit was upon him; but now and again a reaction would seize him, and for days on end he would lie upon the sofa in the sitting-room, hardly uttering a word or moving a muscle from morning to night.' This was surprising enough behaviour in an adult, although Watson seems to have adapted to it with remarkable good humour. In a child, however, the sudden withdrawing into silence and immobility, the days when the young Holmes refused to respond at all to the world around him, were alarming to his parents. Another letter, this one from Sherlock's father to an old college friend, speaks of the boy's 'strange indifference to the daily round of our bucolic life' and of the impossibility of sending him away to school.

There is no doubt that Sherlock Holmes was a difficult and worrying child but is there any evidence that he was, as some ingenious commentators have suggested, autistic? In the mid-nineteenth century autism still awaited clinical definition and description. (The

word was coined in 1911 by the Swiss psychiatrist Eugen Bleuler*
and it was not until the 1940s that detailed case descriptions were
published.) Yet there are certainly similarities between stories of
Holmes, both as a child and as an adult, and modern case histories
of autistic individuals. The odd detachment from the everyday
world, the peculiar fixations on particular objects and the careful
classification of them (his monographs on the 140 different varieties
of pipe, cigar and cigarette tobacco ash, for example), the inability
to understand or empathize fully with other people's emotions and
the heightened acuity of some senses – these all mirror ways in
which the autistic interact with the world. Yet the final judgement
must surely be that Holmes was not autistic in today's definition of
the word. No autistic person would have been able to sustain such
a wide-ranging and demanding career as he did over nearly fifty
years. No autistic person would have reacted with such a sudden
outburst of suppressed emotion as does Holmes in 'The Adventure
of the Three Garridebs' when he believes that Watson has been shot.

As his father's letter shows, however, there could be no question
of Sherlock attending school. In 1860, the thirteen-year-old
Mycroft, previously tutored at home by his father and by local
clergyman William Barnes, was sent south to attend Harrow.
Perhaps surprisingly, he adapted with remarkable ease to the
spartan environment of the school, and favourable reports of his
academic prowess, particularly in mathematics, soon began to
arrive in north Yorkshire. The six-year-old Sherlock was probably
given his first lessons by his mother but they were to be cut short
by tragedy. Violet Mycroft Holmes died on 23 August 1861. On her

---

* Bleuler also invented the word 'schizophrenia' to describe the state of mind of some of his
patients and he used 'autism' to refer to the aloof isolation that was displayed by others in
this group.

death certificate the cause of death is given as 'consumption' and she had no doubt been suffering from what the Victorians often called 'the white death' for years. Indeed, the state of her health may well have contributed to her miscarriages in the early 1850s.

Less than three years later, the family suffered another bereavement. Holmes's grandmother, born Marie-Claude Vernet, died of heart failure on 18 January 1864. She was sixty-five and had lived for more than forty years in the wilds of the Yorkshire Moors, far from the Parisian salons and artists' studios in which she had spent her youth. The losses of both mother and grandmother severely affected the Holmes brothers, but it was the younger Sherlock who was hit the hardest. Fourteen at the time of his mother's death, Mycroft had been attending Harrow for barely a year. He came home for the funeral, returning afterwards to school and, in its bracingly unsentimental atmosphere, was forced to come to terms with the bereavement in order to survive from day to day.

The great public schools in the mid-nineteenth century were slightly more civilized than the self-contained worlds of Hobbesian nastiness and brutishness that they had been before Victoria came to the throne. The reforming zeal of headmasters like the legendary Thomas Arnold at Rugby brought improvements. But they still remained places where only the strong flourished and the weak went to the wall. In 1853, only seven years before Mycroft arrived at Harrow, a monitor at the school had beaten a younger boy so badly, striking him thirty-one times with a cane, that the victim had been permanently disfigured and was obliged to leave. Schools such as Harrow, Eton and Winchester (where a young boy called John H. Watson would soon arrive to study) continued to be places where, in the words of one old Etonian, 'the lads underwent privations that might have broken down a cabin boy, and would be thought inhuman if inflicted on a galley slave.'

Sherlock, seven years younger and still at home, faced perman-ent reminders of his loss. It is all too easy to make speculative psychological diagnoses of historical figures but it is hard to avoid the conclusion that Holmes's suspicion of women is rooted in his response to the deaths of his mother and grandmother. To the child he was at the time, it seemed as if the two women to whom he was most attached had somehow chosen to leave him. When he tells Watson in *The Sign of Four*, 'Women are never to be entirely trusted – not the best of them,' the memory of those traumatic desertions must surely lurk beneath his words.

Reading became an escape for the young Holmes. His father's library was as eccentric as its owner and he found many obscure and unusual volumes on its shelves. Early in their friendship, Watson was to note that Holmes's knowledge of 'sensational literature' was 'immense' and that he appeared to know 'every detail of every horror perpetrated in the century'. Holmes himself claimed that the best thing that Inspector MacDonald in *The Valley of Fear* could do to improve his skills was 'to shut [himself] up for three months and read twelve hours a day at the annals of crime'. In his boyhood, intrigued by his father's volumes of the *Newgate Calendar* – that extraordinarily powerful and often lurid record of the murders, robberies and other crimes of the eighteenth century – this is more or less what Holmes himself had done. In doing so, he had added an array of terrifying pictures to his already powerful imagination but he had also laid the foundations for the mental index of crime that was to prove so useful to him in later life.

Holmes's loneliness and isolation as a boy led him to become an extraordinarily self-contained and fiercely independent man. Watson was to note, in 'The Adventure of the Illustrious Client', the almost neurotic closeness with which Holmes the adult hugged his ideas and thoughts to himself. 'There was a curious secretive streak in the man which led to many dramatic effects, but left even his closest friend guessing as to what his exact plans might be. He pushed to an extreme the axiom that the only safe plotter was he who plotted alone.' Holmes never came to appreciate the delights of society. His reference, in 'The Adventure of the Noble Bachelor', to 'those unwelcome social summonses which call upon a man either to be bored or to lie' reveals the depths of his disdain for ordinary social intercourse. Much of Holmes's strangeness in later life, the feeling he gave people that he dwelt on a different plane to the rest of the workaday world, derived from the peculiarity of his solitary upbringing.

There was only one person who could break through the barriers that the young Sherlock built around himself at an early age. As a boy, he idolized his older brother and traces of this earlier hero-worship can still be read between the lines when he speaks of Mycroft to Watson. But Mycroft, too, deserted him. While his older brother journeyed triumphantly through Harrow, winning scholar-ships and prizes and forming the friendships that were to stand him in such good stead in his future career in the corridors of power, Sherlock, considered too troubled and unusual a child for the hurly-burly of public school, remained at home. In 1866, while Sherlock, aged twelve, was battling with a succession of private tutors at Hutton Hall, Mycroft went up to Christ Church, Oxford, to read Mathematics. Christ Church, of course, had been the college that most male members of the Holmes family had attended for more than three hundred years. A William Holmes, possibly the brother or a cousin of Sir Ralph Holmes, had been among the first students when the college had been founded as Cardinal's College by Wolsey in 1524. Mycroft's father, grandfather and great-grandfather had all studied there. At Harrow the older Holmes brother had already demonstrated his brilliance as a mathematician and he arrived at Christ Church trailing clouds of glory from his school years.

When he took up the scholarship that he had won, the college was going through a period of major change and reform under its relatively new Dean, H. G. Liddell, and in the year after he came up an Act of Parliament was passed to change the college's constitution. Mycroft's tutor at Christ Church was perhaps the most famous don of the nineteenth century, Charles Lutwidge Dodgson, better known as Lewis Carroll. Shy and reserved, Dodgson nonetheless responded warmly to the talent of his new scholar and the two men became close during Mycroft's three years as an undergraduate. Both shared a fondness for logic puzzles as well as a gift for imaginative fantasy and speculation. After the otherwise lackadaisical Mycroft left Christ Church with first-class honours in 1869, he made the effort to keep in touch with his former tutor for decades to come.

The most significant friendship that Mycroft forged at Christ Church, however, was with Archibald Philip Primrose, the future Lord Rosebery, who was his exact contemporary as an undergraduate. At first sight, the two men were unlikely candidates to become friends. Primrose, the heir to an earldom, whose stated aims were to marry an heiress, win the Derby and become Prime Minister, would seem to have little in common with the plump, indolent and intellectual scion of minor Yorkshire gentry. Yet opposites often attract and for a period the two spent many hours in one another's company. Eventually Primrose, offered the choice by the college authorities between abandoning his studies and abandoning a racehorse that he owned (strictly against college regulations), decided that the horse took precedence and left Christ Church. Although the two men cannot have known it at the time, their friendship was to have a dramatic and shaping impact on Mycroft's entire life.

*

Holmes himself once commented: 'I have frequently gained my first real insight into the character of parents by studying their children.' If this is the case, what can we deduce about the otherwise opaque characters of Holmes's father and mother? Sadly, it is almost impossible to rescue any sense of Violet Holmes's character from the oblivion into which the passage of a century and a half has despatched it. She remains a shadowy and imprecise figure, defined, like so many women in the nineteenth century, solely by her relationships with her husband and her two sons. Holmes's father is only slightly less enigmatic, although we do know considerably more about the tracings he left behind him.

William Scott Holmes possessed the dual character that was to mark out his second son. At once conventional country squire and eccentric and erudite scholar, he divided his time between desultory efforts to improve the land he had inherited and wide-ranging, if unconventional, reading of history and philosophy. In the late 1840s, soon after the birth of his son and heir Mycroft, he published, at his own expense, a study of the Glorious Revolution. This briefly attracted the attention of Lord Macaulay, who wrote a blistering review of it in which he remarked that 'one unpardonable fault, the fault of tediousness, pervades the whole of this strange effusion of a disorganised mind' and suggested that 'very few and very weary will be those who persevere to the final page of Mr [sic] Holmes's volume.' It would appear that Macaulay's lofty scorn may well have deterred Holmes's father from daring to publish any further works, as he rapidly moved away from the study of English history into more speculative territory. Much of the second half of his life was devoted to bizarre research into the whereabouts of the Garden of Eden. Struggling in isolation on the Yorkshire Moors, he roamed the world in his imagination and was said to be compiling a massive work of scholarship that would prove conclusively that the Biblical paradise was in fact located in India. Like his son's magnum opus on the whole art of detection, William Scott Holmes's volume was never to see the light of day.

There was much similarity between father and son. It is easy to forget the cranky element in Sherlock Holmes's own intellectual make-up. His belief that the ancient Cornish language was akin to the Chaldean, and had been derived largely from the Phoenician traders in tin who had sailed to Cornwall, is uncomfortably close in spirit to the ideas of those who believe, for example, that the English are descended from the lost tribe of Israel or that by the use of elaborate codes they can prove that Shakespeare's plays were written by Sir Francis Bacon. It is certainly not that far in spirit from the obsession that gripped his father for nearly thirty years.

One consequence of his father's eccentricity was that Sherlock Holmes received an education at home that was very different from the instruction that most members of his class had beaten into them at public school. It was the elder son, Mycroft – destined, in his father's eyes, to inherit the responsibilities of maintaining Hutton Hall and the family estates, shrunken though they were – who was sent south to attend Harrow. Sherlock had to remain in Yorkshire. This had enormous consequences for the development of the latter's unusual personality and curious range of intellectual interests. As an adult, Holmes was radically different from most other members of his social class, in large part because he had not shared the formative experience of public school that had shaped them.

Holmes's sporting interests, for example, did not lie in the team sports, so important in Victorian ideas about education and character development, that he might have played had he attended a major public school. Boxing and fencing, the two sports Watson

mentions as Holmes's particular skills, are activities for the individ-
ualist and egotist. Both were encouraged by his father. For at least
one brief period William Scott Holmes employed fencing instruc-
tor Theodore Dorrington, who had settled in York, to travel out and
stay overnight at Hutton le Moors once a week to teach Sherlock
the art of swordsmanship. Through this teacher Holmes came into
contact with the great tradition of European fencing.

Dorrington, well into his sixties when he was crossing swords with
the teenage Holmes, had himself been taught by the famous Henry
Angelo who ran an academy of fencing in Regency London and
whose pupils included the likes of Byron and the Prince of Wales.
In the young Sherlock, Dorrington found a willing pupil who took
delight in the standard bouts with epée and sabre as well as in the
exercises with singlesticks, the yard-long wooden rods, fitted with a
guard for the hand, that were used in training. Fencing, as we know
from 'The Adventure of the "Gloria Scott"', was one of the few
pastimes that Holmes continued to enjoy during what he saw as his
otherwise desolate exile later on in Cambridge. Dorrington's training in singlestick combat was still paying off more than thirty years
later when, as recorded in 'The Adventure of the Illustrious Client',
Holmes drew on his old expertise to best at least one of the thugs
sent by Baron Adelbert Gruner to assault him.

Boxing was then an unusual pastime for the gentry to practise.
During the Regency period, there was a brief vogue for young
aristocrats to climb into the ring with professional pugilists. Byron,
for example, hired his own trainer in the shape of the professional
fighter, John Jackson. By the 1850s and 1860s, some men of William
Scott Holmes's class were still happy to travel long distances to see
two of their social inferiors knock seven bells out of one another in
bare-knuckle fisticuffs, and to bet large sums of money on the outcome of the fights. They did not, however, usually practise the noble

art themselves, let alone teach it to their sons. Sherlock's father, in contrast, was an unusual man and he may have believed that his younger son would profit from the self-discipline and self-belief that skill in the ring might instil. We have no knowledge of the precise form that Sherlock's early boxing career took – there is no evidence to indicate that a trainer, a pugilistic version of Theodore Dorrington, was employed at Hutton Hall in the 1860s – but there is little doubt that Sherlock took to boxing as readily as he did to fencing.

Although Holmes ceased boxing regularly in the mid-1870s, soon after finally leaving Cambridge, he continued to step into the ring on occasion. Watson had clearly witnessed him fighting, referring to him in 'The Adventure of the Yellow Face' as 'undoubtedly one of the finest boxers of his weight that I have ever seen'. In 1884, Holmes fought three rounds with McMurdo, an ageing prizefighter, at a benefit evening held at Alison's rooms in London. McMurdo, later encountered as a bodyguard for Thaddeus Sholto in *The Sign of Four*, thought well of Holmes's gifts as a fighter. 'You might have aimed high, if you had joined the fancy,' he tells the detective. The only other record we possess of Holmes as a boxer is a passing reference in an obscure 1873 publication titled *Boxiana or the Annals of Modern Pugilism* in which an unidentified writer, comparing the strengths and virtues of boxers ancient and modern, mentions 'young Holmes of Cambridge' who is 'possessed of a gloved right hand as sweetly dangerous as the mighty fist of the late and much lamented Sayers'.* Where the writer saw Holmes fight, unfortunately he does not say.

Two other abiding passions, music and the theatre, also had their origins in Holmes's childhood. Holmes's first violin was given

---

* Tom Sayers, the last of the great bare-knuckle fighters, who died in 1865.

to him for his eighth birthday by his grandmother. In later years Holmes was to become a connoisseur of fine instruments. His own violin, when Watson knew him, was a Stradivarius that was worth 'at least five hundred guineas' and, in *A Study in Scarlet*, he 'prattled away about Cremona fiddles, and the difference between a Stradivarius and an Amati'. This first violin was most likely no more than an old fiddle, bought for a few shillings from a music shop in Pickering, but it was to instil a love of music that would stay with Holmes for the rest of his life. William Scott Holmes was no music lover himself and, we can be fairly certain, refused to employ a music teacher to guide the young Holmes as he scraped his bow across the strings.

Throughout his life Holmes remained an eccentric performer on the violin. Early in their association, Watson describes his habit of 'leaning back in his armchair of an evening' when 'he would close his eyes and scrape carelessly at the fiddle which was thrown across his knee. Sometimes the chords were sonorous and melancholy. Occasionally they were fantastic and cheerful.' Anyone who regularly plays the violin when it is thrown across his knee seems unlikely to have undergone formal training. It sounds like a childish habit that had never been drummed out of him by a tutor. Yet Holmes could play and play well. At Watson's request he plays 'some of Mendelssohn's Lieder' and, in 'The Adventure of the Mazarin Stone', he performs the barcarolle from Offenbach's operetta *The Tales of Hoffman* well enough to fool his audience into believing that they are listening to a professional recording.

Music's appeal was not primarily to his rational self – although his analysis of the polyphonic music of Lassus, of which Watson tells us, would have been a cerebral exercise as demanding as some of his criminal investigations – but to the powerful emotions that lurked beneath Holmes's surface of severe intellectualism. He recognized this himself. 'Do you remember what Darwin says about music?' he asks Watson in *A Study in Scarlet*. 'He claims that the power of producing and appreciating it existed among the human race long before the power of speech was arrived at. Perhaps that is why we are so subtly influenced by it. There are vague memories in our souls of those misty centuries when the world was in its childhood.' Music provided Holmes with the most reliable release from the pressures of work and from the personal restrictions that he had, quite deliberately, imposed upon himself in pursuit of his ambitions. So much is clear from Watson's description of him at a concert. 'All the afternoon,' he wrote in 'The Adventure of the Red-Headed League', 'he sat in the stalls wrapped in the most perfect happiness, gently waving his long, thin fingers in time to the music, while his gently smiling face and languid, dreamy eyes were as unlike those of Holmes, the sleuth-hound Holmes, the relentless, keen-witted, ready-handed criminal agent as it was possible to conceive.' There is a parallel with another great man, born a quarter of a century later than Holmes, who found in music an escape valve from the pressures of work. Albert Einstein also loved music and played the violin throughout his life.

If we are to believe Watson, Holmes did much more than just listen to music and play as an amateur. 'My friend was an enthusiastic musician,' we are told, again in 'The Adventure of the Red-Headed League', 'being himself not only a very capable perfomer but a composer of no ordinary merit.' Yet the most extensive search of music libraries and the yellowing catalogues of music publishers of the period such as Novello and Schott reveals no works by any composer called Sherlock Holmes. Either Holmes published his compositions under a pseudonym (unlikely but possible) or (the most probable explanation) Watson, carried away by feelings of friendship, was merely referring to Holmes's extemporaneous experiments on the violin when he called him 'a composer of no ordinary merit'.

Holmes's love of the theatre was stimulated by the toy theatre bought for him by his grandmother when he was still a small boy. Before he left Yorkshire, more or less for ever, at the age of nineteen, he had had little opportunity to see plays performed on stage but he must have witnessed a few instances of the power of theatrical events. One of William Scott Holmes's few surviving letters refers to a visit to York in early March 1869 to see Dickens give one of the dramatic readings from his own works that made such an impression on contemporary audiences. Dickens, whose life was probably shortened because the emotional and physical intensity of these readings took such a toll on his health, was an extraordinarily theatrical performer. His acting out of the murder of Nancy by Bill Sikes in the novel *Oliver Twist*, one of his regular showstoppers, was mesmeric in its power, often causing the more susceptible members of his audience to faint or have fits. One who managed to remain conscious gave a vivid description of the novelist as barnstorming actor:

Warming with excitement, he flung aside his book and acted the scene of the murder, shrieked the terrified pleadings of the girl, growled the brutal savagery of the murderer ... Then the cries for mercy: 'Bill! dear Bill! for dear God's sake!' ... When the pleading ceases, you open your eyes in relief, in time to see the impersonation of the murderer seizing a heavy club, and striking his victim to the ground.

Although his father makes no mention of his presence, the teenage Holmes was almost certainly in the audience to witness this kind of extraordinarily charged performance by the ailing novelist.

For more than nine years after the death of his grandmother,

Holmes led a strange and secluded life in the sixteenth-century manor house on the edge of the moors. His only companion, apart from servants, was his father who spent much of his time mentally travelling the plains of the Carnatic, searching for signs of the Garden of Eden. Holmes retreated further into the realms of his own imagination, reading obsessively and devoting time to his growing array of idiosyncratic interests. As well as engaging Theodore Dorrington to cross swords with his son, William Scott Holmes employed a sequence of private tutors to teach him the classics he himself loved. None lasted very long. Holmes, imperious and intellectually arrogant even as a boy, cannot have been an easy pupil. The only teacher of whom we have any record is one Thomas Davenport, a young man fresh from a Classics degree at Christ's College, Cambridge, who survived more than six months at Hutton Hall. Davenport, an aspiring poet, published a small volume titled *Lyrics of Love and Life* while he was in Yorkshire, which he dedicated, either from hopeful flattery or genuine admiration, to William Scott Holmes. In a short acknowledgement at the front of the book he refers briefly to 'my pupil, Mr Holmes the younger' whose 'bright intelligence provides a beacon for the future'. If Davenport wished to ingratiate himself with the two Holmeses, father and son, he was out of luck. His employment at Hutton Hall ended only weeks after his poems were published and he disappears henceforth from history.

CHAPTER TWO

'THIS INHOSPITABLE TOWN'

IN THE MICHAELMAS TERM OF 1873, Sherlock Holmes arrived at Sidney Sussex College, Cambridge, to study Natural Sciences. This was not what his father wished. William Scott Holmes wanted his second son to follow both himself and his brother Mycroft to Oxford and he wanted him to read Law. Sherlock, who believed himself overshadowed by his older brother, clearly thought that Oxford, where the memories of Mycroft's academic triumphs would still linger, was not the university for him. Nor did he want to study Law. His father, after lengthy debate, gave way, agreeing with Sherlock's own suggestion that he should go to Cambridge and embark upon a degree in science.

It is unclear how Sherlock's interest in chemistry and the sciences had developed in the rural fastness of the moors. His father, closeted away with his books on ancient history and the geography of India, would not have encouraged it. As far as we know, none of Holmes's private tutors, men who were classicists first and foremost, would have been able to teach him even the most basic scientific knowledge. Yet somehow the young Holmes had stumbled upon a subject that was to fascinate him for the rest of his life. The Natural Sciences tripos had only been introduced at Cambridge in 1851 and, in the 1870s, there were still comparatively few students. 'My line of study was quite distinct from that of the other fellows,' Holmes admits in 'The Adventure of the "Gloria Scott"'.

Disappointment must have hit Holmes hard from his earliest days at Cambridge. He had struggled to persuade his father that neither Oxford nor Law would suit him. He had chosen to study a subject that was still snobbishly regarded by many as a poor relation to the Classics, Mathematics and the Law. Yet, when he arrived at Sidney Sussex, he found that neither the college nor the course of study was to his taste. Never a clubbable man, Holmes joined few societies at Cambridge and seems to have led an almost monastic life. 'I was never a very sociable fellow, Watson,' he admits in 'The Adventure of the "Gloria Scott"', 'always rather fond of moping in my rooms and working out my own little methods of thought, so that I never mixed much with the men of my year.' (The use of the word 'moping' is interesting and is a small indication of just how unhappy Holmes was when he was at Cambridge.)

Given his love of the theatre, Holmes might have become a member of one of the numerous amateur dramatic groups that flourished in 1870s Cambridge. The Amateur Dramatic Club (ADC), the oldest university dramatic society in England, had been founded in 1855 but there is no record of Holmes joining it or any other group. The only club whose meetings we know for certain he attended (the minutes survive in the library of Trinity College) is a surprising one. Holmes, the arch-rationalist, the man later committed to detection as an 'exact science', was a member of a small group, mostly undergraduates, who gathered around the charismatic figure of Edmund Gurney, a young don at Trinity, to undertake what they called psychical research.

Holmes's attitude towards religion, the afterlife and the super-natural was, like so much in his mental make-up, ambiguous. Watson records, in *The Sign of Four*, his friend's admiration for *The Martyrdom of Man* by Winwood Reade ('Let me recommend this book – one of the most remarkable ever penned'), which would suggest that Holmes, having long outgrown these youthful flirta-tions with spiritualism and conventional piety, had little, if any, belief in the traditional comforts of religion. Reade's book, one of those Victorian works that caused enormous debate at the time yet is now almost forgotten, was first published in 1872, three years before its author's death at the age of only thirty-six. A sweeping and idiosyncratic intellectual history of man, from ancient times to the present day, it argued forcefully that religions were cultural con-structs, the work of man not God. Reade, who was himself as remarkable as his book, had travelled widely in Africa and had accompanied British troops as a newspaper correspondent during the Ashanti War of 1873. In all likelihood Holmes had read *The Martyrdom of Man* soon after its publication, when he was at Cambridge. (Watson proved less receptive than Holmes to what he called Reade's 'daring speculations'. More conventional than his friend in all matters, including religion, he had at the time recently been smitten by his future wife Mary Morstan and, as he confesses, 'I sat in the window with the volume in my hand but . . . my mind ran upon our late visitor.')

Yet Holmes, like so many thinking Victorians, remained torn between faith and doubt. 'What is the meaning of it, Watson?' he asks in 'The Adventure of the Cardboard Box'. 'What object is served by this circle of misery and violence and fear? It must tend to some end, or else our universe is ruled by chance, which is unthinkable. But what end? There is the great standing perennial problem to which human reason is as far from an answer as ever.' He could not quite shake off belief in an afterlife in which would be imposed the justice that, he saw only too clearly, was absent in this world. 'The ways of fate are indeed hard to understand,' he remarks in 'The Adventure of the Veiled Lodger'. 'If there is not some compensation hereafter, then the world is a cruel jest.' And, however rigorously he strove to suppress such elements in his personality, it is clear that he failed to shake off completely those traces of mysticism and unorthodox beliefs that led him astray during his time at Cambridge. Soon after meeting Watson, he is regaling him with his ideas about 'vague memories in our souls of those misty centuries when the world was in its childhood', and there were few cases more likely to catch his attention than those that held a hint of the weird or the supernatural. However, the militant scepticism with which he approached the Baskerville case and, later, the stories of the Sussex Vampire and the Creeping Man, hints at the fervour of a former believer fallen into doubt.

Holmes had few fond memories of Cambridge. More than twenty years after he left, when forced to spend a night there in pursuit of the true story behind Godfrey Staunton's disappearance in 'The Adventure of the Missing Three-Quarter', he gloomily refers to it as 'this inhospitable town'. In 1874, a year after going up to the university, Holmes decided, without consulting anyone, that Cambridge was not for him. His future, he concluded, lay not in the academic world but on the stage. The next his father heard of him was a telegram informing the family that he had left Cambridge and was now working as an actor in London. He was appearing on the stage at one of the capital's most famous theatres, the Lyceum, together with the most talked-about actor of the day, Henry Irving.

How Holmes persuaded Irving and the management of the Lyceum theatre that he was of sufficient calibre to join their company remains a mystery. There is a slight possibility that the two had met before Holmes went up to Cambridge (Irving toured the provinces throughout the 1860s and the teenage Holmes might have attended one of these performances) but, in all likelihood, the younger man simply turned up at the theatre and used his eloquence to convince Irving that he should be given a chance.

In the autumn of 1874, Henry Irving was in his mid-thirties. Born John Henry Brodribb in a small Somerset town, he started his working life as a clerk in a London merchant's office. His family had been opposed to him embarking on a stage career (perhaps Holmes's determination to become an actor aroused memories of his own struggle to escape the drudgery of book-keeping) and their doubts had been confirmed by his marked lack of success in his early years as an actor. He had spent the best part of a decade touring the provinces in a variety of down-at-heel repertory companies before gaining his first role in a London production in 1866. He had to wait a further five years for his first major success but, when it arrived in the shape of an over-the-top melodrama titled *The Bells*, it launched Irving on a career that was to make him the archetypal Victorian performer, the first actor to be knighted for his services to the theatre. The opening night of Irving's production of *Hamlet*, on 31 October 1874, was the theatrical event of the season but the actor's muted performance at first puzzled the audience. As Ellen Terry wrote in her memoirs, 'the success on the first night at the Lyceum, in 1874, was not of that electrical, almost hysterical splendour which has greeted the momentous achievements of some actors.' Slowly those lucky enough to be there began to appreciate the subtlety and art of the interpretation and, again according to Terry, 'attention gave place to admiration, admiration to enthusiasm, enthusiasm to triumphant acclaim'.

At this distance in time, it is difficult to know which parts Holmes took during his weeks as a professional actor. It is not even known under what name he acted, although we do know that it was not his own. A trawl through playbills, programmes and theatre reviews from 1874 makes it tempting to speculate on which name hides the identity of the great detective but we cannot be certain. When Holmes arrived at the Lyceum, Irving was at the beginning of his run as Hamlet and it may be that the new recruit to the company was asked to play one of the undemanding but important roles of Hamlet's friends Rosencrantz and Guildenstern. Equally he may just have been a spear-carrier with no speaking part. Certainly he and Irving seem to have hit it off. They continued to meet intermittently until Irving's death in 1905 and, in 1897, when Irving was troubled by the murder of fellow actor William Terriss, it was to Holmes that he turned. Although the case was one in which the murderer was only too obvious, and the crime – despite the glamour imparted by the fame of the victim – not the kind of intellectual challenge that the detective most relished, Holmes was happy enough to give it his time.

There seemed little mystery behind the killing. The perpetrator, Richard Prince, was apprehended even as Terriss lay dying in the street and he offered no resistance. He admitted his guilt to the police, claiming that Terriss had 'kept him out of employment for ten years, and I had either to die in the street or kill him'. Prince, who had clearly reached such a stage of mental distress that he had become incapable of rational thinking, had focused all his frustrations and failures on the unfortunate Terriss whose only real crime was to be successful when Prince was not. At his trial medical evidence proved to the jury's satisfaction that Prince was of unsound mind and not responsible for his actions. He was sentenced to life imprisonment in Broadmoor where he became a mainstay of the asylum's theatre company and orchestra. If the jury was satisfied that the murder was the act of a single, deranged individual, Irving was not. Convinced that there was more to the crime than had emerged at the trial, he wrote to Holmes, asking for his help. Within days Holmes had been able to reassure the over-imaginative actor-knight that the crime was just as common-place as it seemed. It is an indication of the detective's fond memories of his brief acting career that he was willing to spend any time at all on the Terriss murder. It can only have been as a favour to Irving.

How good an actor was Sherlock Holmes? Could he have carved out a career on the stage? 'The best way of successfully acting a part is to be it,' Holmes once remarked, which suggests that he was a method actor before his time. In 'The Adventure of the Dying Detective', the narrative from which this quotation comes, he pushes his method to its limits. In order to pretend to be dying, and thus fool the villainous Culverton Smith, Holmes starves himself until he very nearly is dying. But this is a method with madness in it, as the ever commonsensical Watson points out, and it has little to tell us of his performances at the Lyceum. There are no recorded comments by anyone who actually saw Holmes on stage. However, references in Watson's later narratives to his credibility in roles that he adopt-ed in his investigations (as diverse as those of an Italian priest, a 'drunken-looking groom', a doddering opium smoker and an asth-matic master mariner) suggest that he might well have proved a fine character actor. It was not to be.

In 1874 Mycroft Holmes was living in London. Aged twenty-seven and embarked on his ambiguous career in government, he was also set already in a pattern that would become even more pronounced as the years went by. In later life, as Holmes comments in 'The Adventure of the Bruce-Partington Plans', seeing Mycroft out of his usual haunts was as startling as 'if you met a tramcar coming down a country lane'. In the spring of that year it may not have been quite so surprising to see him outside Whitehall as it would be later, but even then he had established himself as a man of regular habits and routine. These did not include visits to the theatre and Mycroft had no idea that his younger brother was in town until informed of it by the arrival of the telegram from Yorkshire. He immediately set about removing Sherlock from the Lyceum and the influence of Irving. The task was not an easy one. Sherlock did not wish to be removed. He had enjoyed his short stint as an actor and he had no desire to return to the stultifying atmosphere of a university that he felt offered him little.

Holmes's abrupt departure from Cambridge to pursue such a romantic dream of life on the stage is so at odds with the severe rationality of the persona that he later adopted that it demands explanation. Although he never mentions his short stage career to Watson, he remained proud of his thespian skills and he took every opportunity to indulge them, to emphasize them and to draw attention to the effect they had on others. There is an almost childlike boastfulness, for example, in the way that he reports in 'The Adventure of the Mazarin Stone' that 'old Baron Dowson said the night before he was hanged that in my case what the law had gained the stage had lost'. If anything, Holmes's flight from Cambridge to the London stage, not to mention his rescue by Mycroft, echoes Coleridge's departure from the same university, eighty years earlier, to enlist in the dragoons under the unlikely pseudonym of Silas Tomkyn Comberbache. Coleridge proved a disaster in his brief incarnation as a soldier, not least because he could barely ride a horse. His brother George eventually succeeded in persuading the army to discharge the poet on the grounds of insanity. By contrast, it seems that Holmes was a very good actor. Watson was to record how, when in disguise on a case, Holmes's 'very soul seemed to vary with every fresh part that he assumed'. Perhaps the best way of interpreting both stories is to acknowledge that they reveal young men of exceptional genius, trapped in circumstances that they instinctively knew to be wrong for the future development of that genius, and casting around desperately for a means of escape.

The arguments between the brothers were brought to an end by the sobering news from Yorkshire that William Scott Holmes had fallen seriously ill. Both Sherlock and Mycroft hurried north but, by the time they reached Hutton le Moors, it was too late. Their father died on the last day of 1874.

The most pressing concern became the family home of Hutton Hall. Sherlock, all thoughts of an acting career abandoned, returned reluctantly to start the new term at Cambridge. Mycroft, already carving out his unique role in the corridors of power at Whitehall, had no wish to assume the life of a country squire and was eager to return to London.* The decision was taken to sell the house that had been in the family's possession for more than three centuries. (It passed into the hands of Bradford mill-owner Isaac Binns, in whose family it remained until the mid-1920s. In a scandalous act of philistinism, Isaac Binns's great-nephew Benjamin, who had inherited it just after the First World War, had the old house demolished in 1926, despite protests from the Society for the Preservation of Ancient Buildings. There is no record of Holmes's

---

* Upon the death of his father, Holmes's elder brother became a hereditary baronet and was entitled to be addressed as 'Sir Mycroft Holmes'. There is little evidence that Mycroft, who was just as indifferent to worldly honours as his younger brother, ever made much use of his title.

response to news of the destruction of his childhood home. He may not even have known of it.)

Holmes returned to Cambridge under protest, and the authorities at Sidney Sussex needed persuading that he should be allowed to do so, but he seems to have involved himself even less in the life of the college during his second year there than he did during his first. Some time towards the end of 1875 he left Sidney Sussex without a degree, rarely to return, and moved once again to London. For three years we lose sight of him and it is only in the summer of 1878 that he re-emerges from obscurity as 'the world's only consulting detective'. What was Holmes doing in those missing years and how did he settle upon the career that he was to follow for the rest of his life?

Holmes had his own explanation of how this choice came about. According to his own account to Watson, 'the very first thing which ever made me feel that a profession might be made out of what had up to that time been the merest hobby' was the praise lavished on his deductive powers by the father of his college friend, Victor Trevor. Trevor Senior expressed astonishment at Holmes's unnerving ability to use observation and logic to reveal hidden truths, shown in the secrets that the young man unearthed about the elder Trevor's chequered past; this was the catalyst that propelled Holmes into a life of detection. In 'The Adventure of the "Gloria Scott"', following Holmes's revelations about the older man's earlier life, Trevor says, 'I don't know how you manage this, Mr Holmes, but it seems to me that all the detectives of fact and fancy would be children in your hands. That's your line of life, sir, and you may take the word of a man who has seen something of the world.' To this chance remark Holmes traced the beginning of his career. Perhaps, by the time he confided this version of events to Watson, he had himself come to believe the story but the evidence suggests that he was being disingenuous. It seems more likely that Holmes drifted into his life's work rather than making a conscious decision to become a consulting detective.

'When I first came up to London I had rooms in Montague Street, just round the corner from the British Museum, and there I waited, filling in my too abundant leisure time by studying all those branches of science which might make me more efficient.' It may well have been that Holmes was still thinking in those days of a career as a scientist but, self-exiled from academia and unable to gain regular access to a well-equipped laboratory, he could see no way to pursue it successfully. Cases were few and the majority came 'through the introduction of old fellow-students'.

Holmes was always at great pains to emphasize the uniqueness of the profession he had chosen ('I have a trade of my own. I suppose I am the only one in the world. I'm a consulting detective') but, in London in the late 1870s, there were already plenty of men operating as private detectives. In Craig's Court, a small courtyard off a street in Whitehall, there were offices of no fewer than six detective agencies. It is likely that Holmes's insistence that he was not a 'private' but a 'consulting' detective and, as such, unique stemmed from a certain snobbishness and a residual belief that no one from a family and background such as his should be involved in something as vulgar as detective work. The disdain expressed by John Scott Eccles in the narrative that is usually known as 'The Adventure of Wisteria Lodge' ('Private detectives are a class with whom I have absolutely no sympathy') would have been shared by many. For an early twenty-first-century observer, however, it is sometimes difficult to discern the difference between Holmes's role and that of the other 'private' detectives who clustered around Craig's Court. Although he was in a different intellectual league and had more exalted ideas about the value of the work itself, essentially he was doing the same job. Even Holmes seemed to recognize this at some level, since, in one of Watson's later narratives, 'The Adventure of the Missing Three-Quarter', the pretension slips and he calls himself a 'private detective'.

The London of 1878 in which Holmes now lived and where he was to carve out his unique career was the centre of the largest empire the world had ever seen. From its centres of government and corridors of power men controlled the destinies of 400 million people across the globe. Visitors to the city were at once astonished and appalled by the spectacle it presented. London overwhelmed the senses. 'The roar of it comes up to you from all sides,' one observer wrote. 'It is one continual strenuous movement . . . Hour after hour and every day, is the mighty, throbbing life renewed.' For a man of his class and his age (he was twenty-four), Holmes was surprisingly unfamiliar with the capital. His upbringing in the Yorkshire countryside had been secluded and there is no surviving evidence that he had even travelled outside the county before he first journeyed to Cambridge. Even his stint at the Lyceum had been short-lived.

With few clients to take up his time, Holmes began the exploration of the metropolis that was to make him such a knowledgeable guide to it. Tramping the streets from Whitehall to Whitechapel, from Paddington to Peckham, he came to know them intimately, in the process laying the foundations for the mental gazetteer of the city that so impressed Watson. 'Holmes's knowledge of the byways of London,' according to his friend, 'was extraordinary.' In 'The Adventure of the Empty House', Watson records a journey through London with Holmes in which the detective 'passed rapidly and with an assured step through a network of mews and stables, the very existence of which I had never known'. Holmes himself confessed in 'The Adventure of the Red-Headed League', 'It is a hobby of mine to have an exact knowledge of London.' It was more than a hobby, of course. On a number of occasions, it was to prove important to the resolution of his cases and even to save his life. Holmes came to love London and he was never happy, even in the days of his supposed retirement, when he was away from it. As Watson remarked in 'The Adventure of the Resident Patient', 'neither the country nor the sea presented the slightest attraction to him. He loved to lie in the very centre of five millions of people, with his filaments stretching out and running through them, responsive to every little rumour or suspicion of unsolved crime.'

One of Holmes's earliest cases came to him through one of the few acquaintances he had made at Cambridge. Reginald Musgrave had been in the same year as Holmes at Sidney Sussex but they had seen nothing more of one another until, one morning in 1878, Musgrave walked into Holmes's Montague Street rooms with a problem as intriguing as any the detective was to face in later life. After travelling to Musgrave's family home in Sussex, Holmes was able to throw light on the disappearance of the butler Brunton by unlocking the secrets of a strange ritual that had been handed down from Musgrave to Musgrave through many generations. Beyond this story of the Musgrave Ritual, which Watson published in 1893, some time after Holmes had recounted it to him, we have little evidence of the detective's further activities in these early years.

In later life, Holmes referred to the villain Charlie Peace as 'my old friend', which perhaps suggests he was involved in Peace's capture and trial, but it is difficult to reconcile the dates with what little we know of Holmes's life at the time. Peace, one of the most remarkable and notorious criminals of the Victorian era, pursued a dual career as respectable businessman by day and burglar by night throughout much of the 1860s and 1870s. A man of many talents, he was also a sufficiently gifted violinist to appear from time to time as a concert performer. On one occasion, he had been billed as 'the modern Paganini' on a music-hall stage where, like the famous Italian virtuoso, he showed off his talents by playing airs on a single-stringed violin. However, after murdering in 1876 the husband of a woman whom he was determined to seduce, Peace was caught by the police in mid-burglary in October 1878. Originally tried for his house-breaking activities and for attempting to murder the constable who arrested him, Peace was soon accused of the killing of the husband he had wanted to cuckold and was found guilty of that crime at Leeds Assizes in February 1879. He was hanged the same month, although not before admitting to another murder for which an entirely innocent man had already been tried and sentenced. It is just possible that Holmes was drawn into the Peace case early in his career but the dates, and the fact that Peace was caught not through painstaking detective work but by accident, suggest otherwise. Perhaps the two men had met through their mutual love of the violin.

The Farintosh case is mentioned by Helen Stoner in 'The Adventure of the Speckled Band' as a means of introduction to Holmes, who remarks 'I think it was before your time, Watson,' but, beyond the further information that it was 'concerned with an opal tiara', we have no record of it. Among the other cases that Holmes, in 'The Adventure of the Musgrave Ritual', says were 'all done prematurely before my biographer had come to glorify me', there is none that can be firmly tied to the historical record. The Tarleton murders are difficult to identify. The case of Vamberry the wine merchant is equally elusive, although some Sherlockian scholars have suggested that, despite the difference in the spelling of the names, the reference is to the Hungarian scholar Arminius Vámbéry. Vámbéry was primarily known as a student of Oriental languages but he was also a renowned wine connoisseur and he did visit London several times in the 1870s and 1880s. He and Holmes might have met. As for Ricoletti of the club-foot and his abominable wife, it is possible that they are no more than the products of Holmes's mischievous imagination.

One thing that remains clear is that Mycroft, in those early days, steered clients in his brother's direction. Holmes himself admits as much. 'Some of my most interesting cases have come to me ... through Mycroft,' he confesses to Watson in 'The Adventure of the Greek Interpreter'. The two brothers probably saw little of one another in London. Even as early as 1878 there was no possibility of Mycroft veering so far from his self-imposed tracks in Pall Mall and Whitehall as to turn up in Montague Street. Yet this need not have prevented them from staying in regular contact. The telegraph system in Victorian London was astonishingly efficient and both brothers were inveterate despatchers of telegrams. However he communicated with his brother, it is evident that Sherlock Holmes owed much to him, both in those early years and in his later career.

What exactly was the role Mycroft Holmes played in the British government during the last decades of the nineteenth century and the first years of the twentieth? Soon after coming down from Oxford in 1869, Mycroft, uncertain what his future might be and too indolent to make much effort to find employment, was staying in a private hotel in Bloomsbury. Although he had gained the expected first, he had spurned the fellowship (studentship, as it was known at Christ Church) that was offered him. He had no desire to remain at Oxford and none to return to Yorkshire. Spending most of his days engaged in chess problems and desultory research into higher mathematics, he might have passed years in this agreeable idleness if he had not one day met his old college friend Archibald Primrose outside the British Museum. Primrose had succeeded to an earldom on the death of his grandfather the previous year and, although only in his early twenties, was already seen as a coming man in the House of Lords and Liberal Party politics. Rosebery, as he now was, had contacts everywhere within the political establishment and he suggested that Mycroft should exercise his 'extraordinary faculty for figures' in some more immediately useful way than poring over sequences of prime numbers in his hotel room. He found him a post in the Admiralty where he could oversee finances and monitor government expenditure.

Throughout the early 1870s Mycroft established the almost inflexible routine he was to maintain until his death. He took rooms in Pall Mall and, in 1873, together with a group of like-minded loners, he founded the Diogenes Club. This was, as Holmes told Watson, 'the queerest club in London', a club for the unclubbable. He went on:

There are many men in London, you know, who . . . have no wish for the company of their fellows. Yet they are not averse to comfortable chairs and the latest periodicals. It is for the convenience of these that the Diogenes Club was started . . . No member is permitted to take the least notice of any other one. Save in the Stranger's Room, no talking is, under any circumstances, allowed, and three offences, if brought to the notice of the committee, render the talker liable to expulsion.

It was here, in the Diogenes Club, that Mycroft always felt most at ease with the world, restricting to a minimum the intrusions of others into his life. Ostensibly, he continued to audit the books in the Admiralty and other government departments but, within a few short years, his influence extended throughout the interconnected network of Whitehall. No one who met Mycroft could fail to be impressed by his staggering ability to process information of all kinds and soon his unique skills were in demand everywhere within government circles. Sherlock told Watson:

The conclusions of every department are passed to him, and he is the central exchange, the clearing house, which makes out the balance. All other men are specialists, but his specialism is omniscience. We will suppose that a Minister needs information as to a point which involves the Navy, India, Canada and the bi-metallic question; he could get his separate advices from various departments upon each, but only Mycroft can focus them all, and say offhand how each would affect the other.

Holmes, in his lifelong admiration for his brother, may have exaggerated but only a little. Mycroft did make himself essential to the running of the imperial government in all sorts of ways. The civil service was more informal in the early 1870s than it would become in later decades, and once it was recognized by several powerful people that, in Mycroft's great intellect and astonishingly retentive memory, 'everything is pigeon-holed and can be handed out in an instant', the path that he was to follow for nearly fifty years opened before him.

Both the Holmes brothers were, of course, essentially solitary men. Sherlock, an occasional habitué of the Diogenes Club himself, is said, in 'A Scandal in Bohemia', to have 'loathed every form of society with his whole Bohemian soul' and he remained, throughout his life, curiously detached from the rest of the world. 'I was nearer to him than anyone else,' Watson remarks in 'The Adventure of the Illustrious Client', 'and yet I was always conscious of the gap between.' The difference between the two brothers was that Mycroft, through the contacts he had made at Harrow and Christ Church, as well as his subsequent entrée to the corridors of power via Rosebery, always lived within the charmed circle of the establishment. Sherlock, despite his involvement through the years with matters of national and international importance, only ever entered it at his brother's invitation.

Despite the cases that Mycroft must occasionally have passed his way, there is no indication that Holmes's career took off rapidly. Quite the reverse. When he met Watson in 1881, Holmes was still sufficiently underemployed in his detective work that he could devote plenty of time to the continuing experiments in chemistry that he had begun half a dozen years before in Cambridge. One of the reasons for his ample leisure may well have been his reluctance to work with the official forces of law and order in the city.

His reference to 'some bungling villainy even a Scotland Yard official can see through' shows his opinion of the police clearly enough. Holmes's dismissive contempt for Scotland Yard detectives, unhelpful as it was to the furthering of his career, probably had its origin in his earliest professional experience of them in the 1870s.

The Yard was then a demoralized force in disarray. In 1877 it had been rocked by a scandal that, at one point, seemed to threaten the continued existence of the Detective Branch. Following the arrest of Harry Benson and William Kurr, two confidence tricksters who had been fleecing a wealthy French woman of thousands of pounds, questions began to be asked about the ease with which the two men had operated and the difficulties the police had had in tracking them down. Benson and Kurr, facing lengthy terms of imprisonment, were only too pleased to shed some light on the mystery. Half the detectives on the force, it seemed, had been in their pockets. Inspector John Meiklejohn had been receiving backhanders from Kurr since 1873, and more and more of his colleagues had been drawn into the web of corruption. By the time the case came to court in the autumn of 1877, the number of police officers implicated had grown until the entire Detective Branch was fatally compromised.

The Trial of the Detectives as it became known, with Benson and Kurr, already imprisoned for their misdeeds, as the star witnesses against the police, was a sensation, concluding with several of the officers being convicted and sentenced to hard labour. All but twenty of the detective officers of the Metropolitan Police were, by this time, on probation. Something had to be done to restore a semblance of public confidence. The Home Secretary agreed to a commission to look into 'the state, discipline and organization of the Detective Force of the Metropolitan Police'. In the wake of its report, the Criminal Investigation Department was created in 1878. A year later, however, when Holmes was settled in his Montague Street lodgings and had embarked on his career as a 'scientific' detective, Scotland Yard was still struggling to escape the repercussions of the scandal. Changes were made, of course, but Holmes found it difficult to shake off his belief that the force was manned almost exclusively by the incompetent, the unimaginative and the potentially corrupt.

One of the new detectives who had been co-opted into the CID after the reorganization was a young man named George Lestrade. Like Holmes, Lestrade (as his name suggests) had French blood in his ancestry. His family were of Huguenot origin and his ancestors had fled France in the wake of the Revocation of the Edict of Nantes in 1685. Born in 1848 in Spitalfields, he was the son of a weaver with a small workshop in Princelet Street. After leaving school at the age of twelve, George went to work in the family business. However, the 1860s was not a good decade for the small-scale weaving workshops of Spitalfields. It was an industry that had been in decline for much of the century and a commercial treaty of 1860 between Britain and France, which allowed the home market to be flooded with cheaply made but attractive fabrics from across the Channel, dealt it a further severe blow. Thousands of Spitalfields weavers lost their livelihoods in the next few years and among them was Lestrade's father. By 1865, the workshop in Princelet Street had closed.

What Lestrade did in the following four years we do not know but in 1869, aged twenty-one, he joined the police as a constable. (When Watson refers in the early 1880s to Lestrade's twenty years with the CID, he is clearly overestimating both the inspector's age and the length of his service. The CID did not even exist in the early 1860s, quite apart from the fact that Lestrade was then only a teenager.) His entire professional career would be spent in the Metropolitan Police. Although perfunctorily educated, George Lestrade was intelligent and determined, and his superiors soon recognized his qualities. Promoted to sergeant within four years, he was on hand to benefit from the aftermath of the Kurr and Benson corruption scandal. He was made an inspector and transferred to the newly created CID. Whether or not he and Holmes met as early as 1878 or 1879 is not known but their paths were to cross many times in the future. Holmes claimed that Lestrade lacked both imagination and initiative and described him as 'absolutely devoid of reason', but he also grudgingly referred to him as the 'pick of a bad lot' and noted his 'bulldog tenacity'.

Lestrade, keenly aware of the gap in social class as well as the distance between his own plodding intelligence and Holmes's genius, remained wary of the detective. He tried to disguise the inferiority that he always felt in Holmes's presence by a ponderously patronizing attitude to the detective's methods. Yet, by 1902, when the strange case of the six busts of Napoleon unfolded, the relationship between the two men could almost be described as a friendship. Lestrade, then in his mid-fifties and thinking of retirement, had taken to calling unannounced at Baker Street to discuss cases in hand. Holmes in his turn welcomed these visits as a means of keeping in touch with events at Scotland Yard. The days when Holmes had abruptly remarked, 'I do not encourage visitors,' had passed. Any antagonism between the official and the unofficial detectives was at an end, if we are to believe Lestrade: 'We're not jealous of you at Scotland Yard. No, sir, we are very proud of you, and if you come down tomorrow, there's not a man, from the oldest inspector to the youngest constable, who wouldn't be glad to shake you by the hand.'

CHAPTER THREE

'YOU HAVE BEEN IN AFGHANISTAN, I PERCEIVE'

WE KNOW FRUSTRATINGLY LITTLE ABOUT the six years imme-diately following Holmes's departure from Sidney Sussex but he was about to meet his loyal Boswell, the man who would faith-fully record many of his finest cases. The first encounter between Holmes and Watson strikes echoes of the first meeting, in May 1763, between Johnson and Boswell in Thomas Davies's bookshop in Russell Street, Covent Garden. Unremarkable in itself, nonetheless it sowed the seeds of a remarkable partnership. Also, again echoing Johnson and Boswell's meeting, it is now commemorated by a plaque. Affixed to a wall near the pathology laboratory in St Bartholomew's Hospital, the plaque reads:

At this place New Year's Day, 1881 were spoken these deathless words 'You have been in Afghanistan, I perceive' by Mr. Sherlock Holmes in greeting to John H. Watson, M.D. at their first meeting.

John Hamish* Watson was two years older than Holmes. He was born in Southsea on 23 March 1852 and was therefore twenty-eight at the time of the famous meeting in Barts. His father, Henry Moray Watson, was a Scottish engineer who had worked with the famous Stevenson family on the building of lighthouses around the coast of his native country. In 1849 he moved to the south coast of England to supervise the construction of further lighthouses there.† His mother, Mary Elizabeth Watson (née Adam), was the daughter of an Edinburgh lawyer and was distantly related to the Adam family, which, in the previous century, had produced the architect Robert Adam.

Like Holmes, Watson was the second of two sons. His elder brother Henry had been born in 1845 when the Watsons were still living in Scotland. We know even less of Watson's childhood than we do of Holmes's early years. In fact, there are no records of the younger Watson until he was nearly in his teens. What we do know is that John Watson Senior was sufficiently prosperous by the 1860s to send his sons to English public schools. In 1861, Henry, then aged sixteen, was taken away from the local grammar school where he had previously been taught and despatched to Rugby. Showing the gift for wrecking his chances that he was to demonstrate through-out his short life, he was almost immediately expelled. What he did to deserve so drastic a punishment so soon after arriving at the school is unclear but, in view of his future career, it almost certain-ly involved drink, women or some combination of the two. Three

---

* Hamish is, of course, a Scottish variant of the name James and this probably explains the otherwise mysterious moment in 'The Man with the Twisted Lip' when Watson's wife calls him James rather than John.
† John Watson Senior's closest association was with Alan Stevenson, his near-contemporary, and it is probable that he worked with him on the building in 1844 of Skerryvore, often considered to be the world's most elegant and perfect lighthouse.

years later the twelve-year-old John Hamish was sent to Winchester. His stay at public school was as short as his brother's but for a different reason. In July 1865 his father withdrew him from the school in order to take him and his mother halfway around the world.

The Watson family's disastrous journey to Australia is very difficult to explain. Henry Watson Senior was apparently a successful and respected professional man who had carved out a career for himself that was rewarding both financially and intellectually. Why would he have wanted to uproot his family and transport them thousands of miles across the world to a far-off country that had yet to shake off its reputation as nothing more than a dumping ground for convicts and criminals? Yet the Watsons, minus the errant Henry who had made his way to London and was working as a solicitor's clerk, undoubtedly made the long sea voyage. We have the record of their embarkation on Brunel's famous ship the SS *Great Britain*, which made thirty-plus voyages between Liverpool and Melbourne in the 1860s and 1870s, carrying more than 20,000 passengers to Australia. On 24 July 1865, the *Great Britain* sailed from Liverpool with the three Watsons, father, mother and younger son, on board. In later years Watson was to remain conspicuously silent about his time in the Antipodes. 'I have seen something of the sort on the side of a hill near Ballarat, where the prospectors had been at work,' he comments in *The Sign of Four* when faced by the diggings in the grounds of Pondicherry Lodge. Otherwise he never refers his unhappy year in Australia.

The possible inducements to would-be emigrants were many. His father may have believed that even better prospects awaited him as an engineer in Australia than in England. Certainly, the various Australian states, just a few years before the very last transportation of convicts, were eager to attract 'respectable' emigrants with professional skills. Henry Moray Watson may have succumbed to the

blandishments of agents employed by the states in England to pro-
mote the benefits of living in this new land. He was not alone in
dreaming of a better life – Australia's population trebled in the two
decades between 1851 and 1871 – but his dreams came to nothing.
Within a year the family had booked their passage home. On their
return to England in the autumn of 1866, they were greeted by the
news that Henry had been sacked from his job as a clerk for persistent drunkenness. Dispirited, the Watsons struggled to take up the
life that they had deserted so suddenly and mysteriously. While his
father again found work as an engineer, the fourteen-year-old John
Hamish, whose schooling in Australia seems to have been undertaken largely by his father, now began a new term at Winchester.

He must have settled back remarkably smoothly into English
public school life. The only glimpse we have of him during the
next few years is one that he provides himself and it suggests a boy
who had found a way of establishing himself in the school hierarchy. In 'The Adventure of the Naval Treaty' he receives a letter
from Percy Phelps, an old schoolfellow, seeking Holmes's help.
Watson unashamedly recalls the days when he was part of a gang
that used to 'chevy him [Phelps] about the playground and hit him
over the shins with a wicket'. Clearly John Hamish, as a teenager,
had decided that running with the school bullies was a preferable
alternative to becoming one of their victims.

Watson left Winchester in 1870 and, after a brief stay at the family
home, began his studies for the University of London medical
degree. He finally qualified as a doctor in 1878. What do we know
of these years? We know that he was diligent in his medical studies
and that he worked hard to achieve the London degree he received.
The example of his brother's headlong plunge towards the gutter
was always before him. Henry Watson, still only in his late twenties,
was proving incapable of holding down a job for more than a few

months and his relentlessly excessive drinking was already beginning to affect his health. In the spring of 1871 his father paid to send him to take the waters in Malvern, a thinly disguised attempt to force Henry into sobriety, but even at Dr James Gully's Hydropathic Establishment the prodigal son found plenty of opportunities to drink deeply of potations other than the spa waters. He emerged from his 'cure' more broken in health than he had been when he began it.

John had no wish to follow the path his brother had taken. We know that he played rugby, a sport he had enjoyed since his schooldays. 'I believe your friend Watson played Rugby for Blackheath when I was three-quarter for Richmond,' Robert Ferguson says in a letter to Holmes as a means of introduction to him in 'The Adventure of the Sussex Vampire'. Richmond v. Blackheath, first played in 1863, is the oldest regular fixture in club rugby and hidden behind Ferguson's remark is the story of one of the most infamous matches in its early history. Watson and Ferguson were on opposing sides in January 1877 when Blackheath faced Richmond before a large crowd that became increasingly unruly as the match progressed. Large numbers of spectators invaded the pitch and, in the resultant tumult, several of them were injured, as were players on both sides.*

There is a further mystery about Watson's early career, which persists in spite of the attempts by many commentators to ignore it. In 1878, after graduating from the University of London, he joined the Army Medical Corps. Why did so promising a medical man join the army? In the 1870s, the brightest and the best of the profession

---

* Curiously, when he and Watson meet up years later, Ferguson makes no reference to this match but instead recalls another meeting of the two teams at Richmond's ground at the Old Deer Park. Perhaps the near-riot at Blackheath was still too painful a memory for the two ex-players to form the basis of sporting reminiscence.

did not, as a rule, choose to serve in the forces. Quite the contrary. The Army Medical Corps was the refuge for those too idle, dissipated or untalented to pursue a career elsewhere. Watson had already shown that he was a more than competent doctor. After taking his degree at University College, London, he had been a houseman at St Bartholomew's Hospital, a position that would not have been open to any but the most gifted of medical graduates. The explanation can only lie in some scandal that prevented Watson from continuing at Bart's (as it is familiarly known) and diverted him on to the path that was eventually to lead, via a number of false turnings, to Baker Street and Sherlock Holmes.

The image that we have of Watson as the stolid representative of Victorian values, John Bull in a frock coat, is a misleading one. Watson, certainly in his younger days, was both a womanizer and a gambler. Holmes's laconic remark that 'the fair sex is your department' is more than supported by what we know of Watson's tangled love life over the decades. Like his brother, he had an eye for an attractive woman. He himself boasts complacently of 'an experience of women which extends over many nations and three separate continents'. Watson's financial irresponsibility and the urge to gamble beyond his means remained with him into middle age. In 'The Adventure of Shoscombe Old Place' he talks ruefully of paying for his knowledge of the Turf with 'about half my wound pension' and there is the curious incident of the chequebook, locked in Holmes's desk, mentioned so casually in 'The Adventure of the Dancing Men'. It is clear enough from the reference that, as late as 1898, his friend was keeping his chequebook under lock and key and that the doctor had to ask for access to it. Surely, this can only have been a mutually agreed arrangement designed to help Watson overcome the urge to rush out and enrich the bookies at his own considerable expense. It is impossible to be certain of the details of the misdemeanours that derailed Watson's promising career but it seems clear that, if we were to assume that it involved either a woman or a gambling debt, possibly both, we would not be far wrong.

Whatever the reasons for Watson's decision to join the Army Medical Corps – and it is hard to avoid the conclusion that he was forced to it by circumstances – he arrived at Netley in Hampshire in the autumn of 1878. The Army Medical School had been founded at Chatham in 1860 but moved a few years later to Netley where it was to remain until 1902. Once his studies at Netley were complete, he was attached, he tells us, to the 5th Northumberland Fusiliers as Assistant Surgeon. He continues:

The regiment was stationed in India at the time, and before I could join it, the second Afghan war had broken out. On landing at Bombay, I learned that my corps had advanced through the passes, and was already deep in the enemy's country. I followed, however, with many other officers who were in the same situation as myself, and succeeded in reaching Candahar [sic] in safety, where I found my regiment, and at once entered upon my new duties. The campaign brought honours and promotion to many, but for me it had nothing but misfortune and disaster. I was removed from my brigade and attached to the Berkshires, with whom I served at the fatal battle of Maiwand. There I was struck on the shoulder by a Jezail bullet, which shattered the bone and grazed the subclavian artery.* I should have fallen into the hands of the murderous Ghazis had it not been for the devotion

---

* There has been much debate about the exact whereabouts of Watson's wound. Watson himself clearly states, in *The Sign of Four*, that he has to nurse his 'wounded leg' rather than 'wounded arm' and Holmes also refers to his friend's 'tendo achillis' as the site of his troublesome injury. A simple answer to the alleged mystery would be that Watson was wounded in two places and mentioned different wounds in different narratives – perhaps because, at the time of writing, one or the other was making itself most painfully felt – but Holmesian scholars have not always been eager to accept simple answers.

and courage shown by Murray,* my orderly, who threw me across a pack-horse and succeeded in bringing me safely to the British lines.

The Battle of Maiwand is today almost forgotten, one of those innumerable clashes between British troops and restive natives that pepper the history of imperial expansion. At the time, it made front-page news and was seen as a shocking reversal for the British army. Coming so soon after the disastrous defeat inflicted by the Zulus on troops led by Lord Chelmsford at the Battle of Isandhlwana, it was further proof that imperial armies were not invincible.

Maiwand was a small village some fifty miles north-west of Kandahar in Afghanistan where, in July 1880, two armies – a small British force led by General Burrows and a much larger contingent of Afghans led by Ayub Khan – collided. Little went right for the British. Burrows proved braver than he was astute in his tactics and was easily outflanked by the Afghans; his native allies, very sensibly, decided that discretion was the better part of valour and departed the battlefield in droves when they realized how outnumbered the British were. The general and his troops, including Assistant Surgeon John H. Watson, were forced to fall back towards Kandahar. The Berkshires acted as a rearguard for the retreat, losing nearly half their number in the process.

The last stand of the Berkshires has been described by William McGonagall, perhaps the world's worst poet, in his own inimitable style:

---

* This was not the only act of gallantry that Murray performed. Transferred to the 2nd Battalion of the Connaught Rangers and sent to South Africa to fight in the First Boer War, James Murray took part in a skirmish with a small party of Boers at Elandsfontein. After once again rescuing a wounded comrade under fire, Murray was awarded the Victoria Cross. The details can be found on the Victoria Cross website.

Then Ayoub concentrated his whole attack on the Berkshire Regiment,
Which made them no doubt feel rather discontent,
And Jacob's Rifles and the Grenadiers were a confused and struggling
    mass,
Oh heaven! such a confused scene, nothing could it surpass.

McGonagall's scansion, vocabulary and ability to choose an apposite rhyme may be woeful but his short description of the confrontation is accurate enough. The Berkshires might well have suffered even worse casualties, had a relief force in Kandahar, alerted to the unfolding catastrophe by some of the fleeing native troops, not set off for the battlefield. Watson was among those who would, almost certainly, have been overwhelmed by Ayub Khan's men had the relieving troops not arrived.

Invalided out of the army, Watson returned to England in 1881, shaken in both body and soul by his experiences in Afghanistan. He 'had neither kith nor kin in England'. His father had died of pulmonary pneumonia in 1875 and his mother fell victim to a similar respiratory disease a year later. Of his brother Henry, who had last been sighted in Paris by a friend of the family in 1874, he had heard nothing in years. He was uncertain what his future might be. In his own words, he was 'as free as air – or as free as an income of eleven shillings and sixpence a day will permit a man to be', but he had no clear idea what he would do with his freedom. Faced with his dilemma, he 'naturally gravitated to London, that great cesspool into which all the loungers and idlers of the Empire are irresistibly drained'. Staying at a private hotel in the Strand, 'leading a comfortless, meaningless existence, and spending such money as I had, considerably more freely than I ought', he had reached a low point in his life when a chance encounter changed it for ever.

He was standing in the Criterion Bar in Piccadilly when someone tapped him on the shoulder. It was 'young Stamford who had been a dresser under me at Barts'. In the course of their conversation, Watson mentioned that he was looking for a way of leaving his expensive accommodation in the private hotel and finding lodgings. Stamford told him that he knew 'a fellow . . . working at the chemical laboratory up at the hospital' who also wanted someone to go halves with him in sharing a set of rooms in Baker Street. The fellow was Sherlock Holmes.

Stamford warned Watson in advance of Holmes's cold-blooded rationality. 'I could imagine his giving a friend a little pinch of the latest vegetable alkaloid,' he remarked, 'not out of malevolence, you understand, but simply out of a spirit of inquiry in order to have an accurate idea of the effects.' Yet, when the two men met in the laboratory at Barts, Holmes was far from cold-blooded. He was in a state of high excitement. After his offhand observation that Watson had been in Afghanistan, he was full only of what he had just achieved – 'the most practical medico-legal discovery for years'.

Watson and Stamford had arrived just in time to witness a eureka moment. What Holmes had discovered – a reagent precipitated only by haemoglobin – would mean that any police force adopting it had a certain means of detecting blood at a crime scene, even if it was only present in the tiniest of quantities. It is not difficult to understand the frustration he must have felt when, later, he began to realize that the conservatism of the authorities was such that his test would be ignored and overlooked. The method then employed for the detection of blood in other liquids used the resin of the South American guaiacum tree. A tincture of guaiacum when added to a liquid, followed by a solution of ether dissolved in hydrogen peroxide, produced a distinctive blue colour if haemoglobin was present, but Holmes was not alone in believing that the guaiacum test was inadequate and clumsy. Subsequent history suggests, however, that in 1881 he *was* alone in devising a viable, indeed foolproof, alternative.

The first major criminal case in which the forensic detection and analysis of bloodstains found at the crime scene proved important was the murder in 1901 of Lucie Berlin in Germany and it was some years after this that similar evidence was offered in British courts. The scientific evidence on which these cases were built derived from research by scientists such as Bordet and Uhlenhuth whose work dated from the 1890s, at least a decade after Holmes's experiments. 'My name is Sherlock Holmes,' the detective once said, in 'The Adventure of the Blue Carbuncle'. 'It is my business to know what other people don't know.' In this instance, he did indeed know what other people did not but it was to do him no good. There are no further references to his astonishing discovery. We must assume that he could find no one with the imagination to realize what he had achieved. Others must have shared Watson's initial scepticism ('"It is interesting, chemically, no doubt," I answered, "but practically – "'). The Sherlock Holmes Test therefore joined the long list of other discoveries made before the world was ready for them.

This first meeting may have seemed inauspicious, and Holmes and Watson an unlikely pair of men to form a fast friendship, but it was to be the start of a relationship that endured until Holmes's death nearly half a century later. Watson was to remain wary of Holmes. 'His great powers, his masterly manner, and the experience which I had had of his many extraordinary qualities,' he once wrote, 'all made me diffident and backward in crossing him.' Holmes's arrogance ('I cannot agree with those who rank modesty among the virtues') and his strange habits must have made him a difficult person with whom to share lodgings. He cannot have been, by any definition, an easy housemate. Watson makes this only too clear in 'The Adventure of the Musgrave Ritual':

The rough-and-tumble work in Afghanistan, coming on the top of natural Bohemianism of disposition, has made me rather more lax than befits a medical man. But with me there is a limit, and when I find a man who keeps his cigars in the coal-scuttle, his tobacco in the toe end of a Persian slipper, and his unanswered correspondence transfixed by a jack-knife into the very centre of his wooden mantelpiece, then I begin to give myself virtuous airs. I have always held, too, that pistol practice should be distinctly an open-air pastime; and when Holmes, in one of his queer humours, would sit in an armchair with his hair-trigger and a hundred Boxer cartridges and proceed to adorn the opposite wall with a patriotic V. R. done in bullet-pocks, I felt strongly that neither the atmosphere nor the appearance of our room was improved by it.

Holmes, for his part, must often have found Watson's apparent stolidity, common sense and lack of imagination exasperating in the extreme. He responded with satire and flights of fantasy. There is no doubt that Holmes enjoyed pulling Watson's leg and that Watson was to provide a gullible audience for some of the detective's more preposterous claims. Perhaps the most egregious example of Watson being prepared to give credence to almost any story that Holmes fed him occurs soon after they join forces in Baker Street. Watson noted of Holmes:

his ignorance was as remarkable as his knowledge. Of contemporary literature, philosophy and politics he appeared to know next to nothing. Upon my quoting Thomas Carlyle, he inquired in the naivest way who he might be and what he had done. My surprise reached a climax, however, when I found incidentally that he was ignorant of the

Copernican Theory and of the composition of the Solar System. That any civilized human being in this nineteenth century should not be aware that the earth travelled round the sun appeared to me to be such an extraordinary fact that I could hardly realise it.

Even Watson seemed almost prepared to balk at the possibility that Holmes could still hold medieval ideas about the sun being the centre of the universe. To any impartial observer, aware of the detective's almost childish fondness for practical jokes, it is abundantly clear that Holmes was shamming ignorance and looking to find out just how far he could go before his companion grasped that his leg was being pulled. It is inconceivable that Holmes, however poor a student of the sciences at Cambridge, was unaware of Copernicus. In fact, Holmes revealed in later stories a detailed knowledge of astronomy. In 'The Adventure of the Greek Interpreter', for example, he clearly knows more than the average layman about the phenomenon known as the 'obliquity of the ecliptic'.

His supposed ignorance of Carlyle was also a leg-pull. In fact, later he deliberately quotes from one of Carlyle's works, *Frederick the Great* ('They say genius is an infinite capacity for taking pains'), as if tempting Watson to catch him out in his tease. Watson, of course, does no such thing. Instead he goes on to mark the detective's knowledge of literature as 'Nil' although Holmes is, if anything, rather well read. He can quote Shakespeare – he had, after all, played at least one role in Irving's production of *Hamlet* in 1874 – and refers in passing to many of the plays. He twice quotes Goethe. When he is looking for light reading on a train journey, he pulls out his pocket Petrarch. Anyone who can quote from Flaubert's letters to George Sand, published only a few years earlier, is a man who is keeping up with contemporary literature, even if he misremembers the exact words very slightly.* Not only is Holmes familiar with nineteenth-century writers (he can quote Thoreau and George Meredith as well as Flaubert) but he also knows the classics. The private tutors that William Scott Holmes had hired to teach his withdrawn and difficult younger son had done their work well. The poet Horace and the historian Tacitus clearly featured on the syllabus since Holmes quotes them both.

It is also entirely possible that some of the more mysterious cases that Holmes mentions in passing, faithfully transmitted to the reader by Watson, were ones he simply invented. We have already mentioned Ricoletti of the club-foot and his abominable wife. But what of the case of the two Coptic patriarchs or Merridew 'of abominable memory'? Are these real cases? Certainly Holmesian scholars have expended a great deal of time, ink and ingenuity in trying to discover further details of them, but the results have not always been convincing. When students of the detective can seriously suggest, as they have, that Watson misheard Holmes and that 'Ricoletti' is actually a reference to the 'wrinkled yeti' he met in Tibet, the alternative possibility that many of the cases had no existence outside Holmes's playful imagination seems increasingly tempting.

Despite all this, the apparently mismatched couple were launched upon a partnership that was to survive, albeit with hiatuses, for decades. 'We met next day as he had arranged,' Watson tells us,

and inspected the rooms at No. 221B Baker Street, of which he had spoken at our meeting. They consisted of a couple of comfortable bed-

---

* Holmes, in 'The Adventure of the Red-Headed League', remembers it as, 'L'homme c'est rien – l'oeuvre c'est tout.' The actual quote is 'L'homme n'est rien, l'oeuvre – tout.'

rooms and a single large airy sitting-room, cheerfully furnished, and illuminated by two broad windows. So desirable in every way were the apartments, and so moderate did the terms seem when divided between us, that the bargain was concluded upon the spot, and we at once entered into possession. That very evening I moved my things round from the hotel, and on the following morning Sherlock Holmes followed me with several boxes and portmanteaus.

The process by which 221B Baker Street was to become one of the most famous addresses in the world was under way.

CHAPTER FOUR

'HE IS THE NAPOLEON
OF CRIME'

THE 1880s WAS THE DECADE in which Holmes investigated the villainies of Dr Grimesby Roylott and his stepdaughter's fear of the 'speckled band' that had killed her sister. It was also the decade in which he and Watson encountered the five orange pips that marked the murderous persecution of the Openshaw family, pursued Jonathan Small and his Andamanese companion down the Thames in *The Sign of Four* and sought to explain the strange circumstances in which the young engineer Victor Hatherley lost his thumb in a vicious attack. All these cases, and others, are meticulously documented by Watson, yet the doctor records only some two dozen cases in total from the decade. It is a curious fact that Watson chooses to document very few cases from his early association with Holmes. After the initial adventure described in *A Study in Scarlet*, there are no further cases in Watson's archives for two years. 'The Adventure of the Speckled Band', which occurred in 1883, is followed by another hiatus in the annals that is only ended by 'The Adventure of the Beryl Coronet' events in which date from 1886. 'The Adventure of the Resident Patient' and 'The Adventure of the Reigate Squire' both record tales from 1887 and they are followed by a flurry of cases from 1888 and 1889. These two years alone contain nearly a third of the total number of adventures that Watson decided to publish, from the journey to Dartmoor to investigate the disappearance of the racehorse Silver Blaze to the unveiling of Neville St Clair's bizarre profession in 'The Man with the Twisted Lip'. If we assume that each of these cases took, on average, a week of Holmes's time, less than six months of the detective's activities in some ten years are accounted for. The truth is that the reader searches Watson's narratives in vain for more than a passing hint of the three subjects that took up most of Holmes's energies in the 1880s: Ireland, the political and sexual scandals of the ruling classes and the Whitechapel murders. In 'The Adventure of the Bruce-Partington Plans', Watson writes of 'that secret history of a nation which is often so much more intimate and interesting than its public chronicles'. Watson was largely silent about that secret history even when he was implicated in it himself. His silence for much of the decade becomes less surprising when we realize just how far his friend was drawn into the British government's continuing battle against Irish national- ism in all its forms, from the parliamentary campaigns of Parnell and his party to the terrorism of the Fenians and their American supporters.

The Irish question was a running sore on the body politic of Britain throughout the second half of the nineteenth century. Ultimately, it was a question that could not be answered. The Irish, or large numbers of them, wanted independence for their country. The British, or large numbers of those with the power to grant it, did not wish to oblige. There was no compromise to be reached and, until the announcement of Gladstone's conversion to the idea of Irish Home Rule in late 1885, no hope of a settlement. Advocates of Irish independence came in a thousand different hues but there was one broad division within their ranks. On one side of this divide stood those who believed in 'moral force' and peaceful parliamentary means to gain their goal; on the other side were those who thought that only 'physical force' and violent uprising would achieve the desired end. In the course of the 1880s both varieties of Irish nationalist were to take up much of Sherlock Holmes's energies.

The history of Ireland in the nineteenth century was littered with doomed but heroic rebellions against British rule; it was also scarred by the terrible tragedy of the 1840s potato famine. In the years in which Sherlock Holmes had been a teenager at Hutton Hall and his brother had been swapping mathematical puzzles with Lewis Carroll in Oxford, wild plots proliferated on both sides of the Atlantic. The Irish Republican Brotherhood – known as the Fenians after the legendary 'Na Fianna', bodyguards to the old High King of Ireland – was founded in 1858. In 1866 a madcap Fenian scheme to invade Canada with an army of Irish-American patriots, many of them veterans of the American Civil War, ended in fiasco. The following year violence crossed the Atlantic and, in Manchester, a police van carrying Fenian prisoners was ambushed by thirty armed men. One of the police guards was shot dead and the prisoners released. The worst of the Fenian atrocities that year took place in Clerkenwell when an attempt to spring two activists from the prison there resulted in an explosion that killed twelve people and injured dozens more. Another foray across the Canadian border in 1870 was even more disastrous than the first.

Throughout the 1870s physical-force Irish Republicans were largely engaged in licking their wounds and squabbling among themselves, although elaborate and unlikely plans were cooked up to foment trouble throughout the British Empire from South Africa to the frontiers of India. Most sounded more like the plots of boys' adventure stories than serious attempts to undermine British authority. The advocates of peaceful progress towards independence were meanwhile gaining strength. In 1875 the man who was to become the leader of parliamentary Irish nationalism, Charles Stewart Parnell, was elected MP for Meath. In 1879 the Irish National Land League was founded with the aim of forcing reform on absentee landlords in Ireland and, ultimately, transferring Irish land into Irish hands.

It was at this point that Mycroft Holmes entered the Irish arena. One of Mycroft's greatest advocates was Arthur Balfour, a young man with powerful family connections. A year younger than Mycroft, Balfour was the nephew of Robert Gascoyne Cecil, 3rd Marquess of Salisbury (the phrase 'Bob's your uncle' is said to derive from the cosy relationship between them), and, when his uncle was appointed Foreign Secretary in 1878, he became his private secretary. In this role he met Mycroft and was immediately impressed, as so many were, by the extraordinary mind that lurked behind the plump and indolent façade that Holmes's elder brother presented to the world. It was Balfour, with the power of his uncle behind him, who first suggested that Mycroft should turn his thoughts across the Irish Sea, originally with the intention of gaining further information about the Irish National Land League and Parnell's involvement with it. Although the Conservative government was ousted at the 1880 general election, Mycroft, once installed anywhere, usually proved immune to changes of government. Wisely, the incoming Gladstone government decided to allow him a free brief to follow events in Ireland.

By the early 1880s wild rumours about Irish plots were gathering pace in the corridors of Whitehall, as well as in the columns of the more excitable newspapers and periodicals. There were reports from America that hundreds of revolutionists there had formed a secret society, the Knights of Hassan-ben-Sabbah-el-Homari, named after the original founder of the hashish-smoking assassins of eleventh-century Persia. Dedicated to spreading terror through murder, agents of the Knights were preparing to sail the Atlantic and begin their campaigns in Britain. The royal family was at terrible risk. 'Dynamite will be deposited in the coffins in Windsor,' one anonymous correspondent from Chicago reported to the British consulate in that city, 'and blown up with an electric battery when the Queen is staying there.' Ludicrous as these stories might have been, they could not be entirely ignored. Explosions earlier in the year, the work of agents sent from the United States, had shown that there were Irishmen sufficiently committed to their cause to plant bombs in mainland Britain. The assassination of Tsar Alexander II in March 1881 made it clear that not even monarchs – perhaps especially not monarchs – were safe from the danger. Mycroft was more concerned with the escalating troubles in the Irish countryside, sponsored by the Land League, than he was by what were most likely the fantastical products of lengthy drinking sessions in New York bars. Nonetheless he commissioned his brother to travel to Dublin on a largely unofficial investigation into links between firebrands in America and the wilder nationalists in Ireland.

Holmes was not nearly as infallible as Watson's admiring accounts usually suggest and the detective was himself the first to admit this. 'I made a blunder, my dear Watson,' he acknowledges during his 1888 investigation into the disappearance of the racehorse Silver Blaze, 'which is, I am afraid, a more common occurrence than anyone would think who only knew me through your memoirs.' Six years earlier, in Dublin, Holmes had made a more serious blunder and the result was tragedy. Throughout the earlier part of 1882 he spent long periods in the Irish capital, slowly working his way through agents' reports on nationalist activity as they reached the authorities at Dublin Castle and painstakingly building up his own network of contacts. Towards the end of April, word reached him that some kind of dramatic attack on the government in Ireland was in the offing. For reasons that are no longer clear, Holmes came to believe that the most likely target for such an attack was the armoury at Dublin Castle. Throughout the last week of April and the first few days of May, he bombarded Dublin Castle with peremptory instructions, couched in his usual, terse style of address, about defence of the armoury. Many of the senior civil servants in Dublin had, by this time, come to resent what they saw as the interference of this emissary from London, with his ill-defined powers and abrupt manner, but they had also come to appreciate that, somehow, he had the backing of the highest authorities in Whitehall. Most of Holmes's suggestions were acted upon and he felt able to relax, confident that he had thwarted the plans of the potential rebels.

On the night of 6 May he was attending a performance by the Carl Rosa Opera Company of *Maritana*, a then well-known opera by the Irish composer William Vincent Wallace.* We do not know

---

* William Vincent Wallace (1813–65) was an indifferent composer but he had probably the most adventurous life of any musician of the nineteenth century. Born in Waterford in Ireland, he emigrated to Australia as a young man and worked there as a sheep farmer. Abandoning farming for a cruise on a whaling ship, he was involved in mutiny and shipwreck before visiting New Zealand where he was promptly captured by warring Maoris and threatened with execution. Eventually escaping the Maoris he travelled to India and Central America and was chief conductor of the Opera House in Mexico City in the early 1840s. *Maritana*, his one major success as an operatic composer, was first staged in London in 1845.

what Holmes, an admirer of Wagner and German music, made of the saccharine melodies and overblown plot of *Maritana*, a tale of a street singer and her complicated amour with the King of Spain, but the news brought to him by an emissary from Dublin Castle must have sent all thoughts of music flying from his mind. There had been no assault on the armoury. The extreme nationalists had turned to assassination. Earlier that evening, as they walked through Phoenix Park in the city, the new Chief Secretary of Ireland, Lord Frederick Cavendish, and one of his leading civil servants, Thomas Burke, had been confronted by four men wielding surgical knives. Cavendish and Burke were stabbed and slashed at repeatedly. Both died from their wounds. Later reports sent to a Dublin newspaper claimed that a group calling itself the 'Irish Invincibles' was responsible. Although Holmes had been in Dublin, and had had early hints that some major terrorist assault was planned, he had proved powerless to prevent the murders.

In the months following the killings in Phoenix Park, Holmes flitted back and forth between London and Dublin. The official investigation into the assassination, led by Dublin superintendent John Mallon, seemed unable to identify the 'Invincibles' or to track them down. Dozens of men were arrested, interrogated and then released. Mallon appeared no closer to bringing the murderers to justice. Eventually, in January 1883, thanks to the evidence of an informer, thirteen men were brought to trial. Five were sentenced to hang. However, nobody, least of all Holmes and his brother, believed that the true masterminds behind the Phoenix Park killings had been uncovered. Mycroft insisted that Sherlock's investigations in Ireland should continue. Indeed, it was in the second half of 1882, as he struggled to make sense of the labyrinthine politics of Irish nationalism, that Holmes first heard the name Moriarty.

It is often claimed that Watson simply invented Moriarty or that he used the name 'Moriarty' to disguise the identity of the real 'Napoleon of crime', Adam Worth, described by one commentator as 'the outstanding criminal of the Victorian age'. Worth, whose exploits included the daring theft of Gainsborough's portrait of Georgiana, Duchess of Devonshire, from the London art dealers Agnew's in 1876, followed by a succession of inventive scams and frauds, was certainly a remarkable criminal. The system he developed – in which he used a chain of intermediaries as a buffer between himself and the actual commission of the crime, so that those most likely to be caught by the police remained ignorant of the true organizers – certainly sounds very like that employed by Moriarty in his half-criminal, half-political endeavours. However, Worth was not Moriarty. Nor did Watson's portrayal of Moriarty owe much to stories of James Townsend Saward, the barrister and forger known as Jim the Penman who, in the 1850s, used a string of accomplices to cash bad cheques in London banks and was transported to Australia in 1857. Moriarty was no fictional creation nor was he one of the names Watson used to hide another's identity. Moriarty was very much a real person and he was to haunt Holmes for most of the 1880s.

Watson, reporting Holmes's own words, tells us much about Moriarty.

He is a man of good birth and excellent education, endowed by Nature with a phenomenal mathematical faculty. At the age of twenty-one he wrote a treatise upon the Binomial Theorem, which has had a European vogue. On the strength of it, he won the Mathematical Chair at one of our smaller universities, and had, to all appearance, a most brilliant career before him. But the man had hereditary tendencies of the most diabolical kind. A criminal strain ran in his blood, which, instead of being modified, was increased and rendered infinitely more dangerous by his extraordinary mental powers. Dark rumours gathered round him in the university town, and eventually he was compelled to resign his Chair and to come down to London, where he set up as an army coach.

This is a neat thumbnail sketch of his career yet Watson fails to reveal the single most important fact about the criminal mastermind. Moriarty was Irish.*

The name derives from the Gaelic O'Muircheartaigh and, throughout the Middle Ages, the clan was a major power in the west of Ireland. The Moriartys could even claim a twelfth-century King of West Munster among their ancestors. Most Moriartys in the midnineteenth century came from County Kerry but James Nolan Moriarty was born in 1849 in Greystones, a small town on the coastal road between Dublin and Wicklow, the son of an impoverished Catholic land agent in his mid-forties and his much younger wife. (Why Holmes believed that there was a 'criminal strain' running in Moriarty's blood is unclear. James Moriarty Senior was an upstanding, if undistinguished, member of his community and there is no indication that his forebears were anything else.)

What little evidence we have for Moriarty's childhood (two surviving letters written by his mother, a brief reference in a Dublin newspaper of 1858 to a calculating prodigy) reveals that his remarkable mathematical skills were present from an early age. Like Holmes, Moriarty was a difficult child and he was educated largely at home. It is not known who encouraged and fostered his mathematical talent but, by the age of seventeen, he had already published his first academic papers and sought admission to a

---

* Colonel Moran, Moriarty's most ruthless and reliable henchman, also came from a family that was Irish in origin.

university. As a Catholic, Moriarty was unable to enter Trinity College, Dublin, which was an exclusively Protestant establishment. The alternative was the newly founded University College, Dublin, and Moriarty became an undergraduate there in the autumn of 1867. Already his abilities were in a different league to those of his teachers and he seems to have devoted most of his time at UCD to lengthy correspondence with European professors who were better able to follow him into the abstruse mathematical territory he was now entering.

In 1871, having graduated from UCD with the highest first of his year, he published the results of his work over the previous four years or so. Although it appeared under the imprint of a small Dublin publisher, *A Treatise on the Binomial Theorem* made Moriarty's reputation. Carefully sending presentation copies to the mathematicians he had cultivated on the Continent (the treatise was actually dedicated to Carl Gottfried Neumann, a professor at the University of Leipzig), Moriarty nurtured the fame he had gathered and as a result several universities approached him with requests that he join their teaching staff. He had been hoping for a position at either Oxford or Cambridge but, again, his Catholicism stood in the way. Durham, however, although equally committed to the Church of England, seemed prepared to turn a blind eye to his now lapsed religious affiliations.

In the autumn of 1872, aged only twenty-three and still basking in the glory that his treatise had brought him, Moriarty crossed the Irish Sea for the first time and took up his professorship at Durham. The description of Moriarty that Holmes later provides, coloured as it is by the detective's own prejudice against the man, gives a sense of the markedly distinctive figure who was about to become a familiar sight in the streets of Durham. 'He is extremely tall and thin, his forehead domes out in a white curve, and his two eyes are deeply sunken in this head. He is clean-shaven, pale, and ascetic-looking, retaining something of the professor in his features. His shoulders are rounded from much study, and his face protrudes forward, and is forever slowly oscillating from side to side in a curiously reptilian fashion.'

Moriarty remained in the North of England for six years, during which time his mathematical reputation only grew but he was to leave Durham, as Holmes notes, under a cloud. It is unclear what the 'dark rumours' were that gathered there around Moriarty. His name has been carefully excluded from the archives of the university so we must assume that they were very serious indeed. The likelihood is that, at the very least, word reached the authorities of his growing association with the more extreme elements in the Irish nationalist movement. At University College, Dublin, Moriarty had joined the Clan na Gael and, despite moving to England, he had almost certainly maintained contact with its representatives both in Ireland and elsewhere.

Whatever his crime, Moriarty was pressured into resigning his professorship and he moved to London in 1878. He was twenty-nine and at the peak of his mathematical brilliance, yet the only job he could find was as an army coach. One can only speculate whether Moriarty was bitter at being reduced to this but in all likelihood his resentment must have been fierce. Here was one of the great mathematical minds of Europe, a man who had corresponded on equal terms with the likes of Georg Cantor and Carl Neumann, forced to cram the basics of algebra and geometry into the plodding brains of would-be soldiers. Exiled from the intellectual world, he plunged even deeper into the plots and counterplots of those determined to win Irish independence by any means, legal or illegal. Ironically, it was his mathematical genius that made him useful to them. Moriarty became a creator of ciphers and a breaker of codes.

The codes that the Fenians had been using before Moriarty entered their midst had been childishly easy to unravel. Some messages were sent in which the only attempt at secrecy was a half-hearted transposition of one letter for another according to its place in the alphabet. 'B' would substitute for 'A', 'C' for 'B', 'D' for 'C' and so on. Unsurprisingly, even the most unsophisticated police agent was usually able to read supposedly secret communications between the nationalists. Under Moriarty's guidance, and with his exceptional mathematical gifts, the codes became fiendishly complex.

Holmes was an expert on codes. As he said to Watson in 'The Adventure of the Dancing Men', 'I am fairly familiar with all forms of secret writing, and am myself the author of a trifling monograph upon the subject, in which I analyse one hundred and sixty separate ciphers.' His knowledge was practical as well as theoretical. 'There are many ciphers which I would read as easily as I do the apocrypha of the agony column,' he boasted to Watson; 'such crude devices amuse the intelligence without fatiguing it.' In the months since the outrage at Phoenix Park, Holmes had been working on coded communications between the nationalists that the police had intercepted. Soon he began to realize that the ciphers he was now seeing were the work of a mind of a different calibre to those that had produced the earlier codes.

In the wake of the Phoenix Park murders, the rumours of plots and planned assassinations that reached the Foreign Office and soon found their way to Mycroft's desk began once more to grow in number. Princess Louise, one of Victoria's daughters, was to visit Canada and there she would be abducted by a gang of committed Irish nationalists travelling up from New York. Two Sicilians, seasoned experts in the art of political murder, had been hired by a wealthy Irishman to journey to London and do away with the

Prince of Wales. Mycroft, alternately irritated and darkly amused by these largely preposterous stories, was being urged to take action, which of course was not his forte but his brother's. Annoyed though he was by what he continued to believe was Sherlock's negligence in Dublin, he had little hesitation in employing him again. It was time for Holmes to combine his work on the ciphers with more active investigations.

It was a minefield of conflicting loyalties, double agents and secret societies into which Holmes now stepped. Irish nationalism was itself hopelessly divided, not only between those who advocated a peaceful parliamentary pursuit of independence and those who wanted to use physical force to end British rule. The men of violence, in the wake of the disastrous failings of the 1860s, had splintered into numerous small groups, each certain that it, and it alone, was the true torchbearer for the nationalist cause. The Clan na Gael, founded in 1867, squabbled with those loyal to Jeremiah O'Donovan Rossa, a former Fenian prisoner who had been released into American exile in 1871. Irishmen at home in Dublin and Cork resented the interference of the often well-funded activities of those who had emigrated to the United States. One such was General Millen, a Tyrone-born adventurer who had fought with Benito Juarez's armies in Mexico and who had been involved in a dozen plots against British power in Ireland and elsewhere in the 1860s and 1870s. He and men like him were quite prepared to change sides and act as informers for the very government that they were still working to subvert.

Those responsible for protecting Britain and the Empire from Irish terrorism were equally divided. Home Office civil servants bickered with ministers. Ministers failed to agree with the police. The police brooded over the interference of politicians and special agents. In the midst of this the Holmes brothers wove their own web of intrigue. The formation in March 1883 of a new 'Irish Bureau' in the Metropolitan Police, headed by the legendary and flamboyant Chief Inspector Adolphus 'Dolly' Williamson, should have solved many of the problems. Instead, it made them worse. At the heart of the chaos was a man who was soon to become almost as much trouble for the Holmes brothers as Moriarty.

Edward Jenkinson was an ex-Harrovian (he had been at the school a decade before Myroft arrived). In the wake of the Phoenix Park murders this civil servant returned from India and in his new appointment quickly established his own network of spies and double agents who answered to him personally rather than to any government or police authority.* Jenkinson was soon filling much the same role as had Holmes in late 1881 and early 1882, working as a freelance agent with mysterious powers granted by senior figures in Whitehall who could, and would, quite happily wash their hands of him if it became expedient to do so. Both Holmes brothers resented Jenkinson's intrusion into the arena but there was little they could do. He had the backing of the highest authorities.

Whatever the British government did, whatever plots and counterplots were devised by the likes of Jenkinson and Mycroft Holmes, they all seemed to have little effect on the men of violence. Each year in the 1880s saw an increase in Fenian activity. In the spring of 1883, a bomb exploded in the heart of Whitehall. No one was hurt but the bombers had made an impressive display of their ability to reach right into the very heart of the British establishment. In the autumn of the same year, there were two explosions on

---

* One irony is that nearly twenty years later Holmes would adopt precisely the same methods of espionage that he deplored in Jenkinson. In the years immediately after the formation of MI5, Holmes ran an informal network of agents strikingly similar to the one Jenkinson organized and equally beyond the control of the official forces.

underground trains, one on the Metropolitan Line at Paddington, the other on the District Line at Westminster Bridge. Dozens of people were injured, some very seriously. The Holmes brothers may have been engaged in a bitter battle for behind-the-scenes influence with Edward Jenkinson but they would have agreed with him when he wrote in exasperation: 'I *gave* Harcourt [the Home Secretary] warning in the spring that they meant to attack the Underground railway.' Although Mycroft and Sherlock had for some time given clear indications of the threat Moriarty and his colleagues represented, they had met chiefly with bureaucratic frustration.

The circumstantial evidence against the ex-professor remained flimsy. Despite the dubious circumstances in which he had left Durham, Moriarty was still able to maintain a veneer of respectability. As Holmes warned Watson, 'In calling Moriarty a criminal you are uttering libel in the eyes of the law . . . so aloof is he from general suspicion, so immune from criticism, so admirable in his management and self-effacement, that for those very words that you have uttered he could hale you to a court and emerge with your year's pension as a solatium for his wounded character.'

For the authorities the most embarrassing of all the bomb outrages took place on 30 May 1884. The bombers struck, literally, in the police's own backyard. Shortly after nine o'clock at night PC 417 Clark, who had the unenviable job of guarding the public urinal at the rear of Scotland Yard, was blown thirty feet through the air by the explosion of a massive device planted there. The Rising Sun, a pub across the street that was filled with off-duty policemen supping their pints, became a whirlwind of flying glass and splintered wood. Many were injured. Holmes, working night and day on coded communications between the Fenians, most of them the product of Moriarty's fertile mathematical mind, had only succeeded in a partial unravelling of the plot. He was unable to predict the bomb in the Rising Sun but, thanks to his warning, another bomb that had been set to explode at the base of Nelson's column was found before it went off.

The campaign, however, was far from over. The following year, 1885, saw bombs successfully detonated at the Tower of London, London Bridge and the Palace of Westminster. The 'infernal machine' in Parliament was found on 24 January in a black bag by a Mr Green, his wife and sister-in-law, tourists who were wandering, unshepherded, around the chapel of St Mary Undercroft, and reported their discovery to the policeman on duty, a PC Cole. By the time Cole reached the device it was smouldering but, showing courage beyond the call of duty, he picked it up and ran up the stairs to Westminster Hall, preceded by Mr Green yelling, 'Dynamite!' Another police officer, PC Cox, now joined his colleague and, as the two debated what to do, the bomb became too hot for Cole to hold. He dropped it to the ground whereupon it exploded, blowing both the policemen off their feet and leaving the two ladies in Mr Green's party 'bereft of their upper garments'. As others rushed to the scene another device, which had been left in the actual chamber of the House of Commons, also went off. Parliament was in recess and no one was hurt but once again the dynamiters had demonstrated their power to reach into the heart of the government. Holmes, who had been recommending greater security at key locations such as Parliament, was furious. His transcriptions of coded letters between the bombers and their sympathizers – as well as the conclusions he had drawn from them – had been lost in the bureaucratic tangle that surrounded all attempts to deal with the Irish incendiaries.

By this time, Mycroft and Sherlock Holmes were obsessed by Moriarty. There is no question that the professor had been involved in the planning of both the Phoenix Park murders and the bombings of the mid-1880s but it is doubtful whether he was the mastermind that the Holmes brothers believed him to be. The underworld of physical-force Irish nationalism was too fragmented and too divided against itself to allow for the emergence of such a mastermind. There is a sense in which the two brothers were too logical, too committed to tracing a pattern beneath the seeming chaos for their own good. 'Perhaps, when a man has special knowledge and special powers like my own,' Holmes once remarked to Inspector Hopkins in 'The Adventure of the Abbey Grange', 'it rather encourages him to seek a complex explanation when a simpler one is at hand.' He was right in this instance. Watson noted in *The Sign of Four* that, 'through the over-refinement of his logic', Holmes often preferred 'a subtle and bizarre explanation when a plainer and more commonplace one lay ready to hand'. This was a case in point. The simpler truth was that the superficial disorganization of the assorted groups was only a cover for the even deeper disorganization beneath. Mycroft and Sherlock could not accept this and they used the evidence they collected against Moriarty to elevate him to a mastermind status that he did not fully deserve. When Inspector MacDonald, in *The Valley of Fear*, remarks, 'We think in the C. I. D. that you have a wee bit of a bee in your bonnet over this professor,' he may have been right.

Holmes, encouraged by his brother, continued to attach a disproportionate importance to Moriarty. 'He is the Napoleon of crime,' he told Watson. 'He is the organizer of half that is evil and of nearly all that is undetected in this great city. He is a genius, a philosopher, an abstract thinker. He has a brain of the first order. He sits motionless, like a spider in the centre of its web, but that web has a thousand radiations, and he knows well every quiver of each of them.' Yet even as late as 1888, Holmes had never met Moriarty. He had broken into the professor's rooms on a number of occasions and had noted that Moriarty owned a painting by

Greuze, the eighteenth-century French artist who was much admired by the Victorians and whose work fetched high prices. He knew that Moriarty was able to pay his subordinate, Colonel Moran, £6,000 a year, more than the Prime Minister earned. Yet he had never come face to face with him.

As Holmes struggled, over the next two years, to find more concrete proof that Moriarty and the crime organization that he headed were linked with violent Irish nationalism, a parallel investigation was unfolding into events surrounding the Irish parliamentary leader, Charles Parnell. Throughout the 1880s rumours were circulating of Parnell's supposed involvement in all kinds of extremist outrages, from the Phoenix Park murders to the planning of dynamite attacks. The reactions of the Holmes brothers to these rumours were ambivalent. On the one hand, they were both committed to the belief that Ireland should remain under British rule and, for a long period in the 1880s, it seemed as if Parnell had a chance of achieving through constitutional means the Irish independence that they both feared. On the other, they were both convinced, from the very beginning, that the vast majority of the claims made about Parnell were untrue.

Most of the rumours about Parnell could be, and were, dismissed out of hand. The Irish leader was always scrupulous in distancing himself from any connection with terrorism. The biggest threat to his political career came in the shape of a series of letters, allegedly bearing his signature. On 11 April 1887, the sensational contents of the letters began to be unveiled in facsimile in a series of articles in *The Times* with the headline 'Parnellism and Crime'. The most damaging revelation was that Parnell had apparently condoned the Phoenix Park murders, writing, 'Though I regret the accident of Lord F. Cavendish's death, I cannot refuse to admit that Burke got no more than his deserts.' A parliamentary commission was set up to investigate the claims made in the articles. It was to rumble on for the next two years and would force the Holmes brothers to reassess their tactics in their Irish investigations.

Holmes was aware from very early on that the Parnell letters were forged. The man who had brought them to the attention of the British media was a disreputable Irish journalist, Richard Pigott. According to a much later memory of George Bernard Shaw, few people in Ireland had any doubts about Pigott's reliability as a journalist. 'His routine,' said Shaw, 'was to drink himself almost to death, at which point he would write a recklessly seditious article in his paper *The Irishman* and get six months for it. The compulsory abstinence thus enforced restored health and enabled him to begin again.' The 'expert' employed by *The Times* to verify Pigott's letters may have been fooled but Holmes was not. He was a keen student of handwriting, both as a means of revealing character and as a method for deducing more basic information about the writer. In 'The Adventure of the Reigate Squire', he tells his audience, 'You may not be aware that the deduction of a man's age from his writing is one which has been brought to considerable accuracy by experts. In normal cases one can place a man in his true decade with tolerable confidence.' Unlike the man co-opted by *The Times*, Holmes was one of the experts he mentioned. Parnell was forty-six; Pigott, the likely forger if the letters were false, was sixty. Holmes had little difficulty in appreciating, from this one characteristic alone, that the letters could not have been written by Parnell.

After consultation with Mycroft, Holmes had decided that the vindication of Parnell, apart from fitting better with the brothers' sense of justice and fair play, was a better outcome for the British establishment. Distracted as he was by other cases, he nonetheless plunged once more into the investigation of Parnell's and Pigott's affairs. Shortly he discovered a letter written by Pigott three days before the publication of 'Parnellism and Crime' in *The Times*. It provided him with the hook on which to hang the forger. When Pigott appeared before the Parnell commission, the man charged with cross-examining him, Charles Russell QC, later Lord Chief Justice of England, was armed with the information Holmes had unearthed. Holmes suggested that Russell ask Pigott to write several words on a piece of paper as soon as he rose to cross-examine him. One of the words Holmes suggested was 'hesitancy'. Pigott spelled it 'hesitency', just as it had appeared in the Parnell letters. The mistake was a damning one. Pigott was, by this time, at the end of his tether. Under Russell's relentless questioning, he was made to look the rogue and liar he was. The next day, 25 February 1889, the commission was due to sit again and Pigott's crucifixion by cross-examination would continue. The forger, however, was conspicuously absent, having fled the country. He was eventually traced to Madrid but, as the English police entered his hotel intent on questioning him further, he shot himself.

Parnell, thanks in no small part to Holmes's work behind the scenes, had been vindicated. He received compensation from *The Times* as well as a standing ovation, led by Gladstone, when he entered the chamber of the House of Commons.

CHAPTER FIVE

'YOU SHOULD PUBLISH
AN ACCOUNT OF THE CASE'

As HOLMES'S REAL LIFE UNFOLDED, with its catalogue of
murder, espionage and scandal, his extraordinary parallel life
in print was about to be born. Unless Watson is embellishing
his memory retrospectively, the thought of recording his new
friend's cases had occurred to him in the course of the very first
investigation he had witnessed, which he later published as *A Study
in Scarlet*:

'It is wonderful!' I cried. 'Your merits should be publicly recognised. You
should publish an account of the case. If you won't, I will for you.'
    'You may do what you like, Doctor,' he answered.

It may well be that Watson had written down the story of the
Lauriston Gardens mystery soon after Holmes had revealed the
truth behind the deaths of Drebber and, later, Stangerson but,
unable to think of a means of getting it into print, had tucked it

away in a drawer at Baker Street. Now he was to meet the man who could provide him with the opportunity he lacked.

Watson's last-minute decision to attend a doctors' dinner at the Guildhall in November 1885 was to have momentous consequences. Sitting next to him at the table was a physician who had travelled up to town from his home in Southsea near Portsmouth. He was young, Scottish and his name was Arthur Conan Doyle. Conan Doyle, born in Edinburgh on 22 May 1859, came from a family of artists and illustrators – his uncle worked for *Punch* and his grandfather had been a political caricaturist. A Catholic, Doyle had been educated at the Jesuit-run school at Stonyhurst before returning to his home city to study medicine at the University of Edinburgh. Much of Doyle's early life had been overshadowed by the decline of his father, Charles Altamont Doyle, who was a chronic alcoholic. After losing his job as a civil servant, Doyle Senior spent years cloistered in asylums or lodged in the top floor of the family home, an embarrassment to all. After graduating from Edinburgh, Doyle had briefly spent time as a medical officer aboard a ship trading between Liverpool and the west coast of Africa. Eventually he accepted the offer of a fellow Edinburgh graduate, George Turnavine Budd, to join him in a doctor's practice in Plymouth. The decision was a disastrous one. Not only was Budd tantamount to a charlatan, with some idiosyncratic ideas about how to ensure his patients' health, he also had little compunction about using other people's money as if it were his own. Doyle was lucky to escape from Budd's clutches and was able in time to open his own practice in Southsea.

From this very first meeting, Watson and Doyle found they had much in common. Watson's Scottish ancestry and the coincidence of both men having links with Southsea would have provided initial topics of conversation. Although it is unlikely to have come up at this first meeting, Watson and Doyle shared dark secrets. They both knew what it was to have an alcoholic in the family. Drink had ruined Watson's elder brother. Holmes's words in *The Sign of Four* may be intended as one of his self-consciously theatrical demonstrations of deductive skill but they provide a painfully accurate summary of Henry Watson's short and unsuccessful life: 'He was a man of untidy habits – very untidy and careless. He was left with good prospects, but he threw away his chances, lived for some time in poverty with occasional short intervals of prosperity, and finally, taking to drink, he died.' Doyle's father had drowned the artistic talent he possessed in a sea of alcohol and was to die, after years in asylums and private rest homes, in 1893.

At what stage of the evening Watson first mentioned the extraordinary man who was his fellow lodger in Baker Street we cannot know. Doyle, however, would have been instantly intrigued. As well as struggling to establish himself as a doctor, Doyle had literary ambitions. His first story, 'The Mystery of Sasassa Valley', had been published in *Chamber's Journal* in Edinburgh when he was still a student and he had continued to supplement his sometimes meagre earnings as a physician with stories submitted to the enormous range of magazines that existed at the time. When he and Watson met, Doyle's greatest literary success had been a story titled 'J. Habakuk Jephson's Statement', published anonymously in the *Cornhill* magazine in 1883. Unlike his other stories, which had made little impression, this one had aroused controversy. The tale was loosely based on the mysterious, and now legendary, disappearance of the captain and crew of the *Mary Celeste*. A British official who had been involved in the salvage of that vessel in 1872, mistaking fiction for a statement of supposed fact, was outraged by it. By huffing and puffing about the account being 'a fabrication from beginning to end' and by speculating on the damage it might do, the official only made himself look ridiculous. But his reaction was a backhanded tribute to the power of Doyle's imagination and brought 'J. Habakuk Jephson's Statement' more attention than it might otherwise have received. With this experience in mind, Doyle may well have been on the lookout for further true stories that he could embellish with a fictional gloss.

In Watson's strange friend, he may have sensed possibilities. Certainly, in the weeks after his first meeting with Watson, Doyle himself toyed with the idea of writing a story based on what his new acquaintance had told him. Notes exist in Doyle's handwriting in which he records the less than impenetrable pseudonym of Sherrinford Holmes for the detective and Ormond Sacker as a disguise for Watson. After a further dinner with Watson, during which the doctor showed him his own narrative, Doyle, recognizing the worth of what he read, abandoned his own attempt and agreed to act as literary agent for Watson. He probably felt little real concern about relinquishing any ambition to write the Holmes stories himself. Conan Doyle always believed that his true vocation lay in the writing of historical fiction and, to the end of his life, was most proud – not of his association with Holmes and Watson – but of novels such as *The White Company* and *Micah Clarke*. '*The White Company*,' he once wrote, 'was worth a hundred Sherlock Holmes stories.' In an article published in an American magazine as late as 1923 he could still write, 'I believe that if I had never touched Holmes, who has tended to obscure my higher work, my position in literature would at the present moment be a more commanding one.' In the 1880s, however, all the fame and furore that attached themselves to the Holmes name lay in the future. Whatever he claimed later, Conan Doyle was happy enough to take on the task of literary agent for Watson.

Readers today are surprised by Doyle's difficulties in finding a publisher for the manuscript Watson gave him. How could publishers not have seen the potential in the work? Yet *A Study in Scarlet*, as the two men had entitled the narrative, was sent to several publishers in the summer of 1886 without attracting any interest or offers to publish. A publisher by the name of Arrowsmith returned the manuscript in July of that year and Doyle only achieved similar results with others. Watson, who was at this stage uncommitted to the task of publicizing his friend's career and who had received little encouragement from Holmes himself, suggested that they forget the entire scheme but Doyle persisted. Eventually, in October 1886, he received a letter from Ward, Lock & Co: 'Dear Sir – We have read your story and are pleased with it. We could not publish it this year, as the market is flooded at present with cheap fiction, but if you do not object to its being held over till next year, we will give you twenty-five pounds for the copyright.' It was scarcely the ringing endorsement of his work that Watson had hoped for, nor was the money sufficient to excite either of them, but Doyle persuaded his client that they should accept Ward Lock's terms.

The narrative finally appeared in November 1887 in *Beeton's Christmas Annual*, published by Ward Lock and founded several decades earlier by Samuel Orchard Beeton, husband of Mrs Beeton, the famous cook and author of *The Book of Household Management*.

The first publication of Watson's account of his remarkable friend was not without its problems. Early attempts to find a satisfactory illustrator for his memoir had been attended by fiasco and embarrassment. In *Beeton's Christmas Annual*, the narrative had been illustrated by D. H. Friston, an uninspired but competent hack. When Ward Lock reissued *A Study in Scarlet* as a separate paperback in 1888, Doyle, without consulting Watson or Holmes, asked his own father to produce six illustrations. Although a touching demonstration of filial piety, it was also an error of judgement. By this time Charles Altamont Doyle, ravaged by years of alcohol abuse and mental turmoil, was very ill. His son, however, continued to believe in his father's talent. 'My father's life was full of the tragedy of unfulfilled powers and of underdeveloped gifts,' he once wrote. 'He had his weaknesses, as all of us have ours, but he also had some very remarkable and outstanding virtues.' The son remained committed to the hope that he could reveal those unfulfilled powers and the new edition of the Holmes story seemed to offer an ideal opportunity.

Charles Doyle failed to rise to the occasion: the illustrations were very poor. Watson, who knew something of Charles Doyle's history, kept his own counsel. Holmes, who knew nothing of Charles Doyle (and, one suspects, would not have much cared even if he had known the little Watson did), was furious. He had maintained the pretence of lofty indifference to his appearance before the public but, in fact, he had closely followed Doyle's attempts to get the story published. To be shown as he was in Charles Doyle's illustrations – a rather dozy-looking figure, only a few stages beyond a childishly drawn stick-man, who sported a straggling beard – was a severe affront to his considerable *amour propre*. Holmes complained bitterly to Doyle. It was the beginning of the ambivalence that was to characterize their relationship for the next forty years.

The problem of illustrating the Holmes stories was not solved until the first appearance of *The Adventures of Sherlock Holmes* in *The Strand Magazine* in 1891, after Holmes had supposedly disappeared over the Reichenbach Falls. Even then, the solution owed more to chance than careful planning. Walter Paget was a young illustrator with a growing reputation. The art editor of *The Strand* decided to approach him to work on the Holmes stories. Unfortunately for Walter, the letter offering the commission was mistakenly addressed to his older brother Sidney, also an illustrator but a less successful one. Paget was faced by a problem. Watson was insistent that the artist should not base his illustrations too closely on his late friend's real appearance but Paget found it difficult to come up with an adequate image. (Characteristically, Holmes, when he later returned from the dead, was quick to endorse the ban that Watson had placed on the use of his own features, but was equally quick to condemn Paget's work.) The deerstalker, which came to be so closely associated with Holmes, may have been part of Paget's solution to the problem. His other strategy was to base his conception of Holmes on someone he knew very well indeed – his brother Walter, the man who could so easily have become the illustrator of the stories.

In the absence of any indisputably authentic photographs of Holmes, it is difficult to know whether or not Paget preserved anything of the detective's appearance in his illustrations. We are thrown back on the words of those who did know Holmes. According to Conan Doyle, 'He was a more beaky-nosed, hawk-faced man, approaching more to the Red Indian type, than the artist represented him.' The best source, as usual, is Watson. From the many passing descriptions of Holmes in the doctor's narratives, we can build up as accurate a portrait as we can hope to achieve. Holmes was a tall man, 'rather over six feet', thin-faced and with a large forehead. Black-haired (at least until the grey of middle age overtook him), Holmes had piercing, grey eyes, dark and heavy brows and a thin, 'hawklike' nose.

While the early fruits of Watson's and Doyle's collaboration appeared in the late 1880s, Holmes's career was, of course, advancing regardless. Watson records a number of cases from that year. The adventures to which he gives the titles 'The Reigate Squire', 'The Naval Treaty', 'The Crooked Man', 'The Five Orange Pips' and 'The Noble Bachelor' all report events from 1887. By Watson's costive standards this is a positive deluge of material. One case, which Watson only mentions in passing, proves as mysterious as any in Holmes's career. What was the exact nature of the events that took up so much of the detective's energy and resources in the early part of 1887?

Watson leaves us in no doubt that the case of 'Baron Maupertuis' was one of the most exhausting and demanding of Holmes's career. He describes how, in the middle of April 1887, he is summoned by telegram to Lyons where Holmes is lying on his sickbed. 'Even his iron constitution,' Watson tells us, 'had broken down under the strain of an investigation which had extended over two months, during which period he had never worked less than fifteen hours a day and had more than once ... kept to his task for five days at a stretch.' That it was a case that attracted much public attention, Watson also makes clear, writing of 'a time when Europe was ringing with his [Holmes's] name and when his room was literally ankle-deep with congratulatory telegrams'.

The difficulty is that no other records exist of 'the whole question of the Netherland-Sumatra Company and of the colossal schemes of Baron Maupertuis'. Indeed, there is no knowing who Baron Maupertuis was. No Dutch financier or aristocrat of that name figures in the history of late nineteenth-century Europe. No writer of the period other than Watson refers to a financial scandal involving a Netherland-Sumatra Company. Once again, we have to assume that Watson was disguising the true facts of the case beneath aliases and invented names. Indeed, he suggests as much when he refuses to elaborate on the case and tells us that the details of it 'are too intimately concerned with politics and finance to be fitting subjects for this series of sketches'.

The most likely explanation is that Watson was referring to Holmes's investigation of the parlous financing of the Panama

Canal in the 1880s and that he is using the pseudonym Baron Maupertuis to hide the identity of Count Ferdinand de Lesseps, whose attempts to repeat his triumph in building the Suez Canal by dividing Central America with a similar waterway ended in a welter of disease, disaster and financial mismanagement. No other 'colossal schemes', with such international repercussions, fit the bill.

By the middle of 1887, Holmes was obliged to put the terrible exertions of the de Lesseps case behind him. Another, even more potentially world-shattering crime demanded his attention. Walter Bagehot once wrote that the English people 'defer to what we may call the theatrical show of society. A certain state passes before them; a certain pomp of great men; a certain spectacle of beautiful women; a wonderful scene of wealth and enjoyment is displayed, and they are coerced by it . . . The climax of the play is the Queen.' Of no event during Victoria's lifetime could this be more truly said than of the Golden Jubilee, marking fifty years of her reign, but, had it not been for Holmes, the Jubilee could have ended in chaos and tragedy. There is no doubt that Moriarty and his confederates had a sensational act of terrorism planned for the day.

There had been previous attempts on the queen's life. In fact, the many decades of her rule had been peppered by failed assassinations, nearly all the work of those who deserved, and received, incarceration in a lunatic asylum rather than the full penalty that the law decreed for treason. In 1872 there had even been an attack on her that was motivated by British policy in Ireland. A seventeen-year-old relation of the old Chartist leader Feargus O'Connor pointed a pistol at the queen as she was alighting from a carriage outside Buckingham Palace. The weapon was not loaded, however, and the young O'Connor was swiftly overpowered. At his trial, although he persisted in claiming that his aim had been to draw attention to the plight of Fenian prisoners in England – a rational enough motivation – he was deemed insane.

The most recent attack had taken place at Windsor station in 1882, when a young man called Roderick Maclean had fired a pistol at the queen as she sat in her carriage. He was a poor shot and missed. Victoria did not even realize until later what had happened, under the impression that the shot was a noise from the railway engine. Maclean had already spent part of his young life in one asylum and, after a trial at Reading Assizes, he was swiftly returned to another. But the assassination plot now being timed to coincide with the Jubilee was in a different league to these pathetic gestures by deranged and unstable young men.

The procession on 21 June 1887 was to wind through the capital from Buckingham Palace to Westminster Abbey and back. The weather in London that day was glorious and the sun shone from a blue sky. The spectacle in the streets was of a kind that had not been witnessed within living memory. One observer wrote of what seemed like 'a majestic river whose surface glittered incessantly in the powerful rays of the noonday sun' as it flowed through the city. The glitter came from 'sabres and decorations, from the rich trappings and dazzling weapons of the Indian escort, not the least impressive accompaniment of the procession'. Amid all the glamour of the spectacle, Moriarty's hired assassins were poised to strike. Alerted by Holmes, the authorities had sent a coded message to the professor in the shape of an article in *The Times* the previous month, predicting that an attack was planned. The idea had been to warn Moriarty that he had been rumbled but, fuelled by the intellectual arrogance that was central to his character, the professor remained convinced that the assassination attempt should go ahead.

The plan was bold in its simplicity. Today, when heads of state are surrounded by the most elaborate and intensive networks of security, it is difficult to grasp that in the nineteenth century monarchs were often relatively exposed. As Victoria stepped from her coach at the Abbey, she would be in full view of the crowds for several minutes. Moriarty was banking on the security services believing that any attack would be an explosive one. The record of Fenian attacks in London in the 1880s certainly suggested this. He was quite happy for the authorities to undertake, as they did, the most minute search of the Abbey and its environs in search of bombs. He had no intention of planting bombs. His plan was to have two marksmen armed with the latest Lebel rifles, the first weapon in the world to use smokeless gunpowder, in place near the Abbey. One of the marksmen was almost certainly Colonel Sebastian Moran.

Moran, whom we shall encounter several times later in this biography, was born in 1840, the son of the diplomat Sir Augustus Moran, one-time British Minister to Persia, and was educated at Eton and Oxford. He had been recruited into Moriarty's organization some years earlier, when he had returned to London from service in the Indian army. Although he came from a family with Irish connections, Moran's motives for his crimes seem to have been entirely financial. On Jubilee Day 1887 he and an associate, armed with their Lebels, were hidden on an upper floor of the Royal Aquarium opposite Westminster Abbey. The Royal Aquarium was more than its name suggested. Built in 1876 as a palace of entertainment, it contained not only tanks full of fish for the edification of visitors but an array of other facilities, including a skating rink, reading rooms, a theatre and an art gallery. Most conveniently for Moriarty's purpose, the windows on its front elevation provided a clear line of fire at the royal coach.

As the day of the Jubilee dawned, Holmes was just about the only man who still had doubts that any attack on the queen would involve explosives. Plenty of coded messages between Moriarty and his followers had been intercepted but several remained undeciphered. One in particular, in which the same mysterious word was repeated four times, continued to defeat all of Holmes's efforts to decode it. It seems likely that it was only on the very morning of 21 June that he uncovered its meaning. The word was 'aquarium'. Instantly realizing what was planned, Holmes, together with Watson and a hastily assembled group of policemen led by Lestrade, forced entry into the Royal Aquarium even as the queen's coach was setting off on its journey. The two would-be assassins were surprised. Somehow Moran escaped, evading the police in the interconnecting corridors and rooms of the Aquarium, but his associate was captured. The authorities were doubtless expecting him to provide them with valued information about Moriarty's organization. However, it was not to be. Housed temporarily in Pentonville Prison, he was found in his cell with his throat cut. His identity has never been established.

The case of de Lesseps and the Panama Canal, hidden under the disguises Watson uses and the false trails he lays, was a time-consuming and energy-sapping investigation. So too was the race Holmes undertook in that same year to prevent the intended assassination of the queen at the Jubilee celebrations. There were other cases, some of which Watson is happy to relate. The tragic story of the Openshaws and the seemingly harmless orange pips which, delivered in a letter, were harbingers of death, is one. However, there are others to which he refers only in passing. Watson also mentions accounts 'of the adventure of the Paradol Chamber, of the Amateur Mendicant Society, who held a luxurious club in the lower vault of a furniture warehouse, of the facts connected with the loss of the British bark *Sophy Anderson*, of the singular adventures of the Grice Patersons in the island of Uffa, and finally of the Camberwell poisoning case'.

Some of these references are easier to interpret than others. By the Camberwell poisoning case, Watson almost certainly means to refer to the case of Adelaide Bartlett who stood trial in 1886 for murdering her husband with liquid chloroform. Both the date and the London location (the mysterious death of Thomas Edwin Bartlett occurred in Pimlico) correspond closely enough to suggest that Watson was making an attempt, but not a very effective one, to mask Holmes's involvement in that sensational murder trial. His reasons for doing so are unclear but it was not a satisfactory case for anyone connected to the prosecution. Adelaide Bartlett was acquitted of murder, although it seems almost certain that she had in fact killed her husband. After the trial, an eminent surgeon at St Bartholomew's Hospital, Sir James Paget, is reported to have said, 'Now that it is all over, she should tell us, in the interest of science, how she did it.' If Holmes was one of those who had failed to prove Bartlett's guilt, Watson probably felt no desire to draw too much attention to his failure.

Possibly the only benefit to Holmes of the Bartlett case was that it brought him into contact with a man who was to remain a friend for forty years. Sir Edward Clarke was the defence barrister whose skilful cross-examination of prosecution witnesses did much to save his client from the gallows. Whatever his other faults, Holmes was usually appreciative of brilliance in opponents, and he and Clarke seem to have recognized each other's worth. One of the very few surviving letters to Holmes turned up in a Lincolnshire saleroom in the 1950s. It is a short missive written by Clarke in the 1920s in which, in reminiscent mood, he refers to 'our opposing interpretations of that remarkable woman, Mrs Bartlett'. Holmes and Clarke were to meet on other cases in the future.

Other references are more puzzling. The Grice Patersons, whoever they may have been, would have had difficulty in having any adventures, singular or otherwise, on the island of Uffa because no such island exists. It may be that Watson was once again passing on misinformation deliberately, but it seems more likely that he had once again made a mistake. Watson's remark about Holmes's 'summons to Odessa in the case of the Trepoff murder' is another of those enigmatic, offhand comments that pepper his narratives. In 1878, Vera Zassulitch, a young woman outraged by the flogging of a political prisoner, shot the St Petersburg chief of police General Trepoff, wounding him seriously but not fatally. The date, the location, the fact that the general did not die and also that there was little mystery attached to the shooting (Zassulitch was only too keen to claim credit for her action) all suggest that this was not the case Watson had in mind. Yet the possibility remains that the doctor was referring obliquely to a visit to Russia that Holmes had made early in his career. Another of Watson's oblique remarks, to Holmes's 'clearing up of the singular tragedy of the Atkinson brothers at Trincomalee', suggests another journey that the detective made to far-flung places – in this case, Ceylon (now Sri Lanka) – but again we have no independent evidence to confirm this.

We are on firmer ground when it comes to Holmes's involvement in two breakdowns in public order that shocked the authorities in London in the late 1880s. On Monday, 8 February 1886, two left-wing groups, the London United Workmen's Committee and the Social Democratic Federation (a Marxist party led by the eccentric Cambridge-educated journalist H. M. Hyndman), announced meetings in Trafalgar Square to protest against unemployment. Holmes, through the network of contacts he had made as a result of his Irish investigations, was fully aware of the potential for unrest that the meetings represented. He fired off a series of telegraphic warnings to his brother, to the Home Secretary and to anyone else he thought might have the power to act decisively. They were largely ignored. Few believed that trouble might be brewing. To Holmes's exasperation, police preparations were laughably inadequate. The man given the responsibility for maintaining public order, District Superintendent Robert Walker, was in his seventies. His main contribution to the day's proceedings was to get himself lost in the crowds and have his pocket picked.

In Trafalgar Square, the crowds were addressed by Hyndman. The writer Edward Carpenter has left a compelling description of Hyndman as public speaker:

On the platform, with his waving beard and flowing frock-coat, his high and spacious forehead and head somewhat low and weak behind, he gave one rather the impression of a shop whose goods are all in the front window; and though a good and incisive speaker his frequent gusts of invective seemed out of keeping with the obvious natural kindliness of the man and rather suggested the idea that he was lashing himself up with his own tail.

Hyndman's rhetoric on this occasion left large numbers in the crowds roused but unsatisfied and, after the speeches were over, they showed little inclination to disperse. Walker's men proved little better than their commanding officer. As thousands left the square in the direction of fashionable Piccadilly and St James's, intent on smashing windows and intimidating their social superiors, the police stayed put. Still standing close to Nelson's Column, they looked to one sarcastic journalist present as if they were 'propping it up ... lest it should topple, or keeping watch upon the lions for fear they should run away'. Rather to Holmes's satisfaction, no doubt, Black Monday (as it came to be called) cost the Metropolitan Police Commissioner, Sir Edmund Henderson, his job.

Black Monday proved only a dress rehearsal for Bloody Sunday, 13 November 1887. Since the summer, bands of unemployed men had been living rough in Trafalgar Square. The new Commissioner, Sir Herbert Warren, requested a ban on all meetings in the Square to which the Home Secretary eventually agreed. Holmes, whose warnings about police laxity eighteen months earlier had gone unheard, was aware now, as he told Mycroft, that the authorities had swung to the other extreme and that this new decision could prove provocative. However, the warnings of both Holmes brothers had now become little more than irritating background buzzings to the men in real authority. There was little chance of their concerns being given a hearing. Again Hyndman's SDF called a meeting to protest against unemployment and to challenge the ban.

Edward Carpenter was on hand to record the events of that day. This time the police were taking no chances and waded into the crowds without warning.

I was in the Square at the time. The crowd was a most good-humoured, easy going, smiling crowd; but presently it was transformed. A regiment of mounted police came cantering up. The order had gone forth that we were to be kept moving. To keep a crowd moving is I believe a technical term for the process of riding roughshod in all directions, scattering, frightening and batoning the people. I saw my friend Robert

Muirhead seized by the collar by a mounted man and dragged along, apparently towards a police station, while a bobby on foot aided in the arrest. I jumped to the rescue and slanged the two constables, for which I got a whack on the cheek-bone from a baton, but Muirhead was released.

There were more than a hundred casualties and at least two deaths on the day. Holmes, vindicated but disheartened, could only mull over his apparent inability to get his voice heard in Whitehall.

In the year after Bloody Sunday there were plenty of opportunities for Holmes to withdraw from the public role that he had occasionally adopted into a more private arena. In one case, in particular, he returned to a milieu and to people familiar from his undergraduate days. We have seen that, despite the rigorous scepticism he later practised, Holmes had flirted with psychical research during his years at Cambridge and had been an acquaintance of the psychologist Edmund Gurney, a fellow of Trinity College. Gurney, a charismatic figure in Cambridge, was intellectually brilliant, a great athlete and famous for his startling good looks. (George Eliot was so taken by him that, for several days after their first meeting, she could think of nothing else but his handsome features and she is alleged to have used him as the basis for her character Daniel Deronda.) Holmes had put behind him his interest in what he described in *The Hound of the Baskervilles* as that 'realm in which the most acute and most experienced of detectives is helpless' and his later ideas on the subject are indicated clearly enough by the gentle mockery with which he greets Mortimer's concerns about the Hound itself. Gurney, however, continued to look for scientific means to investigate psychic phenomena.

His own interest in any possible survival after death can only have been increased by an appalling tragedy in which three of his sisters drowned when the yacht on which they were sightseeing in Egypt sank in the Nile.

Together with his Cambridge colleagues, F. H. Myers and Henry Sidgwick, Gurney was a founder member of the Society for Psychical Research (SPR) in 1882 and, four years later, he published *Phantasms of the Living*, a monumental volume analysing hundreds of cases of seeming apparitions and ghosts. After their brief collaboration in Cambridge, Holmes and Gurney had, as far as is known, no further contact. Nevertheless, both Myers and Sidgwick knew of Holmes's growing reputation and his past link with Gurney, so when, in June 1888, the latter was found dead in a Brighton hotel in mysterious circumstances, it was unsurprising that his friends and family should invite the detective to make discreet inquiries into the circumstances.

Gurney was only forty-one when he died. He had been summoned to Brighton by a letter from an unknown correspondent and had left home without explaining to his wife, or anyone else, his reasons for going. After signing the register at the Royal Albion Hotel, he had retired for the night and had been found dead in his bed the next morning. A chloroform pad was clamped over his mouth. Gurney was known to make use of chloroform as a painkiller and the first assumption was that he had accidentally overdosed on it. Indeed, the coroner's verdict was one of 'accidental death'. The second thought of many close to him who knew of his slightly depressive personality was that he had killed himself. Neither of these hypotheses explained the mysterious letter that had taken him down to the south coast. Myers and Sidgwick suspected that his death might have been a consequence of his work with the Society for Psychical Research.

Holmes's investigations, although inconclusive, suggested that they were right. He soon found evidence that Gurney had been heavily involved in psychic experimentation with George Albert Smith, a colourful showman. Half charlatan and half genius, Smith was later to become one of the pioneers of British cinema, making a series of short films in the late 1890s that are among the most imaginative produced in those very early days. He began his career, however, as a stage hypnotist and illusionist. How he met Gurney is unclear but, for several years before the tragedy, the two men were in close contact. Naively, the Cambridge academic not only believed that Smith had genuine powers as a mind-reader but had even employed him, in an unofficial capacity, as his private secretary. Holmes was convinced that it was the revelation that Smith had deceived him, and that the work they had done together was valueless, that drove Gurney to take his own life.

Confronted by Holmes, Myers and Sidgwick, Smith confessed that his supposed mind-reading was nothing more than stage trickery but he refused to take any responsibility for Gurney's death. He was in a strong position. Myers and Sidgwick, who had no desire to advertise the fact that their friend's death carried the stigma of suicide, were not going to instigate any legal proceedings against Smith. Indeed, they continued to employ him in SPR work and he was quoted as joint author of a paper published by the Society in the year after Gurney's death. Presumably, Smith was able to use the threat of telling what he knew to put pressure on the two academics. There may even have been darker secrets in Gurney's life which his friends were unwilling to see come to light. It is more than likely that Gurney was homosexual and it is possible that this provided Smith with further ammunition to back up his threats. It was only when his inventive imagination was drawn to the possibilities of magic lantern shows and the new moving pictures that he decided to relinquish his blackmailer's power.*

Immersed in the extraordinary complexities of Irish politics, struggling to deal with the public order problems that had resulted in Black Monday and Bloody Sunday, and drawn into personal investigations such the inquiry into the death of Gurney, Holmes had much to occupy him in the years 1886 to 1888. He was, however, about to be press-ganged unwillingly into the most sensational and longest-remembered crime of the late nineteenth century.

---

* Smith, clearly one of life's survivors, lived on until 1959. When he died, at the age of ninety-five, he had been rediscovered by film historians and, acclaimed as 'the father of British cinema', was made an honorary fellow of the British Film Academy.

CHAPTER SIX

'I'VE HAD TO DO WITH
FIFTY MURDERERS'

ALTHOUGH IT HAS BEEN ARGUED that other, earlier murders in the East End were the work of the man later known as Jack the Ripper, the first undisputed Ripper killing took place on 31 August 1888. The body of Mary Ann Nichols, known as Polly, was found in the early hours of the morning, lying in a narrow, cobbled street that was called Buck's Row at the time and was later renamed Durward Street. Her throat had been cut and her attacker had stabbed her viciously and repeatedly in the abdomen. Polly Nichols had last been seen at 2.30 a.m. by fellow prostitute Emily Holland who reported that she was drunk and looking for a customer to provide her with the few pence she needed to get a bed in a cheap lodging house in Flower and Dean Street. 'I've had my doss money three times today and spent it,' she told her friend before staggering off in search of her last trick.

All of the Ripper victims were drunk, or under the influence of drink, at the time of their deaths. Drink was omnipresent in the slums of the East End. As the writer George Sims noted in his book *Horrible London*:

On a Saturday night, butchers, bakers, greengrocers, clothiers, furniture dealers, all the caterers for the wants of the populace, are open till a late hour; there are hundreds of them trading around and about, but the whole lot do not take as much money as three publicans – that is a fact ghastly enough in all conscience. Enter the public-houses, and you will see them crammed. Here are artisans and labourers drinking away the wages that ought to clothe their little ones. Here are the women squandering the money that would purchase food, for the lack of which the children are dying. The time to see the result of a Saturday night's heavy drinking in a low neighbourhood is after the houses are closed. Then you meet dozens of poor wretches reeling home to their miserable dens; some of them roll across the roadway and fall, cutting themselves till the blood flows. Every penny in some instances has gone in drink.

The killing of Polly Nichols was shocking but, at this stage, seemed no different from other murders that were committed, all too frequently, in the squalid streets of the East End. Just over a week later, however, on 8 September, the body of Annie Chapman was found in a backyard in Hanbury Street. Her throat had also been cut and she had been almost disembowelled by her killer. According to the doctor who examined the body, the injuries to the abdomen were not random slashings but showed that Chapman's murderer possessed considerable anatomical knowledge.

The night of 30 September brought two new murders. Elizabeth Stride, a Swedish woman who had lived in London for more than twenty years, had been seen by witnesses talking to a man on Berner Street at about 12.40 a.m. Twenty minutes later, salesman Louis Diemschutz was driving his pony and cart into

Dutfield's Yard, off Berner Street, when the animal shied abruptly and refused to go on. In the darkness Diemschutz prodded and poked with his whip to see whether there was anything preventing the pony going forward. There was. It was Elizabeth Stride's body. Her throat was cut but there were no further mutilations. In all likelihood, the Ripper was still hiding in the yard when Diemschutz arrived and only escaped after the salesman went for help. Less than an hour later, another body was found. It seemed as if the killer, disturbed by Diemschutz's arrival in the yard but still goaded by whatever inner demons pursued him, had sought out another victim. The unlucky woman was Catherine Eddowes, another of the almost destitute women who turned to prostitution in the streets of the East End. Earlier that evening, Eddowes had been arrested in Aldgate High Street where, outrageously drunk, she had been entertaining passers-by with her imitations of a fire engine's siren. Around 1 a.m., she had sobered sufficiently to be released from Bishopsgate police station, disappearing into the night with a cheery 'Goodnight, old cock' to the policeman who sent her on her way. She was last seen about half an hour later, standing on the corner of Duke Street and talking to an unknown man. Barely fifteen minutes after this, her severely mutilated body was found in Mitre Square.

By this time, hysteria had gripped both the inhabitants of the East End and the journalists and commentators of Fleet Street. This was only fuelled by the letters sent to the police and to George Lusk, the president of the newly formed Whitechapel Vigilance Committee, which supposedly came from the murderer himself. The letter sent to Lusk was particularly horrifying, not least because it accompanied half a human kidney preserved in wine.

From hell.

Mr Lusk,

Sor

I send you half the Kidne I took from one woman and prasarved it for you tother piece I fried and ate it was very nise. I may send you the bloody knif that took it out if you only wate a whil longer

signed

Catch me when you can Mishter Lusk

Despite the atmosphere of fear throughout the city, the prostitutes on the street often remained fatalistic about the prospect of encountering the Ripper and continued to ply their trade as usual. One police inspector in the East End reported that, 'for the sake of fourpence to get drunk on, they will go in any man's company, and run the risk that it is not him.' Often they had little choice. As the inspector continued, 'I tell many of them to go home, but they say they have no home, and when I try to frighten them and speak of the danger they run they'll laugh and say, "Oh, I know what you mean. I ain't afraid of him. It's the Ripper or the bridge with me."'

Along with the hysteria came the kind of half-appalled, half-prurient obsession with the killings that for more than a century has generated a veritable industry of supposition about the Ripper's true identity. By October 1888, when the killer was still roaming the streets and Holmes had yet to be called into the case, an exhibition opened in the East End in which, according to one visitor, 'there is a waxwork show with some horrible pictorial representations of the recent murders, and all the dreadful details are being bleated out into the night, and women with children in their arms are pushing their way to the front with their pennies to see the ghastly objects within.'

The most brutal of all the killings was yet to come. On 9 November the body of a young woman called Mary Kelly was found in a rented room in Miller's Court. Left alone with his victim behind a closed door, the Ripper's desires to mutilate and dismember had been allowed full rein. A short extract from the police surgeon's report on the body reveals only too graphically the extent of the indignities inflicted on Mary Kelly after her death. 'The whole of the surface of the abdomen and thighs was removed and the abdominal cavity emptied of its viscera. The breasts were cut off, the arms mutilated by several jagged wounds and the face hacked beyond recognition of the features. The tissues of the neck were severed all round down to the bone.' The murder of Mary Kelly was to be the last of the Ripper's crimes. Although some students of the case claim that other prostitutes in the East End – Alice McKenzie in July 1889, for example, and Frances Coles in February 1891 – met their deaths at the hands of the same killer, most agree that only five murders (those of Nichols, Chapman, Stride, Eddowes and Kelly) can be definitely ascribed to the Ripper.

Indirectly, it was at the queen's insistence that Holmes was brought into the Ripper investigation. In the days after the butchery and mutilation of Mary Kelly, the police seemed no nearer to tracking down the murderer. Victoria, who had, like so many of her subjects, followed the story of the Whitechapel murders with appalled fascination, was furious at what she saw as police incompetence. Some new initiative was needed and she wrote to the Prime Minister, Lord Salisbury, urging him to make it. 'This new most ghastly murder shows the absolute necessity for some very decided action ... our detectives [must be] improved.' To Salisbury there was only one option available. After nearly twenty years ambling along the corridors of power, Mycroft Holmes had reached a unique and almost unassailable position within Whitehall. Watson's words in 'The Adventure of the Greek Interpreter' provide the best surviving description of Holmes's elder brother as he was in his early forties: 'Mycroft Holmes was a much larger and stouter man than Sherlock. His body was absolutely corpulent, but his face, though massive, had preserved something of the sharpness of expression which was so remarkable in that of his brother. His eyes, which were of a peculiarly light, watery grey, seemed to always retain that far-away, introspective look which I had only observed in Sherlock's when he was exerting his full powers.' This was the man that the Prime Minister now approached. Salisbury knew and respected Mycroft and, although he had never met him, he knew of his younger brother's growing reputation of being able to throw light on the most impenetrably dark mysteries.

Thus, through Mycroft, the suggestion was made that Holmes might consider tracking down Jack the Ripper. The only surprise is that it had taken so long for Holmes to become drawn into the investigation. The probable explanation for this is that, caught up in their continuing investigations into the Fenians and other Irish nationalists, Mycroft and Sherlock were unwilling to be distracted by what they may have seen as a series of murders that, however brutal, were of less significance than threats to national security. Instructions from the widow of Windsor, however, were not to be ignored.

There are more candidates for the true identity of Jack the Ripper than there were dark alleyways in Whitechapel in 1888. The most unlikely and bizarre theories have been put forward to explain the motives behind the murders. Perhaps the most notorious was the claim, entertainingly advanced by Stephen Knight in his 1978 book *Jack the Ripper: The Final Solution*, that the murders were part of a conspiracy to cover up the fact that Prince Albert Victor Christian Edward ('Eddy' to his friends), son of the Prince of Wales and second in line to the throne, had fathered a love-child. The mother was not only an East End prostitute but, even worse, a Roman Catholic. Other prostitutes knew of the child's existence and who he was. To make sure they remained silent, they were all killed and the blame placed on a phantom serial killer. More recently the thriller writer Patricia Cornwell has argued that the painter Walter Sickert was the Ripper and that his dark secret is hidden away in hints and details in his later work. It is no less unlikely than the earlier scenario. Even more preposterous notions have been advanced, presumably in all seriousness, to explain the killings.

One theory claims that the true culprit was Dr Thomas Neill Cream, a deranged abortionist and poisoner who was executed in 1892 for administering strychnine to two prostitutes in South London. Cream is alleged to have been attempting a last-minute confession on the gallows when the executioner pulled the lever and he dropped through the trap. He got as far as, 'I am Jack—' before he fell. The difficulty with this story is that, at the time of the Whitechapel murders, records show that Cream was not only several thousand miles away but behind bars, serving a sentence in Joliet Penitentiary in Illinois. Some researchers, unwilling to relinquish a good story, have got round this apparently conclusive fact by arguing that it was possible that he paid a double to serve his sentence. The most generous assessment of this theory is that it seems implausible. An American researcher once 'proved' that elaborate analysis of the works of Lewis Carroll showed him to be the real Jack the Ripper. Even in the overheated world of Ripperology, this claim was not received with any great enthusiasm.

As for Holmes, his first task was to dispose of the idea that the letters had actually been sent by the murderer. Within days of joining the investigation, he had proved not only that they were fake but that at least one of them was the work of gutter press journalist Tom

Bulling. Although alert to the increasing importance of the press, Holmes was contemptuous of most journalists. He would have agreed with Matthew Arnold's claim that the new journalism of the period was 'full of ability, novelty, variety, sensation, sympathy, generous instinct: its one great failure is that it is feather-brained. It throws out assertions at a venture, because it wishes them to be true ... and to get at the state of things as they truly are, seems to have no concern whatever'. Pressure was placed on Bulling and he collapsed under it, admitting that Holmes was right and that he was the author of one of the most sensational letters. Why this information was not more widely publicized is difficult to fathom but many people today continue to believe that the Ripper letters were genuine.

Holmes carried on with his investigation of the murders but his usual methods of working were soon causing difficulties. When first dragooned into accepting that the consulting detective should investigate the case sub rosa, the Assistant Commissioner of the CID, Robert Anderson, had naively believed that Holmes could be kept firmly under control. Anderson knew Holmes from the work they had both done to combat Irish terrorism earlier in the decade and, to some extent, he liked and trusted him. However, he did not want him 'interfering' (as he saw it) in the Ripper case if it could be avoided. He seemed to expect Holmes to work on the case solely under the narrow guidelines he issued. Holmes, who was not an easy man to work with, had other ideas. 'As sensitive to flattery on the score of his art as any girl could be of her beauty', as he is described in *A Study in Scarlet*, Holmes needed the kind of tactful handling and freedom to manoeuvre that Anderson was not prepared to give. His habit of disappearing into the East End for days at a time, and returning to Scotland Yard dressed as a swaggeringly cocky costermonger to give enigmatic reports of his progress, did not endear him to Anderson and other senior policemen. Yet he did get results where so many had failed.

Trawl through the memoirs of the police officers involved in the Ripper case, from Sir Robert Anderson's to Walter Dew's, and you will find plenty of suggestions that someone, usually the officer whose recollections you are reading, knew who the Ripper was or, at the very least, had a strong suspicion of the killer's identity. Unfortunately, no two officers seem to agree. Often there is speculation that the Ripper committed suicide soon after the murder of Mary Kelly. All these stories can be traced back to Holmes who was the first to become convinced that the killer was himself dead and began to make converts to this theory among the higher echelons of the police. Other apparent murders, particularly those of Rose Mylett in December 1888 and Alice McKenzie, shook many in this belief but not Holmes. He pointed out that Mylett's death was almost certainly not a murder at all and that Alice McKenzie's killer had been left-handed, not, like the Whitechapel murderer, right-handed. To Holmes the evidence was clear and pointed in one direction only.

By the spring of 1889, Holmes was convinced that he knew the identity of the Ripper. The killer who had terrorized the East End was a man called Montague Druitt. The body of Druitt, an Oxford-educated* barrister and schoolmaster with a family history of mental illness, was fished out of the Thames on 31 December 1888. Holmes, newly involved in the investigation, had immediately decided that the Ripper could have committed suicide. With his usual devotion to scouring the more sordid details of the press, he had come across a report of Druitt's demise in the pages of an

---

* Druitt had been at Winchester before going up to Oxford. It is just possible that, although five years younger, he may have attended the school at the same time as Watson.

obscure West London paper and been intrigued. Further investigation into Druitt at first seemed to cast doubt on the possibility that he was indeed the murderer. The barrister was living at Blackheath at the time of the killings and train schedules suggested that it would have been impossible for him to travel freely from there to the East End at the times required. Holmes also discovered that Druitt, a keen sportsman, had played in a cricket match at Blackheath on 8 September a mere six hours after the murder of Annie Chapman. Druitt's legal chambers at 9 King's Bench Walk, however, were within walking distance of Whitechapel and, although unlikely, it was not inconceivable that a psychopathic killer could have been practising his off spin so soon after committing a murder.

Holmes was sufficiently impressed by coincidences of dates between the killings and Druitt's whereabouts, and by the similarity between the barrister's appearance and several of the witness descriptions of a man seen with the victims, to delve more deeply. In one of his forays into the East End in disguise, he seems to have picked up more conclusive proof that Druitt had a taste for the low-life and for slumming in the pubs and dives of Whitechapel. The clinching evidence appears to have come from an interview with Druitt's brother in which it became clear that the barrister's closest surviving relative had suspected, before the killing of Mary Kelly, that Montague was guilty of the murders. Holmes himself, in the wake of this interview, was equally convinced. His difficulty lay in winning over others.

Holmes's maverick approach to the investigation worked against him. By antagonizing Anderson and others in the police, he made it unnecessarily difficult to persuade them that he was right in his identification of Druitt. Eventually he grew weary when what was, to him, blindingly obvious remained, for others, one possibility among many, and he withdrew from the inquiry in disgust. The sole surviving evidence of Holmes's solution to the Jack the Ripper mystery lies in a memorandum written by one of the senior policemen involved in the case, Melville Macnaghten. 'From private information,' Macnaghten writes, referring to Holmes, 'I have little doubt that his own family suspected this man of being the Whitechapel murderer; it was alleged that he was sexually insane.'

For Watson, the Ripper case, however important it was nationally and however much it stretched his friend's resources, was not the most significant event of 1888. In September of that year, Mary Morstan arrived at 221B Baker Street to consult Holmes about the mystery surrounding her father's death.

Mary Morstan was born in 1861 in India, the daughter of an officer in an Indian regiment. Having lost her mother at an early age, she was sent back to England to be educated when still a small girl and lived in a boarding house in Edinburgh. In 1878 the mysterious disappearance of her father left her alone in the world and she was obliged to earn her living as a governess. Enigmatic messages in the advertisement columns of *The Times*, urging her to provide her address, led to the annual delivery of a valuable pearl and, eventually, to a note proposing a meeting with her anonymous benefactor. It was this that was the immediate cause of her arrival in Baker Street. Our only description of her comes through the immediately besotted eyes of Watson but it is clear that Mary Morstan was an attractive and appealing woman:

She was a blonde young lady, small, dainty, well gloved, and dressed in the most perfect taste. There was, however, a plainness and simplicity about her costume which bore with it a suggestion of limited means ... Her face had neither regularity of feature nor beauty of complexion, but her expression was sweet and amiable, and her large blue eyes were singularly spiritual and sympathetic. In an experience of women which extends over many nations and three separate continents, I have never looked upon a face which gave a clearer promise of a refined and sensitive nature.

That Watson was instantly struck by Mary Morstan is clear from his own words. After meeting her he records how he 'sat and mused until such dangerous thoughts came into my head that I hurried away to my desk and plunged furiously into the latest treatise upon pathology'. She also seems to have been impressed by the gallant and kind-hearted doctor. Only circumstances stood in the way of a match that both appear to have desired from the beginning. Throughout the events described in *The Sign of Four* it seems as if a resolution to the mystery surrounding her life will inevitably raise an insurmountable barrier to Watson's hopes. The Agra treasure, which is at the heart of the story, will transform her from a penniless governess to one of the richest heiresses in England and no suitable bride for an ex-army surgeon on a pension. Only when the treasure is lost in the Thames can Watson feel that Mary is within his reach again and make the declaration of his love. Only when the 'golden barrier' between them is removed can they arrange to marry.

After his marriage to Mary Morstan in late 1888, Watson was faced by the problem of how to earn a living. The army pension on which he had happily survived for more than seven years was not sufficient to support a wife. There was only one realistic option. His recent friendship with Conan Doyle and their collaboration on preparing Watson's narratives for publication must have suggested that he could make money from his writings. However, only one of the stories (*A Study in Scarlet*) had appeared and it had shown little sign of making Watson's fortune. He and Doyle had shared the £25 fee between them. He may have daydreamed of a future career as a writer but, in the last months of 1888, there were few indications of the startling success he was to enjoy later. It was inevitable that he would turn again to medicine to support himself and his new wife.

In the years since he had been invalided out of the army, Watson seems to have shown little enthusiasm for returning to work. He was not a particularly ambitious or energetic man and, drawn into the stimulating world of Sherlock Holmes, he had not seen any need for further activity beyond his involvement in his friend's varied cases. Nonetheless, it is clear that he had kept in touch with developments in medical science. As we have seen, in *The Sign of Four* he describes himself leafing through a textbook on pathology and, more surprisingly, in 'The Adventure of the Resident Patient' he is obviously familiar with Dr Percy Trevelyan's monograph upon obscure nervous lesions, a work that even its author believed had sunk into oblivion. Watson could therefore feel confident that, with luck and application, he would thrive as a general practitioner. Thus it was that in December 1888, he bought a practice in Paddington from an old and ailing doctor called Farquhar.

But his literary career was far from ended. Although *A Study in Scarlet* had scarcely set the Thames on fire, Watson and Doyle had enjoyed working together on it and they continued to meet occasionally to discuss the possibility of further collaboration. In August 1889, Doyle, who had published a number of his own stories in America, was contacted by Joseph Stoddart. The publisher of *Lippincott's Monthly Magazine* in Philadelphia, Stoddart was visiting London with the aim of setting up an English edition and recruiting promising young British writers to contribute to it. He invited Doyle to dinner at the Langham Hotel and, on hearing of the arrangement between Doyle and Watson, suggested that Watson should join them. The other guest was Oscar Wilde. What Watson, embodiment of the solid British virtues of dependability and common sense, made of the flamboyant aesthete Wilde is not recorded, but Doyle, at least, was charmed by the Irish wit and raconteur. Years later he was to recall that 'it was indeed a golden evening for me'. Two of the finest pieces of writing of the era – Watson's autobiographical narrative, *The Sign of Four*, and Wilde's fable of good and evil, *The Picture of Dorian Gray* – had their beginnings at this Langham Hotel dinner. It is unsurprising that Watson should have chosen the adventure known as *The Sign of Four** to relate that evening. Not only was the narrative – with its story of missing treasure and Oriental adventure, culminating in the dramatic pursuit of Jonathan Small and Tonga down the Thames – of intrinsic interest but it held a particular significance for him. It had been the means by which he was introduced to his first wife, Mary Morstan.

One of the results of Watson's marriage to Mary Morstan was inevitably that he saw Holmes much less frequently. 'My own complete happiness, and the home-centred interests which rise up around the man who first finds himself master of his own establishment,' he tells us, 'were sufficient to absorb all my attention.' In contrast Holmes 'remained in our lodgings in Baker Street, buried among his old books, and alternating from week to week between cocaine and ambition, the drowsiness of the drug, and the fierce energy of his own keen nature'.

---

* One anomaly in *The Sign of Four* is an intriguing one. Jonathan Small claims that his companions in crime were Sikhs but the names he gives are quite clearly not Sikh names. Why did Watson, who had spent time in India, not realize this?

CHAPTER SEVEN

'THE MANY CAUSES CÉLÈBRES AND SENSATIONAL TRIALS IN WHICH I HAVE FIGURED'

THE YEAR 1889 WAS A busy one for Holmes and, once again, Watson's accounts are as remarkable for those cases that they omit as they are for the ones that they relate. This was the year in which Holmes investigated the strange problem of the engineer Victor Hatherley and the murderous assault that cost him his thumb. It was the year in which the detective revealed the true identity of the beggar, Hugh Boone, whose 'hideous face is one which is familiar to every man who goes much to the City', and in which he shed light on the Boscombe Valley mystery. Watson provides vivid and compelling narratives of these cases. This was also the year in which Holmes was involved in the Cleveland Street scandal and the continuing investigation into the Whitechapel killings. Of these, Watson says not a word. Much of Holmes's work as an in-house detective to the English upper classes in the 1880s and 1890s has gone unrecorded, the victim of Watson's discreet censorship. It was a censorship that Holmes himself welcomed. As he remarks in 'The Adventure of the Copper Beeches':

It is pleasant to me to observe, Watson, that you have so far grasped this truth that in these little records of our cases which you have been good enough to draw up ... you have given prominence not so much to the many causes célèbres and sensational trials in which I have figured but rather to those incidents which may have been trivial in themselves, but which have given room for those faculties of deduction and of logical synthesis which I have made my special province.

We have already considered the role Holmes played in the Ripper murders. It is now time to turn to the Cleveland Street scandal. This was the first major homosexual sensation in Victorian England since 1870 and the trial of Boulton and Park, two androgynous young men who had delighted in donning silk and satin dresses to cruise the theatres and arcades of the Strand as 'Stella' and 'Fanny'. How far was Holmes involved in the cover-up that followed the police raid on 19 Cleveland Street on 6 July 1889? How far – and how discreditably – was he involved in the prosecution case that was brought against a journalist whose only crime seems to have been that he took too seriously his belief that the public had a right to know the truth behind the cover-up?

The Cleveland Street scandal began with an investigation into a possible theft at the Central Telegraph Office and the questioning of Thomas Swinscow, a teenage telegraph boy. Found with an inexplicably large sum of money on him, Swinscow denied any involvement in theft but, under pressure, admitted that he had been given the cash in return for sex with a number of men at a house, 19 Cleveland Street, belonging to one Charles Hammond. A police raid on Hammond's house revealed that he had fled the country (presumably he had been forewarned) but several of his accomplices, most importantly Henry Newlove, another telegraph boy, were later taken into custody.

Newlove chose to talk and, as he did so, police investigators began to shift uneasily in their chairs. Some of the people that he claimed were regular visitors to the house, and regular clients of the platoon of male prostitutes that Hammond entertained there, were prominent members of the social elite of Victorian England. One, Lord Arthur Somerset, was not only a royal equerry and a friend of the Prince of Wales but had served with the forces that were sent, unsuccessfully as it transpired, in 1885 to relieve General Gordon at Khartoum. Another, the Earl of Euston, was descended from Charles II and his mistress Barbara Villiers. Hints began to surface of even closer royal participation in the entertainments at Cleveland Street than mere visits by a descendant of one of the Merry Monarch's by-blows. The name of Prince 'Eddy', the Duke of Clarence and grandson of Queen Victoria, was mentioned.

It was at this point that the political and social establishment began to close ranks and arrange to protect its own. It did so in the shape of Mycroft Holmes, who decided that his brother Sherlock would be a valuable addition to the cover-up operation. Lord Arthur Somerset was hastily despatched abroad and Sherlock Holmes was instructed to make his own discreet inquiries into the affair in parallel with those of the police. All might have been kept under wraps if it had not been for the persistence of one radical journalist. Ernest Parke, editor of the weekly paper *The North London Press*, was unsatisfied by the official story. Describing it as 'a scandal of so horrible and repulsive a character that it would be better unmentioned if it were not necessary to expose the shameless audacity with which officials have contrived to shield the principal criminals', Parke went on the attack. He wondered how Hammond had known in advance of the raid on his Cleveland Street home and why Newlove and others had received such comparatively light sentences. Through contacts within the police, he learned of the allegations that Newlove had made about the involvement of members of the aristocracy in the affair and he even picked up the rumours about Prince Eddy. In November 1889, Parke published a story about the Cleveland Street scandal in which he named both Somerset and the Earl of Euston. In it, he also dropped very broad hints about the involvement of someone even more distinguished and highly placed. Somerset was taking his ease in the spa towns of Europe but the Earl of Euston, despite the urging of Mycroft, had declined to flee the country. He chose, again against the advice of both Holmes brothers, to bring a suit for libel against Parke. Parke honourably refused to name his sources, who had spoken to him in confidence, and was sentenced to a year in prison for contempt of court.

Holmes had undoubtedly played his part in framing the case against Parke – much of the information used to put pressure on the journalist came from him rather than the police – and it is difficult to see his involvement in anything other than an unfavourable light.

As the Cleveland Street case unfolded, Watson continued to create the narratives by which he was to become famous. Holmes himself was only the first of many people to underestimate Watson's skill as a writer and the sophistication with which he manipulated and reshaped the material he used. He may have had 'the impersonal joy of the true artist' in his own work but he was not always able to recognize artistry in someone else, least of all his closest comrade. Yet Watson worked hard to improve the material that reality offered. Presenting Holmes to the reading public was no easy task. Taking the real facts of a case and transforming them to meet the needs of the market – *The Strand Magazine* – that Doyle had found for him was only the first problem. The nature of Holmes's work meant that the details of the cases were often delicate. Discretion and an understanding of the threats implicit in libel law were needed. Sometimes straight reportage of a case was possible. Sometimes the real events in Holmes's career had to be transmogrified in the telling and the identities of real people hidden by false names and elaborate disguises.

Such a case was that of the blackmailer Charles Augustus Milverton. In the story published in *The Strand Magazine* in April 1904, Milverton is an oleaginous villain preying on aristocrats whose marital and amorous indiscretions have come to his attention. Holmes is disgusted by Milverton. 'I've had to do with fifty murderers in my career,' he says, 'but the worst of them never gave me the repulsion which I have for this fellow.' Holmes and Watson, breaking into Milverton's Hampstead home in search of incriminating material on a client, are witnesses to his murder by a woman driven to such a desperate act by his unwillingness to surrender compromising letters.

Much of this narrative, unlike the majority of Watson's tales, is pure fiction. There never was a Charles Augustus Milverton. The names that Watson uses both for the woman who approaches Holmes and for her fiancé (Lady Eva Blackwell and the Earl of Devoncourt respectively) are invented. He admits himself, in the opening lines of the narrative, that he has changed much of the story:

It is years since the incidents of which I speak took place, and yet it is with diffidence that I allude to them. For a long time, even with the utmost discretion and reticence, it would have been impossible to make the facts public; but now the principal person concerned is beyond the reach of human law, and with due suppression the story may be told in such fashion as to injure no one ... The reader will excuse me if I conceal the date or any other fact by which he might trace the actual occurrence.

Yet a real story does lurk beneath the fiction. There may not have been a blackmailer by the name of Charles Augustus Milverton who was murdered by one of his victims but there was one called Charles Augustus Howell who was found, his throat cut, in the gutter outside a Chelsea pub. Howell pursued his criminal trade in a very different milieu to the one evoked in Watson's story but there is little doubt that Watson based his narrative on Holmes's investigation of the man whom James McNeill Whistler once described as 'the genius, the superb liar, the Gil-Blas, the Robinson-Crusoe hero out of his proper time'.

Howell was a man of mystery. Born in Porto around 1840, the son of an English father and a Portuguese mother, he lived in England as a young man and somehow succeeded in ingratiating himself with the great and good of the London art world. During the late 1860s, he worked as secretary to John Ruskin but was dismissed in 1870. Whatever the reasons for his dismissal, Howell continued to maintain his contacts in the art world and acted as an agent for both Whistler and Dante Gabriel Rossetti in the sale of their works. It was Howell who persuaded Rossetti to undertake the bizarre exhumation of his wife's body in order to retrieve the manuscript of some poems that he had deposited in the coffin.

Charming but utterly unscrupulous, Howell was prepared to do almost anything to turn his friendship with these artists into money. After Rossetti's death, Howell and a female confederate produced faked drawings by the late Pre-Raphaelite (the forgeries are the subject of a caricature by Max Beerbohm with the title 'Mr — and Miss — nervously perpetuating the touch of a vanished hand'). Howell also began to exploit his possession of incriminating letters written to him by friends of Rossetti such as the poet Algernon Swinburne. Howell's method was to write to his victims claiming that he had been forced by circumstances to deposit the letters with a pawn-broker and that only payment of a substantial sum to redeem them would prevent the pawnbroker from selling them on to anyone who might be interested. Swinburne in particular, who had written Howell a sequence of indiscreet letters recording his fondness for flagellation, became a regular victim.

Holmes entered the case in the late 1880s, possibly at the request of Swinburne, and was gathering a portfolio of material proving Howell's disreputable dealings when, in 1890, the blackmailer's body was found outside the pub. The whole sordid business was largely hushed up, and Howell was said to have died in a hospital in Fitzroy Square from lung disease. His many victims breathed a collective sigh of relief. Holmes undoubtedly knew who had killed Howell but he chose not to reveal the murderer's identity. Why Watson chose to hide the facts in the Howell case so thoroughly is unclear. The likeliest explanation is that several of the people whom Howell had blackmailed were known to him. He certainly knew Swinburne and he was perhaps unwilling to risk even the slightest possibility that the names of people he respected would be recognized beneath any pseudonyms he might adopt.

Howell left few friends behind him. On hearing of his death, Swinburne wrote a gloating verse about it, which included the lines:

> The foulest soul that lived stinks here no more.
> The stench of hell is fouler than before!

Holmes and Watson would doubtless have agreed.

CHAPTER EIGHT

'I SHOULD NEVER MARRY...'

Holmes's attitude to women was that of an unrecon-structed misogynist. He bemoans women's supposed inability to reason and their assumed dependence on emotional whim and vanity. In 'The Adventure of the Second Stain' he reminds Watson of 'the woman at Margate' whom he suspected of deceit because she chose to sit in a chair with the light at her back so that her face was in shadow. 'No powder on her nose – that proved to be the correct solution. How can you build on such a quicksand? Their most trivial action may mean volumes, or their most extraordinary conduct may depend upon a hairpin or a curling tongs.' The one exception he seems to make is when he crosses swords with an example of the New Woman of the late nineteenth century, confident in her own intelligence and her equality with men.

Probably more nonsense has been written about Holmes's relationship with Irene Adler than any other part of his life. Assorted fantasists, driven to distraction by the thought of Holmes's celibacy, have dreamed up elaborate scenarios about a hidden sex life and, to these people, Irene Adler has proved a godsend. Holmes had an affair with her. Holmes had children with her. These are the stories some writers have committed to paper. It is worth stopping for a minute to consider the shaky foundations on which they have built their baroque edifices. What does Watson, the only real source for Holmes's admiration of Adler, actually say? The story in which she appears, 'A Scandal in Bohemia', was the first that Doyle succeeded in placing in *The Strand Magazine*. It tells of the visit to Baker Street of a European monarch, calling himself the 'King of Bohemia', who wants Holmes to rescue a compromising photograph of him from the possession of one Irene Adler. Holmes goes to great lengths in his attempts to obtain the photograph but, essentially, she outwits him. She even matches him by adopting a disguise in which, unrecognized by the detective, she pays him a mocking farewell. Clearly Irene Adler was, by any standard, a remarkable woman.

Watson does, indeed, comment on the fact that, to Holmes, she was always '*the* woman'. But he also states quite categorically that his friend, who 'never spoke of the softer passions, save with a gibe and a sneer', admired her for her intelligence and daring but never felt 'any emotion akin to love' for her. 'All emotions, and that one particularly,' Watson continues, 'were abhorrent to his cold, precise but admirably balanced mind.' Holmes himself is unambiguous in his dismissal of the 'softer passions'. 'But love is an emotional thing,' he remarks in *The Sign of Four*, 'and whatever is emotional is opposed to that true cold reason which I place above all things. I should never marry myself, lest I bias my judgment.'

Watson later describes the scene in which the 'King of Bohemia', offering Holmes some reward for his efforts on his behalf, is surprised by the detective's request for a photograph of Irene Adler.

Here, claim the romantics, is proof positive of Holmes's feelings for the glamorous adventuress. He wanted nothing from the experience but the image of the woman who had captured his heart. The true reason for the request was probably less sentimental. Holmes, bested for one of the very few times in his career, was more likely to want the photograph for his records – as a means of identification if they met again – than as a keepsake to warm his lonely heart. The stories about a love affair between Holmes and Irene Adler say more about those who continue to believe in them than they do about Holmes himself.

Irene Adler was born in New Jersey in 1858, the daughter of a prosperous inventor and businessman who had made his money from patenting an early form of automatic washing machine in the year before his daughter's birth. Irene grew up in a large and loving household and, like very nearly all women of her class at the time, was educated at home by a series of private tutors. The one who was to make the biggest difference to her life was a music tutor who called himself Signor Enrico Manzoni. Manzoni's real name was Henry Manson and he came not from Naples, as he claimed, but New York. He had changed name and nationality because he assumed, rightly, that the nouveau riche fathers who provided him with employment would have greater faith in an Italian singing teacher than one from the Bronx.

Deceitful he may have been but Manzoni/Manson was a talented musician and, in Irene, he spotted gifts that his other pupils did not possess. Encouraged by him, she determined to make the most of those gifts. Many girls in similar circumstances were given singing lessons as a child. Very few went on to make a career of singing. It is an early indication of the strength of Irene's character that she rode roughshod over all objections raised by her family and, through Manson, was able to appear on stage in 1877 in a performance of Rossini's *La Cenerentola* at the newly built Birch Opera House in Burlington, New Jersey. It was a lucky night on which to make her debut. In the audience, as guest of honour, was Amilcare Ponchielli, the Italian composer of the opera *La Gioconda*, who was touring the United States. Ponchielli was sufficiently impressed by the young Irene that he arranged for her to travel back with him to Europe.

In Europe her career as an operatic contralto initially flourished. She performed at La Scala in Milan and, we are told in 'A Scandal in Bohemia', she became a prima donna of the Imperial Opera of Warsaw before attracting the roving eye of the 'King of Bohemia'. Unfortunately, there are major problems with the mini-biography of her provided in 'A Scandal in Bohemia'. There was no Imperial Opera in Warsaw at the time. More importantly, there was no such ruler as the 'King of Bohemia', nor had there been for centuries. Once again, we are journeying into the shadowlands that Watson created when he mingled fact and fiction in a deliberate attempt to baffle readers in search of the truth. Almost certainly the city that Irene Adler visited after her brief triumph at La Scala was not Warsaw but Sofia, and the 'King of Bohemia' was actually Prince Alexander of Battenberg, at one time the ruler of Bulgaria.

Irene found it difficult to repeat the success that she had had on her first appearances in Italy. For one thing, there were not sufficient leading roles in the repertoire for such a voice as hers. The female singers who attracted the attention of both composers and the opera-going public were sopranos and Irene was a contralto. For another, she herself had lost much of her commitment to a career as a singer. Some time in the early 1880s – the date is unclear – she left Italy and moved to Trieste, then part of the Austro-Hungarian Empire. For a brief period she seems to have been the mistress of Count Lothar von Metternich, a descendant of the famous Austrian statesman. By 1883, she had left Metternich and was living in Sofia where she was once again appearing on the operatic stage. Here she performed before the ruling prince and, within a matter of weeks, had become his lover.

Why did Watson go to such trouble to disguise Prince Alexander's identity but make no attempt to do so in the case of Irene Adler? One reason is that, by the time he came to write up his notes and publish the case, Irene Adler was dead. She died in Venice in 1889, probably during one of the minor epidemics of cholera that still plagued that city in the late nineteenth century. Alexander himself died in 1893, having been ejected from his throne some years earlier (and some years before he travelled to London to consult Holmes about recovering his photograph from Irene Adler). In telling the story of the American diva and the Battenberg prince, Watson used the technique that was to serve him so well in the years to come. Mixing together real cases and real people with individuals whom he disguised under pseudonyms and locations that he altered for his own purposes, he created a narrative in which it is often difficult to disentangle the actuality from the inventions.

The romance between the detective and the opera singer may be no more than a fantasy invented by gullible Holmesians but Holmes was not unattractive to women and he could exercise considerable charm when he chose. 'Holmes had, when he liked, a peculiarly ingratiating way with women,' Watson remarks in 'The Adventure of the Golden Pince-Nez', 'and . . . he very readily established terms of confidence with them.' Nowhere is this clearer than in the strange episode of his engagement, which Watson records in 'The Adventure of Charles Augustus Milverton'. Yet the events also make clear Holmes's indifference to romantic feelings – indeed, his inability to understand them fully. In pursuit of the information he needs for his investigation into the odious Milverton, Holmes adopts the disguise of a plumber called Escott and woos the black-mailer's housemaid. He is so successful that, within days, he is engaged to her. Watson, when told of the ploy, is immediately con-cerned for the feelings of the girl, the unwitting pawn in the chess game. Protesting to Holmes, he is met simply with a shrug of the shoulders. Holmes may be able to play the part of a lover convinc-ingly (the old training with Irving still works) but the idea that love might be more than a game and that real emotions might be involved is obviously beyond him.

There is a similarly astonishing blindness to ordinary human feeling in his surprise at Watson's reaction to his return from the dead. Holmes, theatrical as ever, throws off his disguise as an old bookseller while his friend's back is turned. When he sees a man whom he thought dead suddenly spring to life before him, Watson, not unnaturally, faints. Holmes is taken aback, saying to the doctor as he slowly regains consciousness, 'I owe you a thousand apologies. I had no idea that you would be so affected.' How did he think Watson would react? How would any average man or woman respond to witnessing such a resurrection? Holmes, as he himself admits, has no idea. As Watson remarks in *The Valley of Fear*, 'With-out having a tinge of cruelty in his singular composition, he was undoubtedly callous from long over-stimulation.'

Perhaps this is the place to examine Holmes's sexuality more generally. There are those who are convinced that Holmes's sexual orientation was towards men. One scholar has pointed out similarities between descriptions of Holmes and descriptions of Oscar Wilde as if this was, in itself, sufficient proof of Holmes's homosexuality. It is, however, both difficult and dangerous to apply a twentieth-century word retrospectively to an essentially nineteenth-century man. 'Homosexual' as a description of same-sex attraction was not used at all until the 1860s, when it was coined by the Hungarian writer Károly Mária Kertbeny. Its first recorded use in English dates from an 1892 translation of Richard von Krafft-Ebing's *Psychopathia Sexualis*, first published in 1876. More usual terms in the 1880s and 1890s were 'Uranian', 'Urning' and 'Invert'.

Certainly Holmes knew a number of men who could be described as 'Uranians', from his college acquaintance Edmund Gurney to the German Baron Wilhelm von Gloeden, avid photographer of naked Sicilian boys posed in classical landscapes, for whom the detective investigated a case of blackmail in the mid-1890s. Mycroft's close friend, Lord Rosebery, was attracted to his own sex and, in 1894, narrowly avoided a scandal when Viscount Drumlanrig, the older brother of Oscar Wilde's lover Lord Alfred Douglas, was found dead from a shotgun wound. Drumlanrig owed his career to Rosebery's patronage and it was rumoured that his death, officially adjudged accidental, was actually suicide because he believed his affair with Rosebery was about to be brought to public attention.

Equally certainly, Holmes knew and liked the work of so-called 'decadent' writers and artists of the 1880s and 1890s, many of whom were homosexual. Holmes's aestheticism and appreciation of more adventurous art than the kind admired by the Victorian bourgeoisie are in evidence in the gallery visit that Watson describes in *The Hound of the Baskervilles*. He and Watson go to look at 'pictures of the modern Belgian masters'. From Watson's description, it is clear that Holmes was stimulated and excited by what he saw ('he would talk of nothing but art'). It is also equally clear that Watson, a walking exemplar of the Victorian bourgeoisie, was puzzled by his friend's enthusiasm, dismissively remarking that Holmes had 'the crudest ideas' about art. Who were these modern Belgian masters in whose work Holmes found so much to interest him? James Ensor's strange religious allegories, such as *The Entrance of Christ into Brussels*, and the disturbing, symbolist engravings of Félicien Rops (whose more erotic fantasies would not have been on display) were not to Watson's taste but Holmes clearly found them fascinating. The bizarre appealed to him in art as much as in life. Here is further proof that the detective was far from being a conventional Victorian of his class.

None of this is proof that Holmes was homosexual any more than his admiration for Irene Adler's nerve and intelligence shows that he had an affair with her. It is impossible to rescue from oblivion any sexual relationships that Holmes may or may not have had when he was a young man in London. Perhaps some forgotten actress at the Lyceum shared a bed with him. It is even possible, although unlikely, that he was an occasional visitor to one of the hundreds of brothels that catered for the needs of upper- and middle-class males, both married and unmarried. What seems certain is that, by the time he met Watson, when he was in his late twenties, Holmes had already decided that his life was not to be a sexual one. A historian of nineteenth-century sexuality has written of 'that characteristic Victorian figure, the sexual outsider, the non-participant who viewed the game from the sidelines'. All the evidence suggests that Sherlock Holmes was just such a 'sexual outsider'.

Despite the international intrigues, aristocratic scandals and major crimes in which his work had involved him by 1890, Holmes was still prey to depression and melancholia, convinced that his practice was 'degenerating into an agency for recovering lost lead pencils, and giving advice to ladies from boarding-schools'. The lurking suspicion remained that, for all the acclaim and accolades that he received, his career as a detective was somehow unworthy of him and his exceptional talents. Holmes believed profoundly that the form of detection that he applied was a science and that he was as much a rigorous scientist as any of the great names of the past. As he remarked in 'The Adventure of the Five Orange Pips':

The ideal reasoner would, when he had once been shown a single fact in all its bearings, deduce from it not only all the chain of events which led up to it but also all the results which would follow from it. As Cuvier could correctly describe a whole animal by the contemplation of a single bone, so the observer who has thoroughly understood one link in a series of incidents should be able to accurately state all the other ones, both before and after.

Holmes, the ideal reasoner, was, in his own mind, quite the equal of Georges Cuvier, the great French zoologist of the early nineteenth century. Yet, isolated as he often was in 1890, he was sometimes plagued by self-doubt.

Watson, immured in domestic bliss with Mary Morstan, was no longer so readily available as a colleague in his adventures. 'He still came to me from time to time when he desired a companion in his investigation,' Watson notes, 'but these occasions grew more and more seldom, until I find that in the year 1890 there were only three cases of which I retain any record.' Doyle, whom Holmes had become accustomed to welcoming occasionally to conversations at Baker Street, was also absent for much of 1890. Still committed to his medical career, he had decided that he needed a specialization to help him out of the unproductive rut of general practice. Opting for ophthalmology, he travelled to Vienna. This Continental expedition was an almost unmitigated disaster. Doyle had over-estimated his ability to understand German. The lectures were entirely in that language (unsurprisingly) and Doyle could not follow them. He had intended to stay six months. He remained for only two.

There were, of course, cases to engross Holmes in that year but not all of them ended in success. 'As a rule,' Holmes noted in 'The Adventure of the Red-Headed League', 'the more bizarre a thing is, the less mysterious it proves to be. It is your commonplace, featureless crimes which are really puzzling, just as a commonplace face is the most difficult to identify.' In the same narrative Holmes talks of his 'love of all that is bizarre and outside the conventions and humdrum routine of everyday life'. Few crimes could be more bizarre than that of the movie pioneer Louis le Prince and yet few in Holmes's career proved less susceptible to easy solution.

In 1890 (a full five years before the Lumière brothers organized the world's first public screening of moving pictures) Louis le Prince's wife requested Holmes's assistance in investigating the mysterious disappearance of her husband. Le Prince, born in France in 1842, had moved to England in the 1860s to join the Leeds engineering firm of Whitley Partners and for a number of years had been engaged in experiments into the possibility of moving images. A period spent living in New York, where he had continued his experiments, seemed to bring him closer to success. By the summer of 1890, le Prince, now back in England, was planning to arrange public screenings of his moving pictures. Before he did so, he needed to conclude some family business in France. In September he travelled to meet his brother who was an architect in Dijon. On the 16th of that month he boarded a train in Dijon to return to Paris. He was never seen again.

Holmes joined forces with Francois le Villard, the Brittany-born detective who admired him so much that he had, two years earlier, translated some of his monographs into French,* but, despite their best efforts, le Prince's disappearance was never explained. Le Prince may have committed suicide but, if so, he appeared to have no cause to do so. Holmes and le Villard heard only that he was excited by the prospects of his experiments finally reaching fruition. More significantly, neither they nor the French police could find any trace of his body. He may possibly have been the victim of a rival inventor who was aware that le Prince was about to trump him with the public screenings but, again, the two detectives could discover no evidence to prove this. Le Prince had, in effect, vanished into thin air. Holmes rarely mentioned the case in later years but there may be some echo of it in Watson's reference to the fate of James Phillimore, 'who, stepping back into his own house to get his umbrella, was never more seen in this world'.

One anxiety that might have added to Holmes's fretful state of mind was now a thing of the past. By the time the new decade dawned, Holmes was, by his own admission, financially secure. Gone were the days in Montague Street when he waited impatiently for any case, however slight and inconsequential, to relieve his tedium and augment his purse. 'Between ourselves,' he tells Watson in 'The Adventure of the Final Problem', 'the recent cases in which I have been of assistance to the royal family of Scandinavia, and to the French republic, have left me in such a position that I could continue to live in the quiet fashion which is most con-

---

* Given his French ancestry, Holmes had spoken the language since early childhood and was sufficiently fluent that it was occasionally assumed during his investigations into the activities of Huret, the Boulevard Assassin, that French was his first language. When he saw the letter from the 'King of Bohemia' in 'A Scandal in Bohemia', he knew at once that it was not written by a Frenchman. Despite this fluency, he allowed le Villard to translate the monographs rather than doing so himself, probably for the simple reason that he could not spare the time.

genial to me, and to concentrate my attention upon my chemical researches.' To which cases was Holmes referring? From the evidence of other Watson narratives, it would appear that the detective was employed twice by both the Scandinavian monarchy and the French republic. Indeed, his tracking of Huret, the Boulevard Assassin, for which he received 'an autograph letter of thanks from the French President and the Order of the Legion of Honour', took place after his return from the Great Hiatus and will be considered in a later chapter.

Watson first mentions the king of Scandinavia in 'The Adventure of the Noble Bachelor' where he records Holmes as putting Lord St Simon in his place by telling him, 'My last client of the sort was a king.' When St Simon asks which king, Holmes replies, 'The King of Scandinavia.' This is three years before the events in 'The Adventure of the Final Problem' so it cannot be the case described there as 'recent'. Holmes must have 'been of assistance to the royal family of Scandinavia' on two separate occasions. But who was the king of Scandinavia? There has never been a kingdom of 'Scandinavia'. Here Watson is using one of his less impenetrable pseudonyms and referring to Oskar II, who ruled two Scandinavian countries, Sweden and Norway, at the time.

Born in 1829, Oskar had come to the throne in 1872 and, although married with several children, was renowned, like so many other monarchs of the time, as a womanizer. Again like so many other monarchs past and present, Oskar's particular penchant seems to have been for young actresses. In 1888 he visited London, ostensibly to see the Prime Minister, Lord Salisbury, but his more urgent need was to consult with Holmes. One of Oskar's youthful conquests, the actress Marie Friberg, had returned to haunt him. The problem was that she possessed letters in which Oskar had allowed ardour to outrun discretion in a series of unambiguously phrased endearments. Marie was now threatening to broadcast them to a wider audience. Holmes was obliged to travel to Sweden in order to find an appropriate means of ensuring her silence. He did so but two years later the letters – or one of them, at least – resurfaced. Unwisely, Marie had allowed a subsequent lover, an unscrupulous politician called Olofsson, to see the most outspoken of Oskar's billets-doux and Olofsson was quick to see the advantages that this might offer him. Holmes was once again called to the rescue of the embarrassed Oskar. The evidence that survives suggests that Holmes was able to turn the tables very effectively on Olofsson by uncovering secrets from the politician's own past.

The similarities between the plight of the Swedish king and the indiscreet dalliance of Prince Alexander of Battenberg are such that it is possible that, in telling the story he entitled 'A Scandal in Bohemia', Watson conflated elements of both to produce a narrative that he believed would embarrass neither ruler. (Unusually for a man known for his gallantry to the opposite sex, he seems not to have minded about compromising the reputation of the late Irene Adler. He may have believed that she emerged from the story with such credit that, even had she been alive, she would not have cared whether he used her real name.)

It was not just a Scandinavian monarch who had reason to give thanks to Holmes and his powers in the 1880s. Holmes also accomplished an important mission for the reigning family of Holland that was of such delicacy that he could not confide its details to Watson. Matters of such sensitivity, when they involved royalty, usually also involved unsuitable mistresses and inappropriate clandestine affairs. There must have been times when the notoriously chaste Holmes took a fairly disapproving view of the sexual appetites of princes.

*

Despite all the other alarms and excursions of the year, much of Holmes's energy in 1890 was, in fact, given over to the continuing pursuit of Moriarty. The 1887 plot to use the Jubilee celebrations as the setting for a spectacular, terrorist *coup de théâtre* had been thwarted. Nevertheless the Irishman still posed a major threat and the Holmes brothers continued to be obsessed by him. Despite his criminal activities, Moriarty had not turned his back on science. His reputation with a wider public was as a mathematical genius rather than as a criminal mastermind. To all but the few people who knew of his secret life, he was chiefly remarkable as 'the celebrated author of *The Dynamics of an Asteroid*' which, according to Holmes, was 'a book which ascends to such rarefied heights of pure mathematics that it is said that there was no man in the scientific press capable of criticizing it'.

As his work on asteroids continued, Moriarty corresponded regularly with the French astronomer Auguste Charlois* who, in his laboratory at Nice, had discovered dozens of asteroids in the late 1880s. Holmes learned of this and approached Charlois in the spring of 1890. He even travelled to Nice to interview him. But the Frenchman could throw little light on the non-scientific activities of his correspondent. All Holmes could do was ask Charlois to contact him when Moriarty next succumbed to the temptation to discuss astronomy with one of the few people able to match his own knowledge. Mycroft's old mathematics tutor from Christ Church, Charles Dodgson, had also been in contact with Moriarty. This is surprising since Moriarty was disdainful of Dodgson's abilities as a mathematician. 'It is as well that our friend Dodgson

---

* Death and disaster seemed to pursue those who worked with Moriarty, however innocently, long after the professor's own demise. In 1910, Charlois was murdered by his brother-in-law who was aggrieved that the astronomer had remarried.

has other arrows in his quiver and can conjure up tales of white rabbits and magic potions,' he once wrote to a correspondent in Germany, 'since his grasp of the higher mathematics is so tenuous.' Although Dodgson, knowing of his former student's interest in the renegade mathematician, passed on to Mycroft the details of his brief correspondence with Moriarty, this proved of little help to the Holmes brothers. They were still uncertain of both Moriarty's whereabouts and his future plans. As a new decade opened, the problems posed by the Irishman still loomed large in their minds. At the beginning of the year 1891 they decided that a radical solution was necessary.

CHAPTER NINE

'I TRAVELLED FOR TWO
YEARS IN TIBET'

D ID HOLMES MURDER MORIARTY at the Reichenbach Falls?
That Moriarty met his death there is not in dispute, but was
this the culmination of a carefully premeditated plan? To many
people, these questions will seem perversely contrary. In the accepted version of events, all the premeditation and murderous
intent in the encounter supposedly belong to the professor, furious
with Holmes for thwarting his criminal schemes. It is Moriarty who
pursues a fleeing Holmes from London to Switzerland. Yet, in a
pursuit, the chased might not always choose to evade the chaser
indefinitely. Indeed, the quarry might not only wish to be eventually cornered but also plan the hunt in such a way that a final confrontation, on his terms, is inevitable. As Holmes, accompanied by
a more than usually baffled Watson, zigzagged across Europe in the
late spring of 1891, the intention was to draw the professor away
from the safety of his haunts in London and on to ground where he
was less secure. Watson describes the chase in the narrative he

entitled 'The Adventure of Final Problem' and, in his eyes, we see Holmes's flight from danger until he is confronted by Moriarty at the Falls. However, it needs only a slight change of perspective for us to realize that what Watson is in fact recounting is a subtle campaign to entice Moriarty to commit himself to a face-to-face encounter that he had little chance of surviving.

Holmes, together with his brother, planned in the minutest detail the journey that ended at the brink of the Reichenbach Falls. The death of Moriarty was anticipated from the very beginning. In fact, it was the whole point of the exercise. In London, Moriarty was safe. Holmes knew that the elaborate web woven to capture the professor had failed. Nearly all his associates would fall into it but the main prey would escape. In all likelihood Moriarty would not be brought to trial and, if by any chance this could be accomplished, he would only have been acquitted. Another plan would have to be adopted. Lured out of England, the professor could be eliminated by other means.

The Holmes brothers carefully and coldly planned a sequence of events that would lead Moriarty towards a confrontation with Sherlock. The outcome of hand-to-hand combat between the two men could not be in any doubt. Moriarty placed his trust in brain rather than brawn. In contrast, Holmes, for all his dedication to the life of the mind, not only possessed the strength to bend and unbend iron pokers but was an expert in what Watson calls 'baritsu',*

---

* Watson was referring to 'bartitsu', a method of self-defence devised by the Briton E. W. Barton-Wright who had lived in Japan in the 1890s. Barton-Wright was also interested in the Japanese art of kendo. He published articles on the subject in British magazines, complete with illustrations in which immaculately attired City gentlemen use their umbrellas and walking sticks to disarm and disable assorted blackguards who have had the temerity to attack them. Barton-Wright first demonstrated 'bartitsu' in Britain in 1899 so it cannot have been the method employed by Holmes to send Moriarty over the Reichenbach Falls. Watson, writing years after the events, must have misremembered what Holmes told him and conflated it with what he had recently read about Barton-Wright's technique. Holmes had an interest in Japan and things Japanese that dated back to his undergraduate

a Japanese system of wrestling that was explicitly designed to bring victory at close quarters. The struggle on the brink of the Reichenbach Falls was only ever going to have one outcome. Although it may be hard for any admirer of the Holmes brothers to admit it, when they could not achieve their aims within the law they stepped outside it. The elimination of Moriarty undoubtedly made the world a safer place but equally there is little doubt that, in strictly legal terms, he was murdered.

Once Moriarty disappeared over the precipice at the Reichenbach Falls, the period in Holmes's life known as the Great Hiatus begins. There has been more controversy over these three missing years than any other part of his career. Many students of Holmes have refused to accept the version of events that the detective himself supplied to Watson. Assorted stories, of varying degrees of credibility and involving everything from spying in Germany to a journey to America to solve the Lizzie Borden* murder case, have been put forward to explain the missing years. The only record that Holmes himself left of his experiences during the Great Hiatus is laconic in the extreme. Three years of extra-ordinary activity are summarized in a few brief lines:

I travelled for two years in Tibet, therefore, [he tells Watson] and amused myself by visiting Lhassa, [sic] and spending some days with the head

visit to stay with his friend Victor Trevor, whose father had travelled in Japan. He was also an expert in the European art of singlestick fighting. The two interests – in Japanese culture and single combat – had combined in his own study of Japanese martial arts that owed nothing to Barton-Wright. It was probably ju-jitsu that proved Moriarty's undoing.

* Lizzie Borden was the Massachusetts spinster who, in 1892, allegedly took an axe and gave her mother forty whacks, following this act of matricide, when she saw what she had done, by giving her father forty-one. She was found not guilty of the murders but controversy still rages over who exactly did kill her parents. Holmes took no part in the case. Perhaps, if he had, it would not remain one of the most controversial murder cases in American legal history.

lama. You may have read of the remarkable explorations of a Norwegian named Sigerson, but I am sure that it never occurred to you that you were receiving news of your friend. I then passed through Persia, looked in at Mecca, and paid a short but interesting visit to the Khalifa at Khartoum, the results of which I have communicated to the Foreign Office. Returning to France, I spent some months in a research into the coal-tar derivatives, which I conducted in a laboratory at Montpellier, in the south of France.

Only when he heard of the murder of the Honourable Ronald Adair in the spring of 1894 and realized immediately that Moriarty's deputy, Colonel Sebastian Moran, was the likely murderer, did Holmes choose to return to London and to life.

How likely is it that Holmes made up this tale he told his friend? Certainly, as we have seen, he regularly misled Watson and there is nothing, at first sight, unlikely in the idea that he would invent a story to explain his whereabouts during the Great Hiatus. He may not have anticipated much difficulty in convincing Watson of the truth of the story. Holmes did not expect Watson to ask him pressing questions and Watson rarely surprised him with sudden attacks of ungovernable curiosity. Yet there was little motive for Holmes to deceive Watson quite so spectacularly. Indeed, if the intention was to suppress the doctor's questions about where he spent the years of the Great Hiatus, a less dramatic version would have better served the purpose. If somebody in the twenty-first century disappears for several years and, on his return, tells his friends that he has been on the Moon, he is much more likely to provoke scepticism and curiosity than if he simply says he has been staying in a house that he bought in the Dordogne. To men of the 1890s, a visit to Tibet and Mecca was very nearly as unusual as a lunar trip today. In fact, there are few reasons to doubt Holmes's story enough to invent implausible alternatives and there is plenty of evidence that the detective went exactly where he said he had been. In his crisply concise remarks to his colleague, Holmes was correct in the geography of his travels, if a little cavalier with his dates. However, his honesty about the reasons behind his travels is another matter.

It is easy to forget just how inadequate is the usually accepted explanation for Holmes's three-year disappearance. According to the version he gave on his return from the dead, once the life-and-death struggle at the Reichenbach Falls was over, Holmes realized immediately the opportunities beckoning him. As he told Watson:

The instant that the Professor had disappeared, it struck me what a really extraordinarily lucky chance Fate had placed in my way. I knew that Moriarty was not the only man who had sworn my death. There were at least three others whose desire for vengeance upon me would only be increased by the death of their leader. They were all most dangerous men. One or other would certainly get me. On the other hand, if all the world was convinced that I was dead, they would take liberties, these men, they would soon lay themselves open, and sooner or later I could destroy them. Then it would be time for me to announce that I was still in the land of the living.

This is superficially convincing but it raises as many questions as it answers. Was Holmes's life really in as much peril as he claimed?

His greatest opponent by far, Moriarty, was dead. The professor's replacement, Colonel Moran, intelligent and ruthless though he was, was not a criminal mastermind but an ex-Indian army officer with a taste for women and gambling. Much of the organization that Moriarty had so painstakingly created throughout the 1880s had been destroyed. Both before and after the Reichenbach Falls, Holmes faced equal threats to his life without feeling the need to fake his own death and disappear for three years to the remotest and least-explored corners of the world. Could such an elaborately staged disappearance have been undertaken on the spur of the moment? It seems unlikely in the extreme.

In fact, it becomes clear that Holmes's decision to fake his death had been taken some weeks before he travelled with Watson to Switzerland and that it had been taken in consultation with his brother Mycroft. Mycroft had his own reasons for wanting the world to believe that his younger brother was no longer in the land of the living. Freed from his detective work in London, which Mycroft always believed to be largely a waste of his brother's talents, and assumed by everyone to be dead, Sherlock was in the ideal position to undertake other tasks – tasks that Mycroft considered to be of greater significance than the tracking down of domestic murderers and commonplace criminals, those 'petty puzzles of the police-court' which he is quoted as dismissing so brusquely in 'The Adventure of the Bruce-Partington Plans'.

At first glance, there seems little to connect Holmes's assorted destinations during the three years of his travels beyond the fact that, in the early 1890s, Lhasa, Mecca and Khartoum were all cities barred to Europeans. Why would Holmes have travelled to these places? Even the desire to escape the murderous pursuit of Colonel Sebastian Moran and Moriarty's other henchmen, if that had indeed been his primary motive, need not have driven him so far off the beaten track. The answer to this question, like the answers to so many of the mysteries in Holmes's career, lies in his relationship with his brother Mycroft.

Mycroft's unacknowledged but immensely powerful position at the heart of government – according to Holmes, there were times when his brother '*was* the British government' – meant that he was aware of every shift and change in imperial policy, every cut and thrust in the continual fencing match of great powers diplomacy.

He knew that British interests were at stake in two of these remote cities, far though they were from both the imperial capital and the thoughts of most Britons. (Holmes's reasons for visiting Mecca, as we shall see, probably had little to do with great power politics.) From Tibet, alarming rumours of Russian ambitions to infiltrate the country were reaching London. Khartoum was the capital of an expanding Muslim state which, only a few years earlier, had humiliated the British government by murdering one of its most renowned generals and forcing the withdrawal of a large force of Anglo-Egyptian troops from the country. Reliable intelligence from these 'forbidden' cities was urgently required by the mandarins who decided imperial policy, and what better source than the younger brother of one of them?

'The Great Game', the playing out of the inter-power rivalry between Russia and Britain in Central Asia and the lands that bordered India, was a phrase supposedly coined in the 1840s by Arthur Connolly, an officer of the Bengal Lancers.* It gained its greatest currency through Kipling's novel *Kim*, first published in 1901, but the world-view behind it can be seen in thousands of books, essays and leading articles written in the latter half of the nineteenth century. In 1883, for example, the Victorian historian J. R. Seeley highlighted the anxious scrutiny of far-flung places that the Great Game demanded of Britain:

Every movement in Turkey, every new symptom in Egypt, any stirrings in Persia or Transoxiana or Burmah [sic] or Afghanistan, we are obliged to watch with vigilance. The reason is that we have possession of India, and

---

* Connolly became a victim of the rivalry he had christened. In 1842, he and another officer, Charles Stoddart, were accused of spying by the Emir of Bukhara and, after months imprisoned in a vermin-infested well in the city, were beheaded.

a leading interest in the affairs of all those countries which lie upon the route to India. This and only this involves us in that permanent rivalry with Russia, which is for England of the nineteenth century what the competition with France for the New World was to her in the eighteenth century.

This could be Mycroft speaking. Seeley's words encapsulate the assumptions that governed the thinking of the elder Holmes and dozens of other senior figures in Whitehall. It was the mindset that was to send the younger Holmes thousands of miles across the globe.

On 12 May 1891, just over a week after the fateful struggle at the Reichenbach Falls, Holmes arrived in Florence. The British Consul in the city, alerted to his arrival by a despatch from Mycroft in London, was there to greet him. From the very beginning of his posthumous career, Holmes faced difficulties in retaining his anonymity. Some senior consular officials had to be informed of his real identity if he was to receive the help he needed from them to facilitate his journey. In addition, the colony of expatriate English living a life of *dolce far niente* in Florence was large and included people who might know him from London. Holmes, thanks to Watson and Doyle, was no longer entirely the unknown consulting detective he had once been.

Ironically, his ascent to iconic status in the English-speaking world began after his supposed death when *The Strand Magazine*, prompted by Doyle, agreed to publish some of Watson's shorter narratives. The first of these adventures did not appear until the autumn of 1891, by which time Holmes was in the Himalayas and unaware of his growing fame. The longer stories published by Doyle and Watson as *A Study in Scarlet* and *The Sign of Four* had not been great successes but they had done something to bring Holmes out of the shadows in which he had previously laboured.

There was always the danger that someone in Florence would

recognize him. Holmes, once again adopting the garb of an Italian priest in which he had evaded Moriarty's attention at Victoria Station, left the city at the earliest opportunity and travelled southwards to Brindisi where his arrival coincided with that of a P & O ship travelling to Egypt. Transferring to another P & O steamer at Port Said at the mouth of the Suez Canal, Holmes joined the route that was travelled by thousands of choleric colonels, nervous subalterns and imposing memsahibs in the later decades of the nineteenth century.

A voyage aboard a P & O steamer was a rite of passage for those who built the empire in India and the East. The Peninsular and Oriental Steam Navigation Company, founded by two Scots entrepreneurs in the 1830s, had rapidly become an essential part of the network of communications that held the Empire together. By the early 1890s the journey from Europe to India, once a gruelling marathon of ocean-going that could last months, took little more than a fortnight. After sailing along the Suez Canal, down the Red Sea and across the Indian Ocean, the ship on which Holmes was berthed (probably one of two sister ships, the *Arcadia* and the *Oceana*, which were launched by P & O in 1888 to join the routes to India and Australia) docked at Bombay in early June. It was less than a month since, peering over the brink of the precipice at Reichenbach, he had watched Moriarty fall, strike the rocks and vanish under the water.

For a biographer, tracking Holmes in his passage through India – indeed, following his footsteps throughout the Great Hiatus – can be a frustrating pursuit. Much of the journey has to be made in almost impenetrable darkness. The quarry remains hidden. Only occasionally is he caught in flashes of lightning that illuminate him briefly before he disappears again into the surrounding blackness.

Like a ghost, Holmes passes across vast tracts of territory, leaving no trace whatsoever of his presence. We have no certain record of his time in Bombay but it seems unlikely that he would have stayed long in the city. Mycroft's instructions demanded his presence in Tibet as soon as possible. There was little to be gained from dallying and diversions on the way. There were regular train services from Bombay across the great expanses of central India to Calcutta and we know that Holmes was in the latter city within the week.

In Calcutta itself, the detective emerges briefly from the shadows, as if caught in a faded photograph. On 10 June 1891 a prominent Calcutta citizen makes a cryptic entry in his diary in which he records a meeting at his club with a European traveller bound for Darjeeling. They discuss the work of Bertillon and Sir Francis Galton. The citizen is Edward Henry, newly appointed Inspector General of the Bengali Police, and he is enormously impressed by both the knowledge that the mysterious visitor demonstrates and his keen insights into the past, present and future of police and detective work. The traveller, Henry thinks, is German and he records his name as Siegsohn but there can be little doubt that this was Holmes, already using the persona that he had chosen for his mission.

The detective had long been interested in the possibilities of discovering an infallible physical means of identifying criminals. The two names that Henry mentions – Bertillon and Galton – are evidence that, even under cover and en route to the Himalayas, he could not resist airing his ideas when he chanced upon a sympathetic and knowledgeable listener. Holmes was an admirer of the French criminologist Alphonse Bertillon and of the system of anthropometrical measurements of the human body that he had devised to classify and identify criminals, although he was also aware of the shortcomings of what became known as *bertillonage*. (An exchange between Dr Mortimer and Holmes, recorded in *The*

Hound of the Baskervilles, suggests that the detective was also rather envious of the admiring attention that the Frenchman received.)

Holmes was familiar, too, with the work done by Sir Francis Galton, polymath cousin of Charles Darwin, in devising a method of classifying fingerprints. No police force in the world had yet thought of putting Galton's system at the service of detective work but Holmes, as so often, was ahead of the game. In several of Watson's narratives, thumbmarks and fingermarks have a part to play in the investigations. As early as the mid-1880s there are instances of Holmes emphasizing the potential of such marks as a means of identification. By chance, effectively the only other person in the world who had the foresight and imagination to recognize the opportunities that Galton's system offered law enforcement was the man sitting opposite him in that club in Calcutta on that sultry June night. Edward (later Sir Edward) Henry was already mulling over in his mind the possibility of creating a method of classifying fingerprints that his Bengali police could use. Several years later he would put into practice the ideas that he discussed with the surprisingly well-informed 'German'. Indeed, the fingerprint classification that he devised in 1896 and 1897 is still the basis for most systems in use in the English-speaking world.*

---

* Henry returned to England in 1901 and established Scotland Yard's first fingerprint bureau that year. Appointed Commissioner of the Metropolitan Police two years later, he served fifteen years in the post. He and Holmes met once more, in 1912, when the Commissioner was the intended victim of a half-baked assassination attempt. Albert Bowes, aggrieved because he had been denied a cab licence and convinced that this was somehow Sir Edward's fault, fired three shots at the Commissioner as he stood on the doorstep of his house in Sheffield Terrace, w8. One of them wounded Henry slightly. The police, at first unconvinced that Bowes was nothing more than a deranged loner, asked Holmes to make discreet inquiries into his background. The detective, reporting to a convalescing Sir Edward, made it clear that the assailant was indeed only a madman with a grievance. Whether or not the Commissioner recognized in the distinguished detective the mysterious German, Siegsohn, whom he had met in his Calcutta club twenty years earlier, we do not know.

From Calcutta, Holmes travelled on the Darjeeling Himalayan Railway,* completed only ten years earlier, and arrived in the small hill station and sanatorium town in August 1891. The evidence of Sir Edward Henry's enigmatic diary entry indicates that he had already adopted the persona of the Norwegian explorer Sigerson in Calcutta. Why Holmes chose this particular persona for his travels in the region remains a matter for debate. No explorer named Sigerson, either Norwegian or of any other nationality, is recorded by history. In the 1890s the Swedish traveller, Sven Hedin, did journey into the remote regions where the ill-defined boundaries of Tibet, China, Nepal and British India converged, although he did not reach Tibet until after Holmes had returned to London. The two men cannot have met, but Holmes may have picked up rumours of Hedin's proposed expedition in Calcutta and decided that choosing a Scandinavian identity meant that his own travels might be conveniently confused with those of the Swede. Sigerson, or more properly Sigurdsson, is a common Scandinavian name and one with which Holmes, no stranger to cases in Scandinavia, would have been familiar. (The likelihood is that Holmes used the form 'Sigurdsson' and that Watson misheard and mistranscribed it as 'Sigerson'.)

In Darjeeling, one of Holmes's first ports of call was Lhasa Villa, the home of schoolteacher Sarat Chandra Das. Although Holmes introduced himself under his *nom de voyage* of Sigerson, it is unlikely that Das was under any misapprehension about the purpose behind his visitor's questions and requests for information. If anyone was able to see through the disguises and adopted identities of the Great

---

* Even thirty years after Holmes's visit it remained a difficult, occasionally dangerous, journey. In the 1920s the Calcutta railway authorities received a frantic telegraph message from Tindharia, one of the small stations on the route, which read, 'Tiger eating station master on platform. Please send instructions.'

Game, it was this shrewd and witty scholar from Chittagong in East Bengal. Often claimed as the original model for the character of Hurree Chunder Mookerjee, the 'Babu' in Kipling's *Kim*, Sarat Chandra Das had travelled widely in Tibet, apparently as a pilgrim seeking enlightenment but secretly as a surveyor and geographer for the authorities in British India. In May 1882 he had entered Lhasa and spent two weeks there in lodgings provided by the Panchen Lama. He had even been granted an audience with the six-year-old thirteenth Dalai Lama. 'The Grand Lama,' Das had written, 'is a child . . . with a bright and fair complexion and rosy cheeks. His eyes are large and penetrating, the shape of his face remarkably Aryan, though somewhat marred by the obliquity of his eyes. The thinness of his person was probably due to the fatigue of the Court ceremonies and to the religious duties and ascetic observance of his estate.' There was no one in Darjeeling, or indeed in the whole of the Raj, more qualified to answer 'Sigerson's' questions about Tibet and its mysteries than Das. He not only knew the country but was able to provide the contacts Holmes needed to assist him in his journey. We know that Holmes arrived in Lhasa with two companions. Almost certainly these guides were recommended to him by Das who will also have been the means by which the detective was able to acquire the pack animals and supplies he required.

However, Holmes was not alone in visiting Lhasa Villa that summer. In his autobiographical writings, Das drops hints about 'Sigerson's' visit, although he does not name him, and also implies that the explorer was not the only person who sought him out in his retirement. Again, Das does not name his second mysterious visitor directly but, from what he does say, it is clear not only that this was Colonel Moran, hot-footing it halfway across the world in pursuit of Holmes, but also that Das had come across him before. Both had played the Great Game in the Himalayas in the 1870s.

Paradoxically, by travelling to the very edge of empire, Holmes was entering territory only too familiar to the new head of Moriarty's criminal organization. With Moriarty dead, its leadership had fallen to Colonel Sebastian Moran.* Finding the constraints of Victorian society too restrictive for a man of his tastes and ambitions, Moran had said farewell to England as a young man soon after leaving Oxford and sailed for India. There he joined the Indian army and soon gained the reputation for courage, ruthlessness and hunting expertise that he still retained nearly thirty years later when he had become a card-playing clubman in London. In 'The Adventure of the Empty House', after the Colonel has been arrested for the murder of the Honourable Ronald Adair, Holmes acknowledges that Moran was said to be 'the best shot in India' and assures Watson that 'the story is still told in India' of 'how he crawled down a drain after a wounded man-eating tiger'.

Author of *Heavy Game of the Western Himalayas*, published in 1881, Moran clearly knew the high mountains as well as anyone in the British army. Yet the records of Moran's early career in India and the Empire are curiously patchy. It is only during the Jowaki campaign of 1877, one of the many punitive expeditions sent by the British to subdue unruly tribes on the North-West Frontier, that he enters official records as an officer in a sappers' regiment. By then, Moran was in his late thirties. Thereafter his service in the Second Afghan War is well enough documented until a

---

* For the rest of his life Holmes believed that it was Moran who tried to kill him as he climbed the cliff above the Reichenbach Falls. 'When we were in Switzerland,' he later told Watson, 'he followed us with Moriarty and it was undoubtedly he who gave me that evil five minutes on the Reichenbach ledge.' It seems unlikely. If Moran, one of the Empire's greatest crackshots, had been watching the scene, it is scarcely credible that he would not have been armed with his rifle. He would not have been in a position where his only option was to pelt the climbing Holmes with rocks in the vain hope of dislodging him from the cliff. The assailant was more likely one of Moriarty's lesser-known minions.

mysterious scandal obliged him to retire from the army and return to London.

What, though, was Moran doing in the late 1860s and early 1870s, when his whereabouts are oddly undocumented? The most likely explanation is that he was engaged in intelligence work. And the most likely theatre for this work was the high Himalayas, the poorly explored mountain lands where the boundaries of British India touched those of mysterious independent states such as Sikkim, Nepal and Tibet. Here it was that he and Das would have met one another. Whatever had passed between the two of them, it is clear from Das's autobiographical narrative that he neither liked nor trusted the Colonel. Moran was despatched from Lhasa Villa with a flea in his ear.

Rebuffed by the Bengali scholar, the Colonel needed to find another potential ally in Darjeeling. He chose Dr Austine Waddell, a Scot employed by the Indian Medical Service. Waddell was in addition an expert on the venomous snakes and the birds of the region, as well as being obsessed with discovering all he could about the language and culture of Tibet. During his time in Darjeeling, Waddell had made the acquaintance of several of those Indian pioneers who, like Das, had travelled in the country. 'I heard from their lips,' he wrote, 'the stirring narrative of their adventures.' One of these men, a Sikkimese called Kinthup, accompanied him on a series of expeditions into the heart of the Himalayas.

Waddell's relationship with Das, however, was more fraught than the companionship he enjoyed with Kinthup. The two men disliked one another. Indeed, Waddell seems to have been almost pathologically jealous of the Indian's success in penetrating the mysteries of Tibet and fearful that Das represented a threat to his status as the Raj's self-styled great expert on the country. Ten years later, Das was to say to a friend that Waddell had 'done all in his power to insinuate that I had written the narratives of my journeys as books of fiction' and that he, Das, was nothing more than an 'arch impostor'. If Holmes chose wisely in consulting Sarat Chandra Das, Moran's decision to seek out Austine Waddell was, from his point of view, an equally sensible one. Any friend of Das was unlikely to win the sympathy of Waddell and, with the latter's assistance, Moran was soon able to make his presence in Darjeeling felt.

A town with a population of less than 15,000, Darjeeling was not a place in which new European faces would go unnoticed. Holmes knew of Moran's presence there within hours of the colonel's arrival. Although Holmes would have been instantly on his guard, garbled reports appearing in the Calcutta press in late August suggest that Moran made at least two attempts on the detective's life. Both the *Calcutta Telegraph* and the *Indian Mirror* carried separate accounts of shooting incidents in the hill station involving Europeans. The *Telegraph*, clearly possessed of a better-informed local correspondent, gave the greatest detail, reporting that, under cover of darkness, a mysterious assailant had twice fired upon a man whom the paper described as a 'tea merchant from Northern Europe'. Despite the best efforts of Darjeeling's small police force, the *Telegraph* went on, no motive had been found for the attack but, the paper's correspondent suggested with misplaced confidence, an arrest was expected shortly. It was time for Holmes to move on and, at the beginning of September, he and the two unnamed companions recommended by Das set off for the Tibetan border.

As the lammergeier (the bearded vulture that sweeps over the mountains and plateaus of Tibet) flies, it is only some 250 miles from Darjeeling to Lhasa, but those miles took the traveller from the well-mapped borderlands of the British Raj into what essentially remained, despite the work of dedicated native surveyors like Das and Kinthup, *terra incognita*. To Westerners throughout the nineteenth century, Tibet was a land more of fable than of fact and its capital city of Lhasa became the subject of endless conjecture. Only three Europeans visited the city in the course of the century.

One of these was Thomas Manning. An eccentric Cambridge mathematician and a friend of Charles Lamb, Coleridge and Wordsworth, he had become obsessed by the culture of China and the Far East. In 1811 he managed to travel in disguise to Lhasa. Unsurprisingly, his disguise was soon penetrated but he was allowed to stay in the city for several months and was received by the ninth Dalai Lama, then a small boy. Manning, who had overcome a series of appalling obstacles in order to satisfy his curiosity about the remote city, was unimpressed by much of what he found. 'The avenues are full of dogs,' he wrote, 'some growling and gnawing bits of hide which lie about in profusion and emit a charnel-house smell; others limping and looking livid; others ulcerated; others starved and dying and pecked at by ravens; some dead and preyed upon. In short, everything seemed mean and gloomy . . .'

Thirty-four years later Huc and Gabet, two French priests and missionaries, also succeeded in reaching the city and remained guests of the Tibetans for nearly a year until they were expelled at the insistence of the Chinese imperial commissioner there. During the second half of the nineteenth century, many tried to emulate Manning and the two Frenchmen but none, apart from Holmes, succeeded. If the obstacles of geography were somehow overcome, further difficulties were imposed by the determination of the Tibetans to remain as isolated from the rest of the world as they could. The Polish-Russian aristocrat Nikolai Przhevalski* in the

---

* Przhevalski, almost forgotten today, was probably the greatest of all explorers of Central Asia. One fanciful story about him even claims, on the slender grounds of facial resemblance and a coincidental visit to the right part of Georgia at the right time, that he was Stalin's biological father.

1870s, the French explorer Pierre Bonvalot in the 1880s and an English army captain, Hamilton Bower, in the 1890s were among those intrepid travellers who managed to cross the country's borders but all were turned back before they reached its capital.

In 1892 the English missionary Annie Taylor became the first European woman to enter Tibet and, after a journey of extreme hardship and danger, was within a few days' travel of Lhasa when she was discovered by Tibetan officials. Ejected from the country, she persisted in her belief that it was her destiny to convert the Tibetans to Christianity and she prevailed upon the authorities to let her stay at the border trading-post of Yatung. Perhaps persuaded by the similarity of her first name to the Tibetan word for 'nun', they let her do so and she was still there to greet Younghusband and his expedition twelve years later. By that time, she had made just one convert.

Occasionally, the Tibetans did more than just escort trespassers back to the borders. Sometimes such interlopers were prosecuted more fiercely. In 1897, nearly six years after Holmes first entered the country, Henry Savage Landor, accompanied only by a small group of native servants, set off to reach the forbidden city.* Apprehended by the Tibetans, Landor was first imprisoned and then tortured, forced to ride many miles on a saddle mounted with iron spikes that tore into his flesh. He was eventually released thanks to the intervention of British officials in northern India and Nepal.

---

* Landor, the grandson of the poet and writer Walter Savage Landor, was one of those nonchalantly adventurous travellers so typical of the nineteenth century who journeyed to far-flung places armed with little more than unquenchable self-confidence and a conviction that an English gentleman could overcome all difficulties. He wrote an account of his travails in Tibet titled *In the Forbidden Land* and published a sequence of other books recording his journeys, including *Across Wildest Africa* and *Alone with the Hairy Ainu*, an account of his sojourn with the indigenous people on a remote Japanese island.

Three years earlier, the Frenchman Dutreuil de Rhins had not been so lucky. He was ambushed by bandits and killed.

Tibet, then, was wild and 'uncivilized' territory in which, one might have thought, Western governments, if not their bolder citizens, would have little interest. Nonetheless many late-Victorian British empire-builders were paranoiacally obsessed by the supposed threat offered to the security of India by Russian attempts to infiltrate the country. Tibet might have been a desolate, underpopulated region of high mountains and hidden plateaus but it did share a border with British territory. If the Russians established themselves there, they were on the doorstep of the Raj.

Not all of the British fears were entirely fanciful. The Russians, through Buddhist intermediaries, were making overtures to the Tibetans, to which the Tibetan authorities responded. In 1901, the Dalai Lama sent a letter to the Tsar, Nicholas II, in which the religious leader appeared to be soliciting Russian aid against the British. 'The Buddhist faith of the Tibetan people,' he wrote, 'is threatened by enemies and oppressors from abroad – the English. Be so kind as to instruct my ambassadors how they may be reassured about their pernicious and foul activities.' Yet the co-operation between the Russians and the Tibetans, as well as the scale of the Russian presence in Tibet, were wildly exaggerated by British officials in India, from lowly intelligence agents to the Viceroy, Lord Curzon, who remained convinced that any minor encroachments on Russia's part were all part of a grand scheme for total dominion in Asia.

A more realistic assessment of the threat, as delivered earlier by Holmes's report to Mycroft, was quickly lost amid the frenzied anxiety that characterized the official government position. In 1904, Younghusband and his mission, despatched with Curzon's blessing, fully expected that their advance into Tibet would be met by warriors armed with thousands of up-to-date Russian arms and rifles. In the event, many of the soldiers they faced, carrying only ancient matchlocks and traditional Tibetan swords, seemed to have stepped out of another century. After the one-sided battle at the village of Guru, in which the Tibetans lost nearly 500 killed and wounded, while the expedition suffered no fatalities and less than a dozen wounded, British officers scoured the Tibetan encampment in search of Russian guns. They found three.

Holmes himself left no record of his time in Tibet beyond the brief sentences that Watson preserves in 'The Adventure of the Empty House'. Conan Doyle reveals a passing knowledge of the country in some of his own writings; these may reflect conversations with Holmes in the late 1890s but we cannot be sure. Any documents that exist in government archives have yet to emerge into the public domain. In the absence of firm evidence, all statements about his journeys in the Forbidden Land must, necessarily, be speculative but it seems most likely that he followed the route later travelled by Colonel Francis Younghusband and his military mission to Lhasa. Indeed, Younghusband heard several rumours that a strange, possibly crazed European had travelled through the valley of the Chumbi river a dozen years earlier. This was almost certainly Holmes.

There is no mystery why Tibet remained so isolated from the world for so long. No natural barrier in the world is more formidable than the mountains that surround it. There are few points at which the massive ramparts of the Himalayas can possibly be scaled by men on foot or pack animal. One of them is the Jelep La (Lovely Level) Pass, which leads from the border with Sikkim into the Chumbi Valley and on towards the great Tibetan plateau. It was here that the Younghusband mission entered Tibet and it would have been here, twelve years earlier, that Holmes, together with the two men recommended by Sarat Chandra Das, struggled ever upwards on precipitous paths, often only wide enough to allow progress in single file. This was difficult and demanding terrain to cover, particularly in late autumn when Holmes was travelling, as winter arrives early in the Himalayas. Even a man of his prodigious stamina must have found the going tough.

Although Holmes himself did not note down his reactions to it, others who followed in his footsteps did. One such was Percy Landon, a newspaper correspondent who had attached himself to the Younghusband mission. He recorded the toll that the climb through the Jelep La exacted on men and beasts alike. 'Scarcely anyone,' he wrote, 'even those who rode most of the way, escaped having aching temples and eyeballs; many suffered from actual mountain sickness, and several of the transport animals succumbed on the roadside.' More exacting still was the crossing of the Tang La (Clear Pass), which finally brought them on to the plateau. Landon made the crossing in a blizzard. 'The frozen mist, laced with stinging splinters of ice, was blown horizontally into our faces by the wind that never sleeps over this terrible pass. Men and animals alike were stiff with an armour of ice, and beards and even eyelashes were powdered and hoary with the fine particles of frozen mist. It was difficult to see fifty yards.' We do not know what weather conditions Holmes and his two companions experienced but they may well have undergone the agonies of mountain sickness so graphically described by Landon. 'The brain,' he wrote, 'seems cleft in two, and the wedge, all blunt and splintery, is hammered into it by mallet strokes at every pulsation of the heart. Partial relief is secured by a violent fit of sickness, and through all this you have still to go on, to go on, to go on ...'

Once through the Tang La Pass, Holmes and his two companions had overcome the worst physical obstacles of the journey.

Lhasa was still many miles to the north-east. Other mountain passes and gruelling marches still awaited them but there would be nothing to match the inhospitability of the territory that they had already traversed. Having emerged on to the high Tibetan plateau, the travellers suddenly found themselves surrounded by signs of cultivation and human habitation. One of those who trekked with Younghusband twelve years later described the new, more welcoming landscape that here greeted Holmes. 'We were now,' he wrote, 'in an open bay of the rich plain of the Gyantse Valley, which we could see stretching up and down on either side about two miles ahead of us ... On turning the corner of a spur on our left, the broad plain-like expanse of the fertile valley of Gyantse shot fully into view, dotted over with neat white-washed farmhouses and villas clustered in groves of trees amongst well-cultivated fields.' Fertile valleys and well-cultivated fields meant, of course, more people to witness the arrival of strangers. It is at this point that Holmes and his two men could have expected, like Landor, Annie Taylor and so many other travellers before them, to have been apprehended and turned back. Moran and Waddell, who were in close pursuit, found the disguises they had adopted of little use in fooling the authorities. They were stopped by local headmen, presumably under instructions from a higher authority, and were forced to retrace their steps. By the end of September, records show, Waddell was once more in Darjeeling and we can assume that Moran was with him. (The following year Waddell, together with the Sikkimese hillman Kinthup, again entered Tibet. Gamely, if foolishly, putting his trust in the kind of disguise that had failed him the previous year, he was betrayed by his blue eyes and once more given his marching orders back to the border.) Yet Holmes and his two companions, for whatever reason, were allowed to continue. Riding ever further into the country, they slowly approached its mysterious capital.

On or around 15 October, Holmes entered the city's gate. Lhasa in 1891 was not, by European standards, large. Set on a plain surrounded by the mountains, it was, however, majestic – at least from a distance. The city was overshadowed by the huge mass of the Potala Palace, the temple-residence of the Dalai Lama. Perceval Landon, the newspaper correspondent who travelled with Younghusband, was thunderstruck by his first sight of the Potala.

Simplicity has wrought a marvel in stone, nine hundred feet in length and towering seventy feet higher than the golden cross of St Paul's Cathedral. The Potala would dominate London, Lhasa it simply eclipses. By European standards it is impossible to judge this building: there is nothing there to which comparison can be made ... the central building of the palace, the Phodang Marpo, the private home of the incarnate deity himself, stands out four-square upon and between the wide supporting bulks of masonry a rich-red crimson, and, most perfect touch of all, the glittering golden roofs – a note of glory added with the infinite taste and the sparing hand of the old illumination – recompense the colour scheme from end to end, a sequence of green in three shades, of white, of maroon, of gold, and of pale blue.

Holmes and his travelling companions were, doubtless, as impressed as Landon by their first view of the palace but, as they rode further into the city, they would have seen less to delight the eye. Apart from the Potala and the lesser temples and monasteries that Lhasa supported, the city was little more than an unprepossessing cluster of small clay and brick-built houses, criss-crossed by a spiralling maze of narrow, dirty streets that had changed little in the eighty years since Thomas Manning's visit.

How did Holmes manage to reach Lhasa when so many others had failed, and would continue to fail? How did he surmount the endless obstacles that the Tibetan authorities put in the path of potential travellers? As a whole procession of would-be explorers of the country had proved, there was little or no possibility of travelling in disguise. Europeans could sometimes pass muster when transformed into Hindus or Afghans or, in other parts of the world, Arabs (as Holmes himself would prove later in his journeys). In Tibet, however, these subterfuges would have looked as out of place as any Englishman. Even with his legendary ability to transform his appearance, Holmes would have had difficulty in adopting any suitable camouflage on entering the country. Sven Hedin, making his own bid to reach Lhasa ten years later, shaved his head, removed his moustache and darkened his skin with fat and soot in an attempt to pass himself off as an itinerant lama. Riding past a Tibetan encampment only a few miles over the border, he was immediately spotted as a European because of his height. Hedin was not even particularly tall by European standards. Holmes, described by Watson as 'rather over six feet, and so excessively lean that he seemed to be considerably taller', would have seemed like Gulliver among the Lilliputians.

One other possibility worth considering is that Holmes succeeded in travelling through Tibet without apparent hindrance because the Tibetan religious authorities perceived in him someone out of the ordinary. It was not unknown, for example, for Westerners – even ones with whom the lamas might have been thought to have had little sympathy – to be recognized as the incarnations of holy spirits. Austine Waddell, Moran's companion in the failed attempt to pursue Holmes into Tibet, was the author of a pioneering study on Tibetan Buddhism which argued that the priest-monks of the country were little more than devil-worshippers. Throughout his career, Waddell was dismissive of Tibetan spirituality, arguing that, in his own words, 'Lamaism is only thinly and imperfectly varnished

over with Buddhist symbolism, beneath which the sinister growth
of poly-demonist superstition darkly appears.' Yet many lamas in
Darjeeling and Sikkim hailed him as an incarnation of the Amitabh
Buddha, the Buddha of Infinite Light. Even so, incarnation or not,
Waddell, as we have seen, was unable to reach Lhasa until he travel-
led with Younghusband in 1904.

The most likely explanation for the relative ease with which
Holmes was allowed to travel in Tibet is that he had letters or
passes signed by someone in a senior position within the political
and religious hierarchy of the country. Some powerful person
wanted him in Lhasa. One of the many mysteries surrounding the
detective's visit to Tibet is that Holmes seems so ambiguous in his
passing reference to the important personage he met there. Who
was the 'head lama' with whom he spent several days? Spiritual
power in Tibet had long been invested in the Dalai Lama, chosen
as a small child and assumed to be the reincarnation of the
previous Dalai Lama, but political power belonged to others, most
notably the regent who acted on his behalf until the chosen one
came of age. Most of the Dalai Lamas in the nineteenth century
had signally failed to achieve their majorities. The ninth, tenth,
eleventh and twelfth Dalai Lamas had all died young. Several were
assumed to have been murdered by their regents. (In 1875, the
twelfth Dalai Lama had met an end more extraordinary than most
when his regent arranged for his bedroom ceiling to collapse on his
head, with fatal consequences.)

At the time of Holmes's visit, the thirteenth Dalai Lama was
sixteen years old and still spent his days in seclusion, undergoing
the rigorous training required for the role he might or might not
be allowed to assume. It could not have been he with whom
Holmes conversed. Nor could it have been the Panchen Lama, the
head of the Tashilunpho Monastery who was seen as the second-

in-command in the Tibetan spiritual hierarchy, second only to the Dalai Lama. In 1891, the ninth Panchen Lama was even younger – a boy of eight. Whoever Holmes's 'head lama' was, it must have been he who arranged his passage to Lhasa.

The most likely candidate is the *amban*. He was not a 'lama' at all – Holmes was doubtless being deliberately misleading – but the senior Chinese official in Tibet. It would seem that Mycroft and the British government were not alone in wanting Sherlock Holmes in Lhasa. Keener still was the crumbling power of the Manchu dynasty of China.

CHAPTER TEN

'I THEN PASSED THROUGH PERSIA...'

W HY THE *AMBAN* MADE HOLMES's journey possible and what the two men discussed during the detective's sojourn in the Tibetan capital are matters for debate rather than certainty. The only evidence lies in a number of cryptic references in Foreign Office papers about relations with the Manchu Empire dating to the following year. These make no mention of Holmes by name but the person described as 'our representative in discussions' is almost certainly he. From these Foreign Office documents it is clear that the *amban*, one of those few Chinese officials aware of the true power of European colonial nations, was eager to establish lines of communication with the West. The attempt was doomed to failure. Less than a decade after he and Holmes spoke, the Boxer Rebellion broke out and a joint force of Western powers marched on the Chinese capital to assert its authority.

Holmes remained in the Tibetan capital for nearly six months, giving him plenty of time not only to confer with the *amban* but also

to learn about the country's religion. For a self-proclaimed rationalist, Holmes was always fascinated by the non-rational beliefs of
the faithful of all religions, and Lhasa would have provided him with
many opportunities to satisfy his curiosity. After leaving Lhasa in the
spring of 1892 (we know the date from another reference in a largely
forgotten Foreign Office document), Holmes stages another of
those disappearing acts that punctuate his years abroad. We have
little but his own word as to his whereabouts. As he continues his
narrative to Watson, he tells him, 'I then passed through Persia.'
The idea that Mycroft might have instructed his brother to visit
Tehran if he could is entirely feasible. At the time, dark suspicions
of Russia's ambitions in Persia haunted the minds of British
imperialists as powerfully as did concerns that it would expand into
Afghanistan, Tibet and the remoter steppes of Central Asia. Fears
of Russian influence in Persia were, indeed, more reasonable than
the anxieties that had sent Holmes off the edges of familiar maps
and into the unknown city of Lhasa. For most of the second half of
the nineteenth century, the Persians were keener to maintain friend-
ly relations with the Russians than they were to listen to the voices
of those British ministers to the Shah's court (one of whom was the
father of Colonel Sebastian Moran) who were advocating different
policies. Indeed, in 1856 a dispute about territory to the south of the
country had led to a war that Britain had rapidly won.

In the following decades, determined efforts had been made on
both sides to improve relations. In 1873, the British public had been
treated to a dazzling spectacle of Oriental splendour when the Shah
of Persia, Nasr-ed-Din, visited the country. Dressed, according to
one observer, in 'an astrakhan cap and a long coat embroidered with
gold' and wearing 'as many diamonds and precious stones as his
apparel would bear', the Shah fitted perfectly with 'the precon-
ceived notions people had formed of an Eastern potentate'. His visit

was one of the nine-day wonders of the 1870s. 'Have you seen the Shah?' became a popular catchphrase, endlessly repeated in every-day conversation and in songs performed on the music-hall stages. Darker rumours about Nasr-ed-Din's Oriental despotism also circu-lated. For a brief period, the Shah had stayed at Buckingham Palace while the Queen was away. It was said that he was so angered by the incompetence of one of the servants he had brought with him that he had the man strangled and cremated in the palace garden.

In the two decades since the Shah had made his exotic impact on the British public, however, Russian influence had continued to predominate in Persia. Although Britain had official representatives in Tehran, Mycroft and the mandarins of the Foreign Office may well have wanted the more penetrating and idiosyncratic insights that a visitor such as Holmes could provide. Persia was racked by internal power struggles – the Shah would be assassinated only four years later – and Holmes's reports from Tehran could only have been valuable. In the absence of any evidence to the contrary, we can assume that he spent the summer of 1892 in the country.

According to Holmes, he then 'looked in at Mecca, and paid a short but interesting visit to the Khalifa at Khartoum, the results of which I have communicated to the Foreign Office'. This laconic sentence again raises as many questions as it answers. In the 1890s, Euro-peans did not simply 'look in' at Mecca. It was less than forty years since Sir Richard Burton, the flamboyant adventurer and explorer, had visited the holiest city in the Muslim world. He had travelled disguised as an Afghan doctor, was fluent in Arabic as well as many other Middle Eastern and Oriental languages, yet still risked instant death if his masquerade had been exposed. 'At the pilgrimage season disguise is easy on account of the vast and varied multitudes,' Burton wrote in *Pilgrimage to Al-Medinah and Meccah*, his 1855 best-seller describing his adventures, 'but woe to the unfortunate who happens to be recognised in public as an Infidel.'

Burton liked to suggest that he was the first European to visit Mecca but, as so often in a life of hyperbole and melodramatic extravagance, he was exaggerating. As early as 1503, a Renaissance Italian, Ludovico di Varthema, pretended conversion to Islam and travelled to the city. In the next three and a half centuries, more than a dozen others succeeded not only in getting there but in getting home again to publish accounts of their experiences. John Lewis Burckhardt, an Anglo-Swiss explorer working for the London-based African Association, had obtained access in 1814 and several other nineteenth-century travellers, including a French army officer and a Finnish scholar, had penetrated the city in Arabic dress. Yet there is no denying or underplaying the difficulties involved in the journey. In the forty years since Burton, only a handful of other European travellers had reached Mecca.*

There was no compelling reason for Holmes to travel to Mecca. If he had known of the excursion, Mycroft would almost certainly have disapproved. Two-thirds of Holmes's mission had been completed. Valuable information about Russian intentions in both Tibet and Persia was, thanks to him, now circulating the Foreign Office. His true priority was not a casual and possibly foolhardy trip

---

* One of the most engaging and, in his own way, extraordinary of these was an English suburbanite from Norwood. Herman Bicknell was a convert to Islam and travelled towards Mecca quite openly, dressed in a cheap but well-tailored suit and a starched shirt, before changing into ritual dress known as the *ihram* to enter the city. Holmes, familiar with the works of Burton and Burckhardt, would not have heard of Bicknell, who returned to obscurity in Norwood but, curiously, he had almost certainly read something written by him. After his conversion, Bicknell became interested in Persian literature and his translation of the medieval lyric poet Hafiz was published posthumously in 1875. Holmes knew the work of Hafiz and, according to Watson in 'A Case of Identity', quoted lines by him. There is every likelihood that the version of Hafiz that Holmes knew was by Bicknell, although it has proved difficult to identify the exact line he quotes.

to the Muslim holy city but to get to the Sudan. Perhaps Holmes thought that going to Mecca would provide him with further valuable insights into the religion that he had temporarily adopted, which could only be useful in what threatened to be the most dangerous task that Mycroft had given him. Perhaps he believed that his enhanced status as a hajji, someone who had visited Mecca, could only be an advantage amid the fundamentalist fervour of the Mahdist regime in Khartoum. Most likely, Holmes was simply bored in the aftermath of his Persian adventure and sought to provide himself with the kind of new stimulus that his restless temperament required. 'My life,' as he once remarked, 'is spent in one long effort to escape from the commonplaces of existence.' What could be less commonplace than smuggling himself into the heart of yet another forbidden city?

The only time of the year in which Holmes would have had any chance of making the journey to Mecca would have been during the haj which took place in the late autumn. Amid the vast influx of pilgrims he could, perhaps, pass unnoticed. Thirteen years earlier, Wilfrid Scawen Blunt, a self-consciously Byronic escapee from the confines of English society, had arrived in Arabia with his new wife (one of her attractions for Blunt was that she was not merely Byronic but actually a Byron – she was the poet's granddaughter). Together the Blunts travelled restlessly around the desert and witnessed the passing of a caravan bound for Mecca – a straggling line of pilgrims, nearly five miles long, traversing the desert with the green and red banner of the haj at its fore. Dancing dervishes led the procession across the sands, followed by the mass of less fervent pilgrims, some on the backs of camels and some on foot. One pilgrim, Blunt noted, was smoking a long-tubed narghile as he was carried in a litter. Ten feet ahead of the litter walked a servant who held up the far end of the pipe. It was just such a caravan that

Holmes joined after he had made his way from Tehran to the Arabian peninsula.

Early in the nineteenth century, Domingo Badía-y-Leblich, a Spaniard who had posed as a Muslim, had witnessed the pilgrims arriving in Mecca. He wrote a lyrical account of 'the great spectacle presented by the Haj; the countless thousands from all nations and of all colours, coming through a thousand dangers and hardships from the furthest corners of the earth to worship the same God; the Caucasian giving a helping hand to the African, Indians and Persians fraternising with Algerians and Moroccans: all members of one family, all equal before their creator.' More than eighty years later, this would be the spectacle that Holmes would enjoy as his caravan entered the holy city.

We have no record of Holmes's reaction on achieving his self-imposed task of reaching the heart of Mecca. Richard Burton was overwhelmed when he finally saw the Sacred Mosque and the Ka'bah.

There at last it lay, the bourn of my long, weary pilgrimage, realising the plans and hopes of many and many a year. The mirage medium of Fancy invested the huge catafalque and its gloomy pall with peculiar charms. There were no giant fragments of hoar antiquity as in Egypt, no remains of graceful and harmonious beauty as in Greece and Rome, no barbarous gorgeousness as in the buildings of India; yet the view was strange, unique – and how few have looked upon the celebrated shrine! I may truly say that, of all the worshippers who ... pressed their beating hearts to the stone, none felt for the moment a deeper emotion than did the *hajji* from the far north.

There is no reason to believe that Holmes, a man whose unrelentingly rational exterior concealed a strong streak of mysticism and disguised religious feeling, was any less moved than Burton, the hard-bitten and egocentric adventurer.

Jiddah lies on the eastern coast of the Red Sea. In the 1890s it was, as it still is, the principal port through which Mecca-bound pilgrims travelled. Ships from all over the Muslim world arrived in Jiddah in their thousands during the haj. (In *The Sign of Four*, Jonathan Small and Tonga are picked up by a ship carrying pilgrims to Jiddah.) Jiddah had been home to a British consulate since the 1830s but Mecca, barred to all but the faithful, was only two days' camel ride away and it was from there that Holmes, still travelling as a Muslim pilgrim from North Africa, arrived in early 1893.

From Jiddah, it was easy enough to hire a dhow to cross the Red Sea to the Sudanese port of Suakin, which in 1893 was still held by an Anglo-Egyptian garrison. There Holmes was greeted by despatches from Mycroft in London – the first time he had heard from his elder brother in nearly a year. The urgency of Holmes's task in the Sudan was, if anything, greater than it had been when first outlined to him more than two years earlier. Advice and instructions soon began to descend on Holmes in an unmanageable deluge, most particularly from Horatio Herbert Kitchener, who had been appointed Commander-in-Chief of the Egyptian army the previous year. During the march made towards Khartoum in 1884–5 by troops hoping to relieve the beseiged General Gordon, Kitchener had been an intelligence officer and had himself spent time disguised as an Arab. He was therefore, in his own estimation, something of an expert on the subject of undercover work and he was determined that Holmes should benefit from his expertise. Further – and possibly more useful – information came from a source who had actually been in Omdurman. In 1891 one of the Mahdi's prisoners, the missionary Father Ohrwalder, had escaped and made his way to Egypt. His reports of life at the Khalifa's court had been forwarded to Holmes at Suakin.

From Suakin, on the coast and firmly under British control, Holmes set off inland and towards territory ruled by the Khalifa. Disguised once more as an itinerant trader from Algiers, a role to which he had become accustomed over the previous year, he was probably glad to put behind him both the wearisome bustle of the port and the relentless flow of advice from Kitchener. To visit the Khalifa in Khartoum* was just as dangerous, even suicidal, a mission as any attempt to penetrate the mysteries of Mecca. The Khalifa was the successor to the Mahdi, the Muslim religious leader who had declared a jihad or holy war against Anglo-Egyptian rule in the Sudan and who had, only a few years before Holmes's visit, inspired the forces that took Khartoum and killed General Gordon. The Mahdi had died of typhus six months after the capture of Khartoum. The Khalifa Abdullah, who had been one of his first disciples, emerged from the ensuing chaos as the one man sufficiently ruthless and capable not only to replace him but to hold together the fledgling state he had created.

The Mahdist Sudan, however, was not destined to last long. British and Egyptian forces had withdrawn from the country after the failed attempt to relieve Gordon in Khartoum but it was inevitable that they would return. Public opinion in Britain had been outraged by Gordon's death. Newspaper editors vied with one another in celebrating the general's self-sacrifice and execrating

---

* Holmes, as reported by Watson, claims to have visited the Khalifa in Khartoum. In fact, the Khalifa had established a new settlement at Omdurman a few miles from the old city where Gordon had died. In a very short time the settlement had grown into a thriving city with a population of more than 100,000. Clearly Holmes would have known this but he may have thought that Watson, unfamiliar with the details of Sudanese urban geography, was more likely to recognize the old name.

the government, which, it was claimed, had failed to act quickly enough to save him. Music-hall songs turned the dead Gordon into an icon of Empire. 'His life was England's glory,' according to one; 'his death was England's pride.' Portrait prints, such as the 'newly framed picture of General Gordon' that Watson possessed, sold in their tens of thousands. The Queen bombarded her unfortunate ministers with letters and telegrams demanding that action be taken.

The Prime Minister, Gladstone, was determined not to be drawn into what he saw as a pointless and irrational involvement in a poverty-stricken country that could bring no benefit to Britain. While he remained in power, the Sudan, despite the views of the public and the queen, would be left to the Khalifa to rule. By the late 1890s, however, Gladstone had retired from politics (he died in 1898) and circumstances, both in Britain and in Africa, were such that a renewed campaign was launched to invade the Sudan and avenge Gordon. In the summer of 1898, an Anglo-Egyptian army, led by Major-General Herbert Kitchener, marched deep into the Sudan and inflicted a crippling military defeat on the Mahdist forces of the Khalifa. At the battle of Omdurman, in September of that year, more than 10,000 of the Khalifa's men were killed and upwards of 20,000 wounded or taken prisoner. Kitchener lost 48 men killed and 382 wounded. The Khalifa escaped from the bloody wreckage of his short-lived Muslim state but was killed the following year in another, equally one-sided confrontation. The British and the Egyptians once more ruled the Sudan and would continue to do so until the establishment of the Republic of Sudan in 1956.

Holmes visited Khartoum in 1893, eight years after the death of Gordon and five years before the slaughter at Omdurman. Just as he had done when visiting Mecca, he travelled disguised as an Arab. His mission was to contact the European prisoners held by the

Khalifa and, if possible, to assist their escape. When the Mahdist armies swept through the Sudan, they had captured a number of Europeans who, for various reasons, had been stranded behind their advancing lines. Some were priests and nuns running the religious missions that had been established in the country. Others were members of the makeshift administration that Gordon had set up in the Sudan. Rudolf Slatin was the Khalifa's most prized European captive and the one that Holmes, instructed by Mycroft, was most determined to contact.

Slatin, born in 1857, was an Austrian adventurer who had landed up in Egypt in the mid-1870s. Introduced to Gordon, who had a habit of choosing his subordinates less on conventional merits and more on his own idiosyncratic judgements of character, Slatin was invited to travel with him to the Sudan. By 1879, Slatin Pasha had become the governor of Darfur, a bleak and mountainous region in the west of the country. Captured by the Mahdi's men in 1884, he was held in chains in the Dervish encampment when Khartoum was overrun and Gordon killed. Slatin was obliged to witness the indignities inflicted on the remains of the man who had brought him to the Sudan. He was in the encampment when Gordon's head, impaled on a spear, was brought before the Mahdi and saw it fixed in the fork of a tree where small boys pelted it with stones.

When Holmes arrived in Omdurman, Slatin had been a prisoner for nearly a decade, his fortunes ebbing and flowing with the whims of his captors. Useful to the Khalifa as an interpreter (it was probably Slatin who composed the letter that the Mahdist ruler sent to Queen Victoria, suggesting that she become a Muslim and submit to his overlordship), he had sometimes been allowed a degree of freedom and favour. At other times, he had been returned, for months, to his iron chains. Holmes knew something of the conditions in which Slatin was kept from Father Ohrwalder.

When Holmes, every day in danger of his life, arrived in Omdurman, Slatin was enjoying one of his intermittent periods of relative freedom. When walking in one of the town's markets, he was suddenly addressed by one of the traders in German. His surprise can only be imagined. The trader was, of course, Holmes. He would almost certainly have found an opportunity for a second meeting, at which Slatin was able to pass on as much information as he could to his remarkable visitor. There was no need for note-taking. Holmes's prodigious memory was more than capable of retaining the intelligence until he returned, some months later, to Egypt and Kitchener. Slatin he was unable to help. One European travelling out of Omdurman in disguise was a risky enough venture. Two – one of them already a familiar face to many of the Mahdi's followers – would have proven impossible. The Austrian had to wait a while yet for his release. When Holmes left Omdurman is uncertain. He would not have wanted to tarry in the city but we have no definite knowledge of his whereabouts for the rest of the year 1893.

After the defeat of the Mahdi by Kitchener's forces, the pacification of the country was swift. The Sudan was soon open to tourists as well as imperial soldiers bent on avenging Gordon. In 1900, less than seven years after Holmes's perilous solo mission into territory controlled by the Mahdi, Henry Gaze & Sons, a travel agent with offices just off Trafalgar Square, was offering curious (and wealthy) sightseers a sixteen-day trip from Cairo to Khartoum. Holmes, if he knew of it, was no doubt wryly amused.

As for Slatin, despite his experiences in Omdurman, he returned to the Sudan and worked there as an administrator for many years. He died in 1932, three years after Holmes, by which time he was Major-General Baron von Slatin Pasha KCMG, CB and the recipient of honours from three countries. There is no evidence that he and Holmes met again after their secret conference in the market place of Omdurman in the spring of 1893.

The last of the many mysteries surrounding the Great Hiatus in Holmes's life concerns his time in Montpellier. As several writers on the detective's life have pointed out, his statement to Watson – 'I spent some months in a research into the coal-tar derivatives, which I conducted in a laboratory at Montpellier, in the south of France' – is so imprecise as to be almost meaningless. 'Coal-tar derivatives' could refer to anything from fuel for lamps to Pears' Soap. There is no doubt that Holmes's interest in chemistry continued long after the researches he was conducting at Barts when he and Watson first met. In 1890, a year before Reichenbach, Watson, in 'The Adventure of the Copper Beeches', records him 'settling down to one of those all-night chemical researches which he frequently indulged in, when I would leave him stooping over a retort and a test-tube at night and find him in the same position when I came down to breakfast in the morning'. Yet, if Holmes wished only to recuperate from the stresses and dangers of the previous two and a half years by indulging his passion for chemical research, why did he choose Montpellier? As he would have known, it was Germany, not France, that was at the cutting edge of chemical research, as indeed it was in most fields of science and technology in the 1890s. Montpellier had one of the oldest universities in France, founded in the thirteenth century, but it was renowned more for its school of theology than for its scientific research.

Watson, despite his medical training, was unlikely to show much scepticism about any explanation Holmes gave him for his scientific researches but it seems probable that Holmes's work in those first two months of 1894 was connected with something far more contentious than coal-tar derivatives. What was he investigating in Montpellier? And why Montpellier at all?

The clue lies in the state of his health on his return to London. Watson noticed the difference in his friend. Soon after Holmes's dramatic revelation that he was still alive, he notes that, although the detective 'looked even thinner and keener than of old ... there was a dead-white tinge in his aquiline face which told me that his life recently had not been a healthy one'. Almost certainly, he was conducting research into radioactivity and radiation. Holmes had long been yearning to return to scientific investigations. 'Of late,' he comments in 'The Adventure of Final Problem', 'I have been tempted to look into the problems furnished by nature rather than those more superficial ones for which our artificial state of society is responsible.'

France was chosen over Germany for a variety of reasons, among them Holmes's French ancestry and his fluency in the language. In addition, such was his standing with a number of senior figures in the French government who knew that he had survived the Reichenbach Falls that he was given every assistance in settling anonymously in the country. Most importantly, in Montpellier he had the opportunity to work with the two people who were at the cutting edge of the research he wished to pursue. In the accepted version of the discovery of radium, the momentous news was announced by the husband and wife team of Pierre and Marie Curie in 1898, who had only begun to investigate the properties of radioactive bodies two years earlier. It now seems clear that this chronology is wrong. Their first researches took place some three years earlier and they were undertaken in association with a mysterious English chemist to whom they had been introduced by a high-ranking government official. The rationale for Holmes working in Montpellier now becomes apparent. Pierre's brother,

Laborde Curie, was professor of mineralogy in the university and it was through him that a laboratory was provided.

Yet Holmes's opportunities to indulge in the joys of scientific research were short-lived. Mycroft was already unhappy that his younger brother should remove himself from clandestine government work and he was soon intriguing to have him return to it. The murder of the Honourable Ronald Adair, and the assumed involvement of Moriarty's old henchman Colonel Moran, provided an opportunity to tempt his brother back to England. Holmes, although deep in the work that was eventually to result in the Curies' announcement to the scientific world nearly five years later, succumbed to the temptation. Perhaps he believed that he might return to the mysteries of radioactivity after he had dealt with Moran. Whatever the reason, he chose to leave the laboratory in Montpellier. It was March 1894. Sherlock Holmes, resurrected from the dead, was ready to resume his life in London.

CHAPTER ELEVEN

'I HEAR OF SHERLOCK EVERYWHERE'

D URING THE THREE YEARS IN which Holmes had been absent, Watson's life had been turned on its head. His wife, the former Mary Morstan, had died when only in her early thirties. We do not know the cause. It is possible that she was consumptive but there is no evidence of this in Watson's narratives. Nor is there any evidence that she died giving birth to a stillborn child. For Watson, it meant the loss of the great love of his life. He had loved Mary 'as truly as ever a man loved a woman' and their short marriage had been a source of enormous happiness to them both. Now he was once again alone. As Holmes once said, 'Work is the best antidote to sorrow,' and Watson must have taken this as his motto. He had exchanged his practice in Paddington for one in Kensington the year before Mary's death and now he threw himself into his medical work.

His career as a writer was also taking off. The first of the short narratives about Holmes were published in *The Strand Magazine* in

1891. By the time Doyle came to arrange publication of a second set of stories known as *The Memoirs of Sherlock Holmes* in 1892–3, *The Strand Magazine* was prepared to offer £1,000 (a very substantial sum in the 1890s) for them. Doyle, eager to concentrate on his own literary career, and Watson, with ambivalent feelings about publicizing the career of his supposedly late friend, were both uncertain about whether or not to proceed with another set of adventures but the money was simply too tempting. Neither of them can have anticipated the remarkable success that these tales of the great detective had in the three years when Holmes himself was believed dead.

Watson, who had lost the two people he most loved in less than two years, came to see himself as the guardian of both their memories. In the case of Holmes, this meant that he became overzealous in his determination to protect Holmes's legacy. Watson's exaggerated concern for the reputation of the friend he believed was dead led him and Doyle into some embarrassing situations. As Holmes's fame spread, Watson became convinced that he was doing the detective's memory a disservice and that Holmes, were he alive, would be appalled by the kind of attention he was now attracting.* At a meeting in the Café Royal, the two men agreed on a campaign that they hoped would bamboozle the press and throw doubt on the reality of Holmes's career, indeed on his very existence. As part of the campaign, Doyle began to talk in interviews of his invention of Holmes as a character and the fact that he was based on his old professor at the University of Edinburgh Medical School, Dr Joseph Bell. Doyle had been reminded of Bell during his very first conversation with Watson about Sherlock Holmes. Bell

---

* Watson was almost certainly wrong. Although Holmes made noises about the vulgarity of the attention Watson's stories brought him, the evidence strongly indicates that he was largely delighted by the publicity.

was renowned not only for his skill as a diagnostician but also for his uncanny ability to deduce personal details of the history, nationality and occupation of patients during his examination of them. In later writings Doyle quotes examples of Bell in action and he certainly does sound remarkably like Holmes:

Ah,' he would say to one of the patients, 'you are a soldier, and a non-commissioned officer at that. You have served in Bermuda. Now how do I know that, gentlemen? Because he came into the room without even taking his hat off as he would go into an orderly room. He was a soldier. A slight, authoritative air, combined with his age, shows that he was a non-commissioned officer. A rash on his forehead tells me he was in Bermuda and subject to a certain rash known only there.

It must have seemed a brilliant idea to suggest that Holmes was inspired by Bell but the plan backfired almost immediately. The press began to pursue Bell and Doyle was obliged to write a letter to him, apologizing for the intrusions.

When he returned in the spring of 1894 from beyond the grave, Holmes found himself in a strange and anomalous position. Thanks to the success of *The Adventures of Sherlock Holmes* and *The Memoirs of Sherlock Holmes*, the detective was one of the most famous men in Britain. Yet, also thanks to Watson and his account of the confrontation at the Reichenbach Falls, he was assumed by the majority of the population to be dead. As it was the kind of situation to appeal strongly to Holmes's sardonic sense of humour, he did not encourage Watson to spread the news that he was very much alive. For the best part of a decade, he refused to allow his Boswell to publish any word of his survival. *The Hound of the Baskervilles*, published in 1901, told of a case from the late 1880s and it was only in

1903 that the sensational news was revealed to the public, via the pages of *The Strand Magazine*, that Sherlock Holmes was still alive and still practising the art of scientific detection. During those years there were, of course, hundreds of people who knew the truth.

Yet, despite this fact and despite the detective's growing fame, word that Holmes had emerged unscathed from the encounter at the Reichenbach Falls did not become general knowledge. There is no doubt that, for the majority of those who read 'The Adventure of the Empty House' when it appeared in *The Strand Magazine* in 1903, the revelation came as a genuine surprise. How was it possible that the secret of his survival was kept from so many for so long? Clearly such an elaborate subterfuge could not work today. Yet, in the late nineteenth century, the mass media were still in their infancy. There was no radio and no television. The press, though increasingly powerful, was not as all pervasive as it is in the early twenty-first century. Those journalists in possession of the truth could be pressured into keeping it quiet. Mycroft had powerful friends. Scotland Yard, which had a vested interest in maintaining the charade, would also have had ways of silencing any pressmen too eager to break ranks and shout the news from the rooftops.

In the short term, when Holmes returned to London, there was the question of the man whose presence had brought him back to the capital. Holmes had used an elaborate charade to tempt Moran out of cover, in which a waxwork figure of the detective had invited the marksman to shoot at what he imagined to be Holmes's head silhouetted against the light in 221B Baker Street. As a consequence, Colonel Moran was finally caught but the evidence to put him away for any length of time, let alone hang him, was surprisingly thin. What is more, Moran in custody was almost as big an embarrassment to the government as Moran roaming Central Asia and northern India. His card-playing exploits had brought him into contact with the highest in the land. The name of Lord Balmoral, one of those from whom (as Watson records in 'The Adventure of the Empty House') Moran and the unfortunate Ronald Adair had won 'as much as four hundred and twenty pounds in a sitting', almost certainly hides the identity of the Prince of Wales.

The prince had already been involved in one scandal over cards. A few years earlier, the Tranby Croft affair had brought the Prince of Wales into the courtrooms, subpoenaed as a witness in a civil action brought by Sir William Gordon-Cumming. In 1890, Gordon-Cumming had been caught cheating at baccarat during an evening game played at Tranby Croft, the home of wealthy shipbuilder Arthur Wilson. The other players, including the prince, had come to a gentlemen's agreement with Gordon-Cumming whereby he would renounce gambling in return for their silence over his very ungentlemanly conduct. When rumours about him nonetheless began to circulate, Gordon-Cumming very foolishly decided to bring an action for slander against his accusers. When the case was heard in June 1891, the prince was forced to take the witness stand.

It was not the first time that the heir to the throne had been obliged to make an embarrassing appearance in a court of law. Twenty years earlier an aristocratic young woman, Lady Frances Mordaunt, had made a tearful confession to her husband, Sir Charles Mordaunt, that she had been 'very wicked' and 'done very wrong'. When he pressed her to be more specific, she claimed to have committed adultery, 'often, and in open day', with a wide range of his acquaintances including the Prince of Wales. At the court case that followed this astounding confession, the prince was required to stand in the witness box and answer a series of questions not customarily addressed to a senior member of the royal family.

In an atmosphere of hushed excitement, he was asked, 'Has there ever been any improper familiarity or criminal act between yourself and Lady Mordaunt?' When he replied firmly, 'There has not,' he may well have been telling the truth. All of Lady Mordaunt's claims were at least partially undermined by the fact that she was very disturbed and was later certified insane. Yet, whatever the circumstances in which the accusation was made, the heir to the throne had been dragged unwillingly into the mire and some of the mud had stuck. Now, two decades later, his private life was again to be put under the spotlight.

In the Tranby Croft case, it is difficult to see that Bertie, as the prince was known, had done anything morally untoward himself but, cross-examined with merciless efficiency by Gordon-Cumming's counsel, Holmes's friend Sir Edward Clarke, he was made to appear, not for the first time, as an idle reprobate with a taste for gambling and the high life. It was, after all, the prince who had suggested, indeed insisted upon, the game that had tempted Gordon-Cumming into cheating. In addition he had acted as banker and so practised a player was he that he owned a set of special, custom-made counters, adorned with the Prince of Wales's feathers. The press seized upon the case with huge delight. Then, as now, few stories provided a greater guarantee of increased sales than a juicy royal scandal. When the prince ventured out to Ascot, he was greeted with impertinent shouts from some of the spectators of 'Have you brought your counters?' and 'If you can't back a horse, baccarat.' The famous political cartoonist Sir John Tenniel showed naughty schoolboy Bertie listening to his mother Victoria, carpet beater in hand ready to chastise him as she listed his many shortcomings. On his jacket the Prince of Wales's motto reads not 'Ich Dien' but 'Ich Deal'.

Gordon-Cumming lost the case and retired in disgrace to his

estate in Scotland* but the damage had been done. Three years later, the very last thing the authorities wanted was public revelation of the prince's involvement in another shady game of cards. Moran needed to be persuaded that it was in his own best interests to keep quiet about his connection with the heir to the throne, and putting him on trial for his life for the attempted murder of Holmes was unlikely to have that effect. Holmes had finally cornered the colonel, but there must have been those in authority who wished he had not. Finally Moran struck a deal in which he avoided the capital charges. If we are to believe a hint in a later Watson narrative, the colonel was still alive twenty years later, presumably in prison.

Holmes's renown soon began to spread beyond the pages of *The Strand Magazine*. The first representation of Holmes on stage took place in 1893 while he was still assumed to be dead. Charles Brookfield played the detective in a short skit he had written himself titled 'Under the Clock' – 'an extravaganza in one act', as he dubbed it. Brookfield was a Cambridge-educated actor, playwright and journalist, three years younger than Holmes, who had performed with some of those actors, including Irving, whom Holmes had known in his own brief stage career. Watson, who was at the Royal Court Theatre on at least one occasion to see Brookfield's performance, was appalled by the way his late friend was portrayed but there was little he could do about it. Fame, then as now, has its own momentum.

By the mid-1890s, Holmes's apparently posthumous prestige was such that advertisers were prepared to pay to make use of his name. In 1894, Beechams, the pill manufacturers, in the clear knowledge

---

* The estate was Gordonstoun, later to be the site of the famous boarding school.

that he was very much alive, sent a representative to Baker Street to sound Holmes out on the possibility of gaining his endorsement in their advertising. There was a growing use of celebrities to endorse the most unlikely goods and services that had moved beyond those stars of stage and music hall who for decades had been lending their names to the puffing of products. Oscar Wilde, who, like Holmes, had a prescient understanding of the power of personality, gave his name to publicity for Madame Fontaine's Bosom Beautifier. 'Just so sure as the sun will rise tomorrow, just as sure it will enlarge and beautify the bosom,' ran the copy on the advertisement. Although perhaps only Madame Fontaine knew why Wilde was deemed a suitable front man for it, he earned good money from the campaign. Not long afterwards, Robert Baden-Powell, hero of Mafeking, and poet and writer Rudyard Kipling were both tempted to sing the praises of Bovril in public print.

The advertisers of the late Victorian period were also pioneers in the art of merchandising. Novels and plays that became popular spawned a whole array of associated goods. Trilby hats owe their name to George du Maurier's amazingly successful 1894 novel of artistic life in the Latin Quarter of Paris, entitled *Trilby*, but fans of the book could also purchase Trilby sausages, Trilby ice-cream moulds, Trilby lapel pins and Trilby bars of soap. Now it was Holmes's turn to be transformed into a selling tool.

Initially, Holmes dismissed Beechams' unfortunate representative with a flea in his ear. However, he was sufficiently intrigued to approach Conan Doyle and ask him to look into the commercial potential of the idea. Doyle, by this time more interested in his own literary career than in working as Watson's and Holmes's agent, was not best pleased, yet he was aware that his reputation and his income still depended heavily on the two men in Baker Street. He opened negotiations with Beechams and the result was that the

Illustrated London News of 20 July 1894 carried a half-page advertisement in which a letter, supposedly from Holmes to Watson, was featured. 'Dear Friend,' the letter began,

Mystery follows mystery; but the most mysterious thing of all is what has become of the part of my system which has almost taken the form of my second nature. I was especially cautious to provide myself with the indispensable before leaving home, but it has disappeared and I have lost all trace. I have unravelled many of other people's losses, but here is one of my own which has thrown me on my beam ends. I would not have troubled you, but in this benighted spot – although you will scarcely credit it – I cannot procure what I much need; so send by <u>first</u> post, as my movements are uncertain, one large box of Beecham's Pills. Note my assumed name and enclosed address, which I beg of you to destroy, as I do not wish my whereabouts to be known.

Yours,

S.H.

Years afterwards, Watson recalled the advertisement with amusement and, perhaps remembering the later occasion when Holmes sent him a telegram reading, 'Come at once if convenient – if inconvenient come all the same,' reportedly remarked to Doyle that his friend would not have been so prolix. He would simply have telegraphed, 'Require Beecham's Pills. Send by first post,' and expected Watson to spring into action. There is no record of what Holmes thought then or later. He may have appreciated the fee that Doyle had negotiated but was probably unimpressed by the quality of Beechams' copywriters.

'A name which is destined to be in everybody's mouth,' Oscar Wilde once wrote, 'must not be too long. It comes so expensive in the advertisements.' Holmes was lucky in that his name, combining as it did an exotic Christian name with a commonplace surname, was found to be doubly memorable. In the last decades of the nineteenth century, the growth of the mass media had created a cult of celebrity that we would recognize today. Newspapers and magazines vied with one another to produce profiles of the well known, relaxing in their own homes, illustrated with photo portraits and studded with their thoughts on a wide range of topics. *The Strand Magazine*, for example, ran a series titled 'Portraits of Celebrities at Different Times of their Lives' that featured everybody who was anybody, from the Lord Bishop of Peterborough to Miss Rosina Brandram, star of the Savoy operas. For the first time in history, famous people were instantly recognizable by the man or woman on the street. Holmes was there to benefit from this kind of celebrity but he was also resolute in maintaining his privacy. Ill-phrased and rather embarrassing advertising campaigns there might have been but there was little chance of Sherlock Holmes welcoming journalists into the Baker Street lodgings and expounding his ideas on New Scotland Yard or modern drama as Mrs Hudson hurried to provide afternoon tea.

The resurrected Holmes was as much in demand as ever. As Watson records, 'From the years 1894 to 1901 inclusive, Mr Sherlock Holmes was a very busy man. It is safe to say that there was no public case of any difficulty in which he was not consulted during those eight years, and there were hundreds of private cases, some of them of the most intricate and extraordinary character, in which he played a prominent part.' Through both choice and necessity, his Boswell was able to write down no more than a handful of these cases. 'There are some,' he confesses, 'which involve the secrets of private families to an extent which would mean consternation in many exalted quarters if it were thought possible that they might find their

way into print.' Yet he does admit to 'three massive manuscript volumes', which contained the details of Holmes's work in the months
immediately after his return, and he mentions a handful of the cases
that engaged his attention.

As I turn over the pages, I see my notes upon the repulsive story of the
red leech and the terrible death of Crosby, the banker. Here also I find an
account of the Addleton tragedy, and the singular contents of the ancient
British barrow. The famous Smith-Mortimer succession case comes also
within this period, and so too does the tracking and arrest of Huret, the
Boulevard assassin – an exploit which won for Holmes an autograph
letter of thanks from the French President and the Order of the Legion
of Honour.

Some of these cases are irretrievably lost to the historian. There are
no records extant of the Addleton tragedy or the terrible death of
the banker Crosby, while the fame of the Smith-Mortimer succession case has faded into oblivion. Perhaps Watson was once again
exercising that discretion that can be so infuriating for the modern
researcher into Holmes's life and career, disguising real cases behind
false names and invented aliases.

   When it comes to Huret, the Boulevard Assassin, however, we are
on firmer ground. The 1890s was a decade in which the great and
the good throughout the world seemed peculiarly vulnerable to the
anarchist assassin. In September 1898, the Empress Elizabeth of
Austria, staying near Lake Geneva, was fatally stabbed by the
Italian anarchist Luigi Luccheni. In 1894 in France, in the same year
in which Watson places Holmes's tracking and arrest of Huret, the
French president, Sadi Carnot, was killed after making a speech at
a public banquet. The murderer was another young Italian
anarchist. Sante Jeronimo Caserio, according to the reports issued

by the French government after the assassination, was a seriously disturbed individual who had been prompted to commit his crime as much by his own inner demons as by any coherent political philosophy. It seems, however, that this was a smokescreen designed to conceal from the public the fact that there was in existence a small cell of ruthlessly dedicated and violent men, committed to the overthrow of society. The leader of the cell was a Frenchman from Lyons, one Eugène Huret.

Born in 1868, the son of a weaver in the city, Huret had been a brilliant pupil at the local *lycée* and had won a place at the Ecole Normale Supérieure in Paris in 1887. Once in Paris, he had largely neglected his studies and gravitated towards those cafés of the Left Bank where politics and poetry were discussed with the kind of fervour and intensity that only French intellectuals can devote to them. At first, Huret was more interested in poetry than politics and in 1889 he even published a small volume of ghoulish *vers libre* entitled *Les Enfants de la Mort* (*The Children of Death*). In view of Huret's later career, it is interesting to read these immature and derivative verses, poor imitations of Rimbaud's more lurid visions, with their death-obsession and neurotic lingering on disease and suffering.

Huret first came to the police's attention as a member of a small circle of self-proclaimed anarchists centred on the journal *Le Drapeau Noir* (*The Black Flag*), who met in the cafés of Montmartre and talked of days to come when the blood of aristocrats, priests and capitalists would flow in the Parisian streets. The group's most prominent figure was Leo Ferry, a veteran of the Paris Commune. Huret and others, however, soon grew weary of Ferry's endless posturing and speechifying and began to demand action. In 1892, they broke away from *The Black Flag*, set up their own, even smaller-circulation newspaper, *L'Ami du Peuple* (*The People's Friend*), and began to plot an act of terror that would attract a blaze of publicity.

Their target was to be the head of the French state and their stooge the half-crazed Italian, Caserio.

With Carnot dead, the new president, Jean Paul Pierre Casimir-Perier, was clearly the next target of Huret's cell. Even before accepting the presidency, Casimir-Perier had been hated by the anarchists. As a minister he had been relentless in pressing the police into prosecutions aimed at destroying the very kind of groups in which Huret was so prominent. Only too aware of his vulnerability, Casimir-Perier himself asked that Holmes should be invited to France. The detective agreed to cross the Channel but he insisted on an entirely free hand in organizing his investigation. For several weeks, making use of his fluent French and his own aptitude for bohemian living, he mingled with the poets and anarchists of Montmartre. Only when he was certain that the real threat to law and order in the French capital came from the fanaticism of one man – Eugène Huret – did he call in the French police. The arrest was bungled by the Sûreté. It was intended that Huret should be seized in his own run-down apartment in Montmartre but an overeager officer attempted to arrest him as he walked along the Boulevard Raspail. Huret did not submit meekly and, in the ensuing exchange of gunfire between himself and French police officers, three passers-by were shot. One of them later died. The legend of the Boulevard Assassin was born.

Holmes's part in the thwarting of Huret's plans was downplayed. Watson does record an 1894 case in which Holmes crosses swords with European anarchists in 'The Adventure of the Golden Pince-Nez'. With its echoes of Russian revolutionary activity in the previous decade and its story of Professor Coram's wife stalking her traitorous husband (one of many who did so, he almost certainly gave evidence against the terrorists who assassinated the Russian Tsar Alexander II in 1881), it is, however, only a substitute for the far more interesting case of Huret. The encounter with the latter Watson feels able to mention only in passing.

Perhaps it was due to the difficulties of readjustment to London life. Perhaps it was the the result of the stress of his undercover work in Paris. But, within months of his return from his travels, Holmes's addiction to cocaine had once again taken hold. Some commentators on the detective's life have chosen to play down his dependence on drugs but there is little doubt that it became a serious problem in the latter half of 1894.

If nothing else, we have Watson's account of his own mounting concern for his friend's well-being. Originally content to accept that Holmes's use of morphine and cocaine was little more than another of his bohemian eccentricities, Watson soon became anxious about the effects of his regular intake. In *The Sign of Four*, a case dating from 1888, he watches Holmes prepare to inject his 'seven-per-cent solution' with ill-concealed irritation, noting 'the sinewy forearm and wrist, all dotted and scarred with innumerable puncture-marks', suggestive of persistent use. Eventually he feels obliged to protest.

'But consider!' I said earnestly. 'Count the cost! Your brain may, as you say, be roused and excited, but it is a pathological and morbid process which involves increased tissue-change and may at least leave a permanent weakness. You know, too, what a black reaction comes upon you. Surely the game is hardly worth the candle. Why should you, for a mere passing pleasure, risk the loss of those great powers with which you have been endowed? Remember that I speak not only as one comrade to another but as a medical man to one for whose constitution he is to some extent answerable.'

Holmes, unsurprisingly, is unmoved, merely pointing out, not for the first time, his abhorrence of the dull routine that descends when he has no case in hand and his need for artificial stimulation. By the time of 'The Adventure of the Missing Three-Quarter', which takes place in 1896 but was not published until 1904, Watson was referring to the 'drug mania which had threatened once to check his remarkable career'.

Holmes had his own explanation for his dependence on drugs. 'Give me problems, give me work, give me the most abstruse crypto-gram or the most intricate analysis, and I am in my own proper atmosphere,' he said in *The Sign of Four*. 'I can dispense then with artificial stimulants. But I abhor the dull routine of existence. I crave for mental exaltation.' Perhaps the departure of his greatest enemy had dulled Holmes's enthusiasm for his work. 'London has become a singularly uninteresting city since the death of the late lamented Professor Moriarty,' he tells Watson at the beginning of 'The Adventure of the Norwood Builder'. Whatever the reason, he clear-ly turned more and more to drugs.

How Holmes first encountered his favourite stimulants is not known. In all likelihood, he began to take them either as a student or during his thwarted career as an actor. Nineteenth-century Britain was unembarrassed about its drug-taking. Opium was avail-able over the pharmacist's counter. Hundreds of thousands – per-haps millions – of people took it as a painkiller or as a recreational stimulant. Gladstone took laudanum, a mixture of opium and alcohol, to calm his nerves before major speeches in the House of Commons. Dickens was another user. His friend Wilkie Collins was so inured to the stuff that, for years before his death, he was taking enough to fell twelve less seasoned addicts. Even babies were given preparations that included opium, which rejoiced in names like Godfrey's Cordial and Mother Bailey's Quieting Syrup. Cocaine was similarly commonplace.

Watson's concern about Holmes's use of the drug shows him to be ahead of the standard medical opinion of the time. In the 1880s and 1890s, few doctors would have condemned it as unequivocally as he does. Indeed, for many, cocaine was beneficial, a kind of wonder drug to be prescribed for all sorts of complaints from depression to impotence. Most famously, Holmes's and Doyle's acquaintance from Vienna, Sigmund Freud, was for a number of years an enthusiastic advocate of cocaine's miraculous powers, taking it himself and recommending it to everyone he knew, including both his father and his fiancée, Martha Bernays. 'I take very small doses of it regularly against depression and against indigestion, and with the most brilliant success,' he wrote to Martha in 1884. It was only when one of Freud's friends, Ernst von Fleischl-Marxow, after taking the drug regularly to ease the pain of chronic illness, became quite obviously addicted to cocaine (he imagined white snakes crawling all over his skin if he withdrew from it) that Freud began to wonder whether it was quite such a 'magical drug' as he had thought. However, many physicians continued to view cocaine as completely safe and it remained entirely legal. In America, when John Pemberton launched a new soft drink in 1886, one of its ingredients was cocaine. The drink was Coca-Cola.

Perhaps Watson, deeply distressed by his elder brother's descent into incurable dipsomania and then by his death in 1888, was more alert than most to the signs of encroaching addiction. In persuading Holmes to look after his health, Watson faced an uphill struggle. As he acknowledged in 'The Adventure of the Devil's Foot', it 'was not a matter in which he took the faintest interest'. Holmes was, of course, also a prodigious consumer of tobacco. Pipe or cigarettes were always to hand. The famous rooms in Baker Street must have reeked of tobacco and a haze of smoke hung forever in the air. As we learn in 'The Adventure of the Engineer's Thumb', Holmes had the true addict's habit of recycling the remains of the previous day's smoking, his before-breakfast pipe consisting of 'all the plugs and dottles left from his smokes of the day before, all carefully dried and collected on the corner of the mantelpiece'. Here again, Watson made fruitless attempts to persuade Holmes to look after his health. In 'The Adventure of the Devil's Foot', Holmes refers to 'that course of tobacco-poisoning which you have so often and so justly condemned'. There is, however, little indication that he took the condemnation seriously.

CHAPTER TWELVE

'OCCASIONAL INDISCRETIONS
OF HIS OWN'

B Y THE SPRING OF 1895, a combination of Watson's tactful care
and Holmes's own iron constitution had ensured that the
detective's health was much improved. In 'The Adventure of the
Black Peter', written and published nearly a decade after the events
it described, Watson's relief can still be felt in his remark that he had
'never known my friend to be in better form, both mental and physical, than in the year '95'.

That year was to see several other cases that Watson recorded for
posterity. The murder of Aloysius Garcia, and the tangled web of
revenge and conspiracy surrounding the deposed dictator Don Juan
Murillo, 'the Tiger of San Pedro', are detailed in the narrative that
later became known as 'The Adventure of Wisteria Lodge'.*

---

* As published, the narrative known as 'The Adventure of Wisteria Lodge' provides the
clearest of all examples of Watson's unreliability with dates. 'I find it recorded in my
notebook that it was a bleak and windy day towards the end of March in the year 1892,'
begins his account. 'Holmes had received a telegram while we sat at our lunch, and he had

Holmes and Watson travel to 'one of our great university towns' in 'The Adventure of the Three Students' and are drawn into an investigation of potential cheating in an upcoming examination for the prestigious Fortescue Scholarship. In 'The Adventure of the Solitary Cyclist', Violet Smith consults Holmes about the mysterious bicycle-riding stalker who follows her through the Surrey countryside.

These are private cases, just a handful of the 'hundreds' in which Watson acknowledges that Holmes plays a prominent part in the years between his return from the dead and the demise of Queen Victoria. Of the public cases, Watson, as we have come to expect, says very little. The case involving the theft of the plans for the Bruce-Partington submarine and the murder of the unfortunate Arthur Cadogan West is the only one that Watson records from 1895 that could be so described, although he does drop hints and asides about even more illustrious clients.

Leaving England for only the second time since the adventures of the Great Hiatus, Holmes journeyed to Rome, at the express desire of the Pope, to investigate the sudden death of Cardinal Tosca. Leo XIII had succeeded Pius IX in 1878 and remained pontiff until his death a quarter of a century later. He already had reason to appreciate Holmes's remarkable skills (in the 1880s the detective had solved the mystery surrounding the disappearance of a valuable set of quattrocento cameos from the Vatican collection). Therefore when one of his cardinals died in circumstances that some said suggested foul play, he had no doubts about the best man to undertake a discreet investigation.

---

scribbled a reply.' In March 1892, Holmes was in Tibet and in no position either to receive a telegram or to scribble any reply to it. How Watson could make this mistake is a mystery. How Doyle, preparing the manuscript for *The Strand Magazine*, could miss it is equally inexplicable.

Watson, in referring obliquely to the case, was equally discreet. Cardinal Tosca* is one of the aliases that Watson invents for certain characters. The cardinal in question was actually Cardinal Luigi Ruffo-Scilla, one of a family of Sicilian noblemen and high church-men, who collapsed and died in Rome at the end of May 1895. Still only in his mid-fifties at the time of his death – positively youthful by the standards of the cardinalate – Ruffo-Scilla had made enemies within the Curia, and rumours that he had been poisoned were soon drifting dangerously along the corridors of the Vatican Palace. In the short time that he was in Rome – he was probably there no more than a few days – Holmes was able to prove conclu-sively that the cardinal had died a natural death. The rumours were scotched and the Pope was once again impressed by the English detective's acumen and resourcefulness.

There were cases in 1895 nearer to home that Holmes felt unable to accept. In the spring of that year, Oscar Wilde instituted pro-ceedings for libel against the Marquess of Queensberry. Wilde was involved with the Marquess's son, Lord Alfred Douglas, and the Marquess, a dangerously unstable personality, had pursued the writer around London, uttering threats and insults at every oppor-tunity. Matters came to a head when Queensberry left a card at Wilde's club, addressed 'To Oscar Wilde posing as a somdomite [sic]'. Wilde, pressured by the equally unstable Douglas, took legal action and sued for libel. It was a foolhardy move. Wilde's private

---

* In using the name Tosca as an alias, Watson is probably not referring to Puccini's opera, as a modern reader might believe – it was not premièred until 1900 – but to the original play by the French dramatist Victorien Sardou. The play had been seen in London in 1891, with Sarah Bernhardt in the role of Tosca. Her performance had stunned audiences used to the more sedate acting style of English players. 'The cries of the despairing Tosca, as her lover is being tortured,' wrote one critic, 'literally sent a shudder of horror round the house.' Watson had probably been in the audience at Her Majesty's Theatre. The death of the cardinal, occurring just a few years later, recalled, for some reason, the emotions of that night.

life was not the kind that could bear the scrutiny necessarily applied during a court case. Casting around for some way out of his terrible predicament, Wilde remembered Watson from the meeting some years earlier at the Langham Hotel and recalled his stories of the remarkable powers of his friend Sherlock Holmes. He contacted Watson. Could Holmes, Wilde wondered, be persuaded to work on his behalf?

Holmes could not. From his army of contacts in the criminal and sexual underworlds of the capital, he knew enough of Wilde's doings and of the life of Alfred Taylor, who had procured young men for Wilde and was to stand trial with him later, to realize that the game was up for the charismatic Irishman. His advice was short and to the point. Wilde should flee the country. This was what many of Wilde's friends were urging. Wilde, encouraged by Lord Alfred to contest his father's case and paralysed by a strange fatalism, chose to stay. In April, Holmes, like thousands of other Londoners, read in the papers of Wilde's arrest at the Cadogan Hotel.

Although he declined to provide Wilde with any assistance other than advice that the writer ignored, Holmes had strong connections with the era's 'decadent' artists. He had, for example, been briefly employed by the poet Ernest Dowson in 1895, the same year that Wilde's life and career plunged into the abyss, when Dowson had been searching for the truth about the deaths of his mother and father. Dowson Senior had succumbed to an overdose of chloral, a highly addictive drug used by Victorians as a sleeping potion, and his wife had hanged herself a couple of months later. The younger Dowson was possessed of a richly morbid imagination that permeated his life and work. Even in a love poem to a mistress, he could not resist the temptation to point out, 'For all too soon we twain shall tread/The bitter pastures of the dead.' He became convinced that his father had been poisoned by some unknown enemy. However,

Holmes found no evidence of anything other than addiction, accident and an urge to self-destruction in the Dowson family's tragic history.

There were other cases in that year of which we know little. One example must suffice. The memoirs of Charles Alcock, who was secretary of the Football Association for twenty-five years and who was responsible for the creation of the FA Cup competition in the early 1870s, carry a small hint that Holmes was involved in the search for the Cup when it was stolen from the window of the Birmingham sports outfitters, William Shillcock, on 11 September 1895. Mention of a 'legendary private investigator' hired by the FA certainly suggests Holmes but we cannot be sure. Presumably, Holmes, if it was he, failed to find the thief, although the possibility exists that he did identify him and that there was insufficient evidence to take the case to court. The Cup was never found but, in 1963, an octogenarian confessed to the crime on his deathbed and admitted that he had melted down the trophy to create counterfeit half-crowns. Did Holmes know who the thief was? We shall never know. Alcock makes no more than his single, enigmatic reference to the private detective.

Watson records only three cases in 1896 and again he avoids all mention of those events with international repercussions that took up so much of his friend's time in that year. 'The Adventure of the Veiled Lodger', in which Holmes discovers the true identity of the mysterious woman who rents a room in the house of Mrs Merrilow, is a tale of domestic tragedy. So too is 'The Adventure of the Sussex Vampire', with its story of a woman desperately attempting to hide an awful truth from her husband and arousing his darkest suspicions in the process, and also 'The Adventure of the Missing Three-Quarter', in which Godfrey

Staunton's reasons for missing the Varsity Rugby match are revealed.

In early 1897, Holmes's health again threatened to give way and he was obliged, unwillingly, to undertake a rest cure before he was able to return to his work. Watson is, for once, rather circumspect in describing the symptoms and causes of his friend's breakdown – he refers euphemistically to Holmes's ill health being 'aggravated, perhaps, by occasional indiscretions of his own' – but it is clear enough that Holmes had succumbed once more to his addiction to cocaine. The Harley Street doctor, Moore Agar, no doubt an early specialist in the treatment of drug dependence, recommended Cornwall as a refuge from the excitements and temptations of London. Holmes, alarmed by Agar's suggestion that he might otherwise become 'permanently disqualified from work', agreed to go. Even at the furthest extremity of England, however, murder and mystery pursued Holmes. It was here that the dramatic events recorded in 'The Adventure of the Devil's Foot' unfolded and the detective uncovered the truth behind the bizarre deaths of several members of the Tregennis family.

Watson records only one other case in 1897: 'The Adventure of the Abbey Grange',* in which Sir Eustace Brackenstall is apparently murdered during a burglary. Holmes reveals how he actually met his death. These incidents almost certainly pre-date the visit to Cornwall, so the detective's activities for much of the year remain a mystery. The frustration for a biographer continues for the next three years. As the new century approached, we can assume that

---

* Holmes was a keen student of the Newgate Calendar and cannot have failed to recognize similarities between the murder with which he was faced at the Abbey Grange and the murder in 1813 of the elderly merchant Thomson Bonar and his wife. As Holmes himself remarked in *The Valley of Fear*, 'Everything comes in circles ... The old wheel turns and the same spoke comes up. It's all been done before and will be again.'

Holmes was as stretched as he had ever been, yet Watson records only four cases for the years 1898, 1899 and 1900. For 1898 we have 'The Adventure of the Dancing Men' in which the English squire Hilton Cubitt seeks Holmes's help in solving the mystery of the strange, chalked stickmen that have been drawn on the doors and window frames of his house. It is not one of Holmes's greatest successes. Although he manages to understand the messages from the hidden past encoded in the figures, he cannot prevent the tragedy that they portend. Cubitt is murdered.

The following year Watson records two cases – the double murder that he entitles 'The Adventure of the Retired Colourman', and the excursion to Hampstead that ends in the death of the blackmailer Charles Augustus Milverton. And, as we have seen, the story of Milverton is an almost entirely fictional variation on a real-life case that took place a decade earlier. For 1900, we again have only a single case: 'The Adventure of the Six Napoleons', in which Holmes unravels the story behind the apparently mindless destruction of a series of plaster busts of the Emperor Napoleon. It is one of the detective's most imaginative triumphs, yet it is again curious that Watson can find no other cases of that year to record for posterity. Holmes might well have had cause to berate his Boswell for idleness but there may have been reasons why he would in fact have been happy that his activities at the turn of the century should go unrecorded. The continuing pretence that he had died at the Reichenbach Falls was becoming well nigh impossible to sustain. Too many people were privy to the secret. Holmes's mind was turning to other means of maintaining the anonymity that he believed essential to his work.

By 1900, the collaboration between Watson and Conan Doyle, which had brought the detective into the public eye, had persisted for more than a decade. The result of a chance meeting and idle conversation at dinner, it had been a happy association. Watson, largely uninterested in the literary world, had welcomed Doyle's willingness to undertake the mundane business of selling the stories and dealing with editors and publishers, as well as his occasional advice on writing. Doyle had seen his own stumbling literary career flourish as a consequence of his involvement with the stories about Holmes's exploits.

The only fly in the ointment had been Holmes himself. Although the detective was mostly content to ignore his appearances before the reading public, he had periods when, idle and bored, his attention would turn to the adventures that had been published while he was supposedly dead. On these occasions he would usually find himself displeased, either with the writing itself or the process of publication. Doyle became used to intermittent volleys of telegrams in which Holmes, never reconciled to the idea that the chronicles had appeared in *The Strand Magazine*, would offer peremptory advice on the ways in which they could have been placed in more intellectually reputable journals. But Doyle soon learned that, if he ignored these communications, a new case of interest would rapidly distract Holmes's attention and the detective would appear to forget his dissatisfaction. It was Watson who bore the brunt of his friend's literary criticism.

Holmes was consistently dismissive of the narratives Watson wrote. Over and over again, he refuses to acknowledge the demands of the readership that Watson and Doyle had found for them, preferring to believe that there was some more discriminating forum awaiting them, if only they would cater for it. 'You have degraded what should have been a course of lectures into a series of tales,' he complains in 'The Adventure of the Copper Beeches' and in another story, 'The Adventure of the Abbey Grange', he inveighs against Watson's 'fatal habit of looking at everything from the point of view of a story instead of as a scientific exercise', which, he says, 'has ruined what might have been an instructive and even classical series of demonstrations'. As he warms to his theme, and as Watson no doubt wearily prepares himself to hear strictures that he has heard a hundred times before, Holmes sounds like a fastidiously intellectual don unexpectedly confronted by a penny dreadful: 'You slur over work of the utmost finesse and delicacy, in order to dwell upon sensational details which may excite, but cannot possibly instruct, the reader.'*

In fact, the collaboration between Watson and Doyle had, by the end of the century, become so close that, at their regular meetings over dinner at Simpson's in the Strand, they swapped and shared stories without any of the competitive paranoia that has characterized so many other literary relationships. Watson was often remarkably unpossessive about the narrative material that his adventures with Holmes had provided. (For the second half of the 1890s, of course, Holmes had placed a ban on publication of information about his current work and Watson may not have believed that the accounts he was occasionally outlining would ever see the light of day.) 'The Adventure of the Abbey Grange', recounting events that had occurred 'towards the end of the winter of '97', was not published until 1904 but Watson had clearly given Doyle an outline of them much earlier and was untroubled by the younger writer's use of some of the details in a tale that Doyle published in

---

* An irony, which Holmes would not have appreciated but Watson might, is that when, in 'The Adventure of the Blanched Soldier' and 'The Adventure of the Lion's Mane', the detective recorded cases in first-person narratives, the style is often indistinguishable from that of his colleague and friend. Indeed, in the preamble to the first of these stories, Holmes is forced to admit that Watson's method of constructing a story had its strengths. 'Having taken my pen in my hand,' he confesses, 'I do begin to realise that the matter must be presented in such a way as may interest the reader.'

1899. To any Holmesian, the close similarities between the case of Lady Brackenstall and the Conan Doyle story 'B.24', which appeared in *The Strand Magazine* in March of that year, are immediately apparent.

Although no word of Holmes's activities reached the wider public between his return from the dead in 1894 and the turn of the century, his celebrity was undimmed. Watson often misread his friend's ambivalent feelings about his continuing fame. To Watson, Holmes seemed always a reluctant public figure. 'In recording from time to time some of the curious experiences and interesting recollections which I associate with my long and intimate friendship with Mr Sherlock Holmes,' he noted in 'The Adventure of the Devil's Foot', 'I have continually been faced by difficulties caused by his own aversion to publicity.' Watson tended to take at face value Holmes's lectures on the vulgarity of public prominence, continuing to believe that 'to his sombre and cynical spirit all popular applause was always abhorrent', even when there was clear evidence to the contrary. In truth, Holmes was one of those men who enjoyed backing into the limelight.

By the early years of the new century, Holmes was beginning to gain that extraordinary worldwide fame that his contradictory nature both craved and abhorred. Thanks largely to Doyle, Watson's stories were well known on both sides of the Atlantic. Theatrical versions of them had begun to appear and the finest actors in the country thought seriously about bringing the detective to the stage. Both Sir Henry Irving, Holmes's old friend, and Herbert Beerbohm Tree considered staging the Sherlock Holmes play that Doyle, perhaps with Watson's help, had devised. While they were debating, the rights were bought for the American actor William Gillette.

The sale had not been an easy one. Negotiations dragged on for some months and all three of the principals concerned grew weary of the saga. When Gillette proposed substantial alterations to the text and even cabled from America with the rather astonishing suggestion that Holmes might marry in his drama, Watson and Doyle had almost passed the point of caring. Holmes meanwhile, as so often, feigned magnificent indifference to his public reputation. Doyle cabled back: 'You may marry him, murder him, or do anything you like to him.' Gillette, now working with Doyle's full if exasperated approval, produced the play. He was to perform it more than a thousand times over the next few decades.* In 1901 the play, with Gillette again in the title role, began a run at the Lyceum in London, the very theatre in which Holmes had appeared with Irving's company nearly thirty years earlier.

The fledgling cinema industry had brought Holmes to the screen as early as 1900, with the brief film *Sherlock Holmes Baffled*. It lasted all of forty-nine seconds. Perhaps the most ambiguous tribute to Holmes's growing renown was that at least one criminal was inspired by his reading of Watson's stories to create his own inventive scam. What 'Killer' Evans probably did not anticipate was that the crime that he committed would itself be investigated by Holmes but it is very clear that the mastermind behind 'The Adventure of the Three Garridebs' had taken note of the deceptions recorded in 'The Adventure of the Red-Headed League' and 'The Adventure of the Stockbroker's Clerk'.

*

---

* Gillette wrote, produced and starred in other Holmes productions, including a brief sketch titled 'The Painful Predicament of Sherlock Holmes' in which an entirely silent Holmes confronts a garrulous woman intent on gaining his attention. There were rumours at the time that Holmes came to an arrangement with Gillette to play himself on stage and it may have been in this non-speaking role that the detective appeared on the London stage for the first time since 1874.

Holmes was now probably as busy as ever but, once again, Watson records only a few of his cases. From 1901 we have three. The mysterious disappearance of Lady Frances Carfax, which sent Watson careering across Europe, was one; the strange circumstances surrounding the death of Mrs Neil Gibson at Thor Bridge another. The most revealing one is perhaps the narrative that Watson titles 'The Adventure of the Priory School'.

Superficially, throughout his career, Holmes acts like a man for whom the mundane and trivial business of earning a living is of negligible interest. Yet his attitude to money is more complex than it first seems. Partly he is still hamstrung by his belief that being a professional detective is somehow beneath a gentleman of ancient family like himself. When he airily tells Helen Stoner, in 'The Adventure of the Speckled Band', that she is 'at liberty to defray whatever expense I may be put to, at the time which suits you best', we catch sight of the man who would prefer to be the disinterested amateur of crime. At other times Holmes falls back on a supposedly strict system of remuneration that he claims to use. 'My professional charges are upon a fixed scale. I do not vary them, save when I remit them altogether.' This is manifestly untrue, as is clear from the events that Watson describes in 'The Adventure of the Priory School'. The cheque from the 'Duke of Holdernesse' that Holmes pockets so complacently is for an enormous sum of money. Although Holmes's claim to be 'a poor man' is ironic (he had been financially secure since at least 1890), £6,000 was the equivalent of almost £500,000 in today's terms. If we are looking for the means by which Holmes was later able to purchase his cottage on the Sussex Downs, we need look no further.

Watson's records for 1902 are more extensive than his circumstances might have suggested. In that year he married for a second time and once again set up in medical practice, this time in Queen Anne Street. Although the doctor had, in Holmes's words, 'deserted him for a wife', Watson was still a frequent visitor to Baker Street but the friendship, now more than twenty years old, had changed. By the time he published 'The Adventure of the Creeping Man' in 1923, Watson, then in his early seventies, had leisure to review earlier times and recognize that Holmes was constitutionally incapable of genuine intimacy. The relationship had always been one in which the doctor gave far more of himself than he ever received in return. When he recalls that 'as an institution I was like the violin, the shag tobacco, the old black pipe, the index books, and others perhaps less excusable' and that many of Holmes's remarks 'would have been as appropriately addressed to his bedstead', his remark may be lightly tinged with resentment and bitterness at the way Holmes had treated him over the years. Nevertheless it remains an honest and clear-eyed assessment.

Yet, although this year saw Watson record more adventures than his altered position at Baker Street might dictate, there are still only five cases extant from 1902. In the very last case that he and Doyle arranged for publication, 'The Adventure of Shoscombe Old Place', Watson looks back more than two decades to Holmes's investigation into the strange behaviour of Sir Robert Norberton and his sister Lady Beatrice Falder. 'The Adventure of the Three Garridebs', with its ironic echoes of Holmes's own earlier cases, and 'The Adventure of the Three Gables', in which an unpublished novel is the focus of feverish attempts to possess it, are also both cases from this year, which Watson recollects from the vantage point of his old age.

'The Adventure of the Red Circle', another 1902 case, is perhaps most interesting because of the proof it provides of Holmes's linguistic abilities – he clearly understands Italian well enough to unravel secret communications in that language – and the hidden evidence of Watson's wariness in writing about the Italian secret societies of the late nineteenth century. In the manuscript of the adventure, which has survived, the organization concerned is quite clearly identified as the Camorra but, by the time Watson and Doyle have finished their editorial work and the story is published in *The Strand Magazine*, discretion has replaced candour. The still-flourishing Camorra has become the Carbonari, which, by the beginning of the twentieth century, was for Italians nothing more than an echo from history.

One more event in 1902 of which we have some details demands attention. In June 1902, Holmes refused a knighthood. Had he accepted, he would have appeared in the same honours list as his agent and friend Arthur Conan Doyle, who had been knighted for his services in the Boer War. Why did Holmes refuse the title?

True, he had always claimed an indifference to public honours. When Mycroft, in 'The Adventure of the Bruce-Partington Plans', suggests that he might have a fancy to see his name in the next honours list, Holmes merely smiles, shakes his head and remarks, 'I play the game for the game's own sake.' Seven years earlier, his services in the case of the Bruce-Partington submarine had won him a private audience with Victoria and a royal gift of an emerald tiepin. The 1902 honours list was one of the first drawn up by her son, the new king, Edward VII, for whom Holmes had little respect, regarding him as a selfish and egocentric wastrel. In the previous two decades, he had been employed several times, not always willingly, to help rescue the then Prince of Wales from the consequences of his own indiscretions. Three months after his refusal of Edward's proffered knighthood, Holmes was once again drawn into the monarch's private affairs. The 'illustrious client' in the adventure of that name is almost certainly the king. Yet Holmes's spurning of the knighthood can have had little to do with his personal opinion of Edward.

The true explanation must lie in the fact that, in 1902, the detective was still officially dead. As we have seen already, the fiction that Holmes had perished at the Reichenbach Falls had been severely compromised during the late 1890s. Inevitably, many people now knew that he had survived but Holmes, for his own, enigmatic reasons, still insisted on maintaining his cover. Accepting an honour such as a knighthood would have dealt a final blow to the pretence that he was no longer in the land of the living. At the same time, Holmes was contemplating another elaborate charade to maintain what anonymity he could. He was planning his supposed 'retirement'.

CHAPTER THIRTEEN

'A SMALL FARM UPON
THE DOWNS'

IN 'THE ADVENTURE OF THE LION'S MANE', a story that Holmes himself tells, he describes the setting for his 'retirement'. 'My villa,' he reports, 'is situated upon the southern slope of the downs, commanding a great view of the Channel . . . My house is lonely. I, my old housekeeper, and my bees have the estate all to ourselves.' Watson describes it as 'a small farm upon the downs five miles from Eastbourne'. This, then, is the setting for what we are supposed to accept is Holmes's retirement from active life in 1903. The events as described by Watson are – to put it bluntly – incredible. Are we really expected to believe that a man of Holmes's intense energy and commitment to his work would simply quit London at the age of forty-nine in order to spend the last quarter of a century and more of his life pottering around the Sussex Downs, looking after bees while signally failing to write a magnum opus on the art of detection? This, after all, is the man whom Watson himself describes as driven almost insane by lack of mental stimulation.

This is the man who once said, in *The Sign of Four*, 'I never remember feeling tired by work though idleness exhausts me completely.' This is the man who, in 'The Adventure of Wisteria Lodge', referred to his mind as 'like a racing engine, tearing itself to pieces because it is not connected up with the work for which it was built'.

When Holmes claims that, in his retirement, he has given himself up entirely 'to that soothing life of Nature for which I had so often yearned during the long years spent amid the gloom of London', the reader's only appropriate response has to be a hollow laugh. Holmes had had more than enough of Nature's supposed balm during the loneliness of his upbringing in Hutton le Moors and there is no other evidence that he ever pined for it again after his departure from his family home in 1873. On the contrary, we have Watson's word that 'appreciation of nature found no place among his many gifts'. We can therefore safely assume that Holmes would have found permanent retirement to the Downs an exile from all that for him was most interesting and stimulating.

Certainly, Holmes did indeed buy the 'small farm upon the Downs' that Watson described and he did spend long periods of secluded study there. Certainly, some of his time in the years between 1903 and 1910 was spent in the passions he claimed to be pursuing. His *Practical Handbook of Bee Culture, with Some Observations upon the Segregation of the Queen*, the 'fruit of pensive nights and laborious days', was undoubtedly published during these years, although it is an exceptionally rare volume that hardly ever appears in the catalogues of antiquarian book dealers. But Holmes had not given up his lodgings in Baker Street, nor had he relinquished the work that gave meaning to his life. In fact, he continued to involve himself in crime investigation until he was close to seventy and the decade after his supposed retirement to the Downs was one of the busiest of his career.

Watson added to the mystification surrounding Holmes's retirement, presumably deliberately, by some of the contradictory statements he made on the subject over the years. In 'The Adventure of the Second Stain', first published in 1904, he claims that he has been slow to allow his narratives into print because of

the reluctance which Mr. Holmes has shown to the continued publication of his experiences. So long as he was in actual professional practice, the records of his successes were of some practical value to him, but since he has definitely retired from London and betaken himself to study and bee-farming on the Sussex Downs, notoriety has become hateful to him, and he has peremptorily requested that his wishes in this matter should be strictly observed.

The facts make a nonsense of this comment: 1903, the year in which Holmes supposedly retired and notoriety became hateful to him, was, of course, the very year in which Watson began a new series of short autobiographical narratives for *The Strand Magazine*. It was also the very year in which it was revealed to the world at large, rather than just to the privileged few, that Holmes had survived the Reichenbach Falls and had been practising his science of detection in London for nearly a decade.

What is more, we know of plenty of cases in which Holmes interested himself long after his supposed retirement. The only case from 1907 recorded in the narratives that appeared in *The Strand Magazine* preserves the convenient fiction that Holmes had retired. Written by Holmes himself (although one is forced when reading it to suspect the editorial interventions of both Watson and Doyle), 'The Adventure of the Lion's Mane' tells of his emergence from retirement to investigate the terrible death of a schoolmaster on a

Sussex beach. Yet in the same year we know, from references in the unpublished letters of Arthur Symons, that Holmes was commissioned to find the publisher Leonard Smithers, who had disappeared from his usual haunts in Paris and London.

Smithers was a key figure in literary circles in the 1890s and had published many of the most significant writers of the day from Ernest Dowson to Oscar Wilde. The latter, referring to the publisher's taste for pre-pubescent girls and his commitment to disseminating literature that was not so much daringly unconventional as pornographic, said of Smithers, 'He loves first editions, especially of women: little girls are his passion. He is the most learned erotomaniac in Europe.' Symons, the man who approached Holmes, was a poet whose early volumes of verse Smithers had published when no one else would. Holmes traced the missing Smithers but he was too late. Alone in a suburban home in Parson's Green, the publisher had succumbed to chronic lung disease and his taste for an opium-based medicine marketed as Dr Collis Browne's Chlorodyne. Holmes found little in the house apart from Smithers's naked body and an array of empty bottles of his favourite poison.*

We also know of the detective's involvement in a more celebrated case that same year. The Camden Town murder seemed at first a commonplace, if brutal, crime, a case to prove that, in Holmes's words in another context, 'man, or at least criminal man, has lost all enterprise and originality.' On 12 September 1907 a young woman,

---

* Holmes had other acquaintances in the strange subterranean world of publishing where undoubted pornography and adventurous avant-garde literature rubbed shoulders. Some years earlier, he had come across a man who worked under a variety of aliases ranging from Dr Sinclair Roland and Roland de Villiers to George Ferdinand Springmuhl von Weissenfeld. In his imagination 'de Villiers' had endowed Watford with a university and had published *Sexual Inversion* by Havelock Ellis and John Addington Symonds at the 'Watford University Press'. The attempt at academic respectability had failed and booksellers had been prosecuted for selling a book that was considered 'grossly obscene'.

Emily Dimmock, was found with her throat cut in her home in St Paul's Road, North London. Emily's past life had been chequered and she had spent periods working as a prostitute, but at the time of her death she was living as common-law wife to one Bert Shaw. A chef on Midland Railway trains, Shaw spent several nights a week away from London. On the night of the murder he was in Derby and could not have been responsible for the crime, but the police did have a suspect. Robert Wood, a young man with artistic pretensions and a taste for the seedier side of London life, was arrested and charged with Emily Dimmock's murder. There was no dispute that Wood knew Dimmock. He had met her in a pub a few days before the murder and a postcard that he had written arranging a further meeting was found in her room. Several people gave evidence that he was the last person to be seen with her, leaving a Camden pub on the evening of 11 September. While Bert Shaw was away, Emily, it seemed, had returned to her former trade.

The evidence against Wood, however, was flimsy. Much of the police case rested on the identification of him as a man seen in the early hours of the morning leaving the house in which Emily's body was later found. Robert McCowan, out and about in St Paul's Road at 5 a.m., identified Wood as the man he had seen because of Wood's peculiarly distinctive way of walking. Holmes was brought into the case by an old acquaintance, Edward Marshall Hall, the legendary QC who had taken on Wood's defence. As Holmes and

In 1902, Holmes heard that de Villiers had been tracked down to a suburban house in Cambridge where he had had a secret passage built, hidden behind apparently ordinary wall panelling. When the police, interested in his more extreme publishing ventures, came to visit, de Villiers retired to his lair but was dragged from it, brandishing a revolver, by an intrepid constable who had realized that there was more to the house than met the eye. Just as he was about to be taken away to the local cells, de Villiers was seized by a sudden apoplexy and dropped down dead. Self-administered poison was suspected but never proved.

Hall both clearly saw, McCowan's evidence was central to the police case. Cast doubt on McCowan and Wood was saved. Holmes set about doing just that. Most tellingly, he found another man who had been in St Paul's Road at the right time and, in the kind of *coup de théâtre* he loved so much, revealed to Hall that this man, William Westcott, was a former professional boxer. From his days in the ring, he walked with a noticeable rolling gait. It could just as easily have been Westcott that McCowan saw. Turning to the alibi that Wood had provided, Holmes showed, to his and Hall's satisfaction, that the young man had actually constructed one that was weakest for the very time that Emily Dimmock died. Logic dictated that no one who was guilty would have provided an alibi that failed to cover adequately the period of time when it was most needed. Armed with the material Holmes had gathered, Hall gave one of his most barnstorming and theatrical speeches in defence and Wood was acquitted by the jury after only fifteen minutes' deliberation. It has never been proved who did kill Emily Dimmock, although passing remarks in Hall's autobiography, published years later, suggest that he and Holmes strongly suspected that a pimp from Emily's less salubrious past was the murderer. The man fled to Australia before the police could act on Holmes's suspicions.*

If any clinching evidence was needed that Holmes was active in criminal investigations after his reported retirement, we have it in two well-documented cases where he worked in tandem with his old friend Conan Doyle. By 1906, Arthur Conan Doyle had acted as literary agent for Watson and Holmes for nearly twenty years. The

---

* The Camden Town murder is now perhaps best known through the work of Walter Sickert. The artist, who lived close to the scene of the murder, created a number of dark paintings that seem to refer to the case.

arrangement had proved satisfying for all of them, not least financially. Watson had seen his narratives reach an astonishingly large readership. Holmes had been able to watch his fame growing world-wide while losing little of the freedom to conduct his life and his career as he wished. Doyle had been transformed from one of the army of late-Victorian writers for magazines into a respected and best-selling author, largely on the back of his connection with the Holmes stories. None of the three very different partners had any major cause to complain. (This did not, of course, prevent Holmes from regularly chastising Watson for his 'sensationalism' and Doyle for selling the stories to magazines in America that the detective considered vulgar and populist.) In all these years, Doyle had never called upon Holmes's professional skills himself – although he had recommended to others that they use his services. This changed late in 1906 when Doyle, outraged by a blatant miscarriage of justice, became involved in the case of George Edalji. He asked Holmes for help in reviewing the evidence against the accused man. Luckily the case was an interesting one, characterized by just the kind of bizarre detail and odd circumstance that so appealed to the great detective.

George Edalji's father was an Indian, a Parsee who had con-verted to Anglicanism, married an Englishwoman and become a vicar with a parish at Great Wyrley to the north of Birmingham. George was the eldest child of the marriage. At the time that his nightmare began, he was a solicitor with a practice in Newhall Street in Birmingham. A specialist in transport law, he was the author of a book entitled *Railway Law for the Man in the Train: Chiefly Intended as a Guide for the Travelling Public on all points likely to arise in con-nexion with the Railways.* In 1903, farm animals in the countryside around Great Wyrley were found mutilated in the fields. Sheep, cows and horses had their stomachs sliced open and were left to bleed to death. Police investigating the crimes were sent anonymous letters accusing the respectable young solicitor, George Edalji, of being the sadist responsible for the attacks. The evidence against him, apart from the anonymous letters, was pathetically inadequate, largely based on ignorance and racial prejudice. Ludicrous motives for the crimes (for instance, that he was sacrificing animals in some religious ritual) were ascribed to him. Despite the flimsiness of the evidence, Edalji was convicted and sentenced to seven years' hard labour. Released in October 1906, and still barred from practising as a solicitor, Edalji began to campaign to have his conviction overturned. It was at this point that Doyle and Holmes took an interest in his case.

Holmes, always alert to the report of any more unusual crimes, had read about Edalji's trial in 1903 and had told Watson that the accused was clearly innocent. However, Holmes had had no time to pursue the case. Now he and Doyle travelled to Birmingham. It was Holmes's first visit to the city since the events surrounding Hall Pycroft's mysterious employment there, recorded by Watson in the narrative he entitled 'The Adventure of the Stockbroker's Clerk'. For Doyle, Birmingham was more familiar territory. As a young man, he had lived and worked in Aston for several months in the early 1880s.

The evidence for Edalji's innocence was not hard to find. The young solicitor was exceptionally short-sighted and when Holmes and Doyle attempted to reconstruct the crimes, it soon became clear that it was extremely unlikely that Edalji had been guilty of them. As Doyle later wrote, 'It did not take any elaborate deduction to come to the conclusion that a man who is practically blind did not make a journey at night which involved crossing a main line of railway, and would have tested a trained athlete had he been called upon to do it in the time.'

The arrival of the two men in Birmingham did, however,

create a stir. Soon Holmes and Doyle were themselves receiving anonymous letters threatening dire consequences if they persisted in their enquiries.

Desperate men have sworn their Bible oath to scoop out your liver and kidneys ... and there are those who say you have not long to live. I know from a detective of Scotland Yard that if you write to Gladstone* and say you find Edalji is guilty after all, and you were mistaken and promise to do no more for him, they will make you a lord next year. Is it not better to be a lord than to run the risk of losing kidneys and liver?

There was more of the same. Holmes had faced worse threats in the past than the scooping out of his liver and kidneys and he treated the whole incident as a huge joke. Doyle was merely indignant. They continued their investigations and soon had shown, to their own satisfaction, that Edalji was entirely innocent.

Despite their achievements in the Edalji case, the trip to Birmingham was not a success. Thrown together for several days, Holmes and Doyle got on one another's nerves. Doyle wrote to Watson, 'I do not wish to be ungrateful to Holmes, who has been a good friend to me in many ways. If I have sometimes been inclined to weary of him, it is because his character admits of no light or shade.' Yet, a few years later, another case of manifest injustice brought the two men together again as an investigative team. Holmes and Doyle could count themselves largely successful in their endeavours on behalf of George Edalji. In the later case of Oscar Slater, their efforts to prove that an innocent man languished in prison were less effective.

---

* The reference is to Herbert Gladstone, fourth son of the great nineteenth-century Prime Minister, who was Home Secretary at the time.

Within days of the murder of an elderly woman, Marion Gilchrist, in her Glasgow home, the police had been convinced that they knew who was responsible. Their suspicions fell on the German Jew, Oscar Slater, a small-time crook and gambler who had been living in Glasgow for several months at the time of the killing. He had recently pawned a diamond brooch and, soon after the crime took place, he had boarded the liner *Lusitania* to New York, travelling under an alias. The Scottish police contacted the authorities in America, and Slater was arrested when the *Lusitania* docked. Baffled by the charges against him, he readily agreed to return to Scotland to clear his name. It was a major mistake. In court, he was found guilty. Slater was condemned for who and what he was rather than on the basis of the evidence against him. This had always been circumstantial and was based on dubious testimony, identifying him as a man seen near Marion Gilchrist's flat just before her body was discovered. Oscar Slater was sentenced to death in May 1909. Two days before he was due to die, his sentence was commuted to life imprisonment.

Together Holmes and Doyle painstakingly gathered fresh evidence and revealed the flimsiness of the prosecution case. Slater had been travelling to the States under an assumed name because he was conducting a clandestine affair and his mistress was accompanying him. The brooch that he had pawned was nothing like the one stolen from the Gilchrist flat. The hammer that the police claimed was the murder weapon could not have inflicted the injuries Marion Gilchrist received. One of the witnesses who had identified Slater had earlier named another man. Most tellingly, Holmes was able to deduce that the old lady had opened the door herself to her attacker and had therefore known him. She had never met Oscar Slater. In 1912, Conan Doyle published a short work, *The Case of Oscar Slater*, outlining what he and Holmes had unearthed. The authorities ignored it and a request for a retrial was refused. Doyle was furious. 'How the verdict could be that there was no fresh cause for reversing the conviction is incomprehensible,' he wrote. 'The whole case will, in my opinion, remain immortal in the classics of crime as the supreme example of official incompetence and obstinacy.'

Holmes, already deeply involved in the undercover work that led to the thwarting of the German agent Von Bork, had long lost interest in the case but Doyle persisted in proclaiming Slater's innocence whenever he got the chance. The authorities continued to maintain, in the face of all the evidence, that justice had been done. Slater eventually served eighteen years in prison before being released, although not pardoned, in the autumn of 1927. Even then, there was no happy ending to the saga. As Doyle wrote in a letter to the ageing and ailing Holmes, by this time more or less confined to his cottage on the Downs by rheumatism and ill health, Slater was a difficult man to like. Although he was eventually cleared of the crime in a retrial and awarded financial compensation, Slater refused to reimburse any of the considerable monies that Conan Doyle had advanced to help him. Doyle scarcely needed the money but he was distressed by what he saw as Slater's dishonourable dealings with him. Indignantly, he wrote to Slater, saying, 'You seem to have taken leave of your senses. If you are indeed responsible for your actions, then you are the most ungrateful as well as the most foolish person whom I have ever known.'*

Holmes's involvement with the Edalji and Slater cases has long been suspected. It was always thought unlikely that Doyle, intent

---

* Slater died in 1948 but not before suffering another period of imprisonment. As a German, he was held in an internment camp during the Second World War.

on proving the innocence of the two men, would not have turned to the man best qualified to help him. It is less certain whether or not the detective contributed to other famous criminal cases of the Edwardian era but there is now little doubt that Holmes made his presence felt in both the Crippen murder and the serial killings commonly called the 'Brides in the Bath' murders.

Holmes, according to Watson, once remarked, 'When a doctor does go wrong he is the first of criminals. He has nerve and he has knowledge.' As a general rule of thumb this might be true but, in the case of Dr Crippen, we seem to have hit upon the exception to the rule. Far from demonstrating nerve and skill, Crippen seemed to be the most pusillanimous and pathetic of murderers. Yet Crippen so very nearly escaped the hangman's noose. Had Holmes had his way, he would have done. For the great detective believed, to the end of his life, that Crippen was innocent. More than that, he believed that he, Holmes, had uncovered the proof of his innocence and that the police, for reasons of their own, had chosen to ignore it.

Nearly a hundred years after the events, the outline of the Crippen case remains familiar. The unfortunate and bumbling doctor, more quack than true physician (his medical degree was self-awarded), has become one of the great bogeymen of English criminal history. Dozens of books have been written on the case and at least three films have told the story. Crippen's eerily compelling wax likeness is still on display in Madame Tussaud's Chamber of Horrors.

In February 1910, Crippen's blowsy and boisterous wife Cora, formerly an unsuccessful music-hall singer known as 'Belle Elmore', disappeared from the family home in Hilldrop Crescent, Camden. Her husband claimed that she had moved back to America, suffering from some unspecific but life-threatening illness. Mournfully he issued a series of reports to Cora's friends, chronicling her failing health and, finally, her death. When pressed for details of where she had died, he could say no more than that it was in 'some little town near San Francisco, with a Spanish name'. Unsurprisingly, Cora's friends grew suspicious. Their suspicions became stronger when Ethel Le Neve, Crippen's young secretary, appeared to have moved into Hilldrop Crescent. Ethel accompanied Crippen to a ball given by the Music Hall Benevolent Fund and was seen wearing a brooch known to have belonged to Cora.

At the end of June 1910, more than four months after Mrs Crippen was last seen, John and Lillian Nash, two jobbing actors who were close friends of the missing woman, took their misgivings to Scotland Yard. When confronted in his house by police officers, Crippen immediately changed his story. Cora was not dead. She had run off to the States with former prizefighter Bruce Miller, and Crippen had been too humiliated to admit the truth. The police, unconvinced but with little evidence to go on, left. Crippen, however, panicked. When the police returned to Hilldrop Crescent a few days later, there was no sign of him. Down in the cellar of the house they found the headless remains of a woman. A major hunt for Crippen and Le Neve was launched, first in Britain and then worldwide.

On 22 July the captain of the SS *Montrose*, a passenger ship crossing the Atlantic, was reading a newspaper when he was struck by photographs of the fugitives on its front page. They looked strangely familiar. He used the new Marconi telegraph to wire back to his ship's owners: 'Have strong suspicion that Crippen London Cellar murderer and accomplice are amongst saloon passengers. Moustache shaved off, growing a beard. Accomplice dressed as a boy. Voice, manner and build undoubtedly a girl.'

The owners forwarded the report to Scotland Yard. Chief

Inspector Walter Dew swiftly travelled to Liverpool to board the SS *Laurentic* in pursuit of the doctor and his mistress. The speedier *Laurentic* outpaced the *Montrose* across the Atlantic and when the latter ship arrived at the mouth of the St Lawrence, Dew, masquerading as a river pilot, was ready to board it. Confronting the surprised fugitives, he greeted them with the words, 'Good afternoon, Dr Crippen, remember me? I'm Inspector Dew with Scotland Yard.' After a moment's pause, Crippen replied, 'Thank God it's all over,' and held out his hands for the cuffs. Taken back to Britain, he faced trial at the Old Bailey.

Holmes's involvement in the case had begun before anyone at Scotland Yard had heard the name Crippen. On 15 June, a fortnight before they approached the police, the Nashes, acting on the recommendation of a friend, had visited Baker Street. It is not clear what Holmes made of the case at this early stage but he may well have been instrumental in persuading the Nashes to take their suspicions to Scotland Yard. By the time Dew returned from his Atlantic passage with his prisoner in tow, Holmes had almost certainly come to his own conclusions about the case, which he passed on to the Scotland Yard inspector. Holmes had come across Dew many years before. As a young police constable, Dew had been stationed in Whitechapel at the time of the Ripper murders and had even been present when Mary Kelly's mutilated body had been found, 'the most gruesome memory of the whole of my police career', as he described it in his memoirs. Despite their old acquaintance, however, Dew was unwilling to act upon the theory that Holmes outlined.

In 'The Adventure of the Lion's Mane', Holmes acknowledges, 'I hold a vast store of out-of-the-way knowledge without scientific system, but very available for the needs of my work. My mind is like a crowded box-room with packets of all sorts stowed away therein

– so many that I may well have but a vague perception of what was there.' One of these packets of out-of-the-way knowledge contained information about the uses sometimes made of hyoscine, the drug that had caused Cora Crippen's death. It was a sexual depressant. Holmes was certain of what had happened. Cora had indeed taken hyoscine but she had done so unwittingly. Crippen, however, had never intended to kill his wife. He was secretly administering the drug to her in an attempt to depress her sexual appetite. All had gone horribly wrong and the unfortunate Crippen had been faced by his wife's corpse. Panicking, he had attempted to dispose of the body and then concocted the story about her flight to America.

As Holmes struggled to persuade the police of the truth of this scenario, he had much need of what Watson, in 'The Adventure of the Missing Three-Quarter', called that 'half comic and wholly philosophical view which was natural to him when his affairs were going awry'. Dew, who had a sneaking liking for Crippen, was prepared to listen sympathetically but he was convinced that the doctor had intended from the beginning to kill his wife and that he should face not a manslaughter charge but a capital one. To Holmes's profound distress and anger, the murder case against Crippen went ahead. He was found guilty and, on 28 November 1910, he was hanged. On the eve of his execution, he sent a last message to his mistress Ethel Le Neve.* 'We shall meet again in another life,' he wrote. 'We have always been so entirely one in heart and soul, thought and deed, even in flesh and spirit, I cannot believe otherwise but we shall be together in that other life I am going to soon.'

Despite his other preoccupations, Holmes remained an avid reader of the more sensational pages of the newspapers. No account of-

---

* Ethel Le Neve changed her name after the trial. She married in 1916 and lived on until 1967.

murder or robbery, no coroner's report on a sudden and mysterious death escaped his attention. On 23 July 1912 he read of an inquest into the death of Bessie Williams, née Mundy, who had been found drowned in her bath in the small resort town of Herne Bay on the north Kent coast. The doctor who had attended Bessie Williams believed that she had suffered an epileptic fit while in her bath. Perusing the details of the case, Holmes knew immediately that the doctor was wrong. Was it not suspicious that only days before her death she had made a will that bequeathed her entire savings (£2,579 13s 7d) to her husband? How was it possible for an apparently healthy woman, even one subject to epileptic fits, to drown in the way the doctor stated she had? After one reading of the report Holmes was convinced that Bessie's husband, a man calling himself Henry Williams, was a cunning and heartless murderer who had escaped detection.

Holmes no longer had the contacts in Scotland Yard that he had once had. Lestrade and Gregson were retired. His more recent associate, Walter Dew, had also left the force – ironically, to become a private detective. Holmes, in semi-retirement himself, found that, although new men at the Yard listened politely to his ideas, they did little to follow up on the case. To them, the case of Bessie Williams was a closed book which they had no wish to open solely on the say-so of an ageing private investigator, no matter how distinguished his earlier record. Distracted by his secret service work and about to be plunged into the long, undercover investigation that culminated in the exposure of the German agent Von Bork, Holmes had no time to pursue the truth. It was an omission that he would live to regret.

Henry Williams, whose real name was George Joseph Smith, had discovered what he believed to be a foolproof method for disposing of unwanted wives, once he had persuaded them to make him the sole beneficiary in their wills. A serial bigamist with a string of aliases, Smith went on to murder at least two more wives by drowning them in the bath. For the rest of his life Holmes was to berate himself for failing to act more forcefully on his immediate realization that murder was being committed.

CHAPTER FOURTEEN

'THERE'S AN EAST WIND COMING'

IN THE YEARS OF EDWARD VII'S REIGN, between 1901 and 1910, Holmes largely stepped back from the kind of criminal investigations in which he had made his name. The trip to Birmingham to unravel the mystery surrounding George Edalji was a favour to an old friend. The case known as 'The Adventure of the Lion's Mane' had thrust itself upon his attention while he was resting and recuperating at his cottage on the Downs. Holmes maintained his interest in the criminal world but from a distance. In 1905, he must have smiled wryly when he read of the Stratton case, in which two brothers were tried and found guilty of murder on the evidence of a thumbprint found at the scene. It was the first capital case in which the prosecution had depended on a system of identification that Holmes had been advocating for more than twenty years. He must have recalled the events of June 1891 and his late-night discussion of fingerprints with the Inspector General of the Bengali Police, Edward Henry. It was Henry, returning to London as Assistant

Commissioner at Scotland Yard, who had established the Finger-print Bureau.

When he was not spending time in sight of the Sussex coast, Holmes was being drawn more and more into the work of the fledg-ling MI5 and MI6. Other than 'His Last Bow', the story of the detect-ive's thwarting of the German agent Von Bork, Watson records three cases in Holmes's career in which the detective is drawn into the murky world where international diplomacy and espionage met. One, 'The Adventure of the Naval Treaty', took place in 1887, before the Great Hiatus; two more, 'The Adventure of the Second Stain' and 'The Adventure of the Bruce-Partington Plans', date from the years immediately after the detective's return to London. In 'The Adventure of the Naval Treaty', a former schoolfellow of Watson, Percy Phelps, finds his glittering career in the Foreign Office at risk when important state documents are stolen from his office. The opportunist thief turns out to be his fiancée's brother who aims to lessen his financial problems by selling the details of the treaty to a foreign power. There was a secret treaty between Britain and Italy, known as the 'Mediterranean Agreements', in force between 1887 and 1896, and it may well be a behind-the-scenes crisis connected to this treaty that Watson works into the narrative he published.

According to Watson, 'The Adventure of the Second Stain' takes place 'in a year, and even in a decade, that shall be nameless' and begins when 'two visitors of European fame' (the Prime Minister, referred to as 'Lord Bellinger', and the 'Secretary for European Affairs') visit Baker Street. Once again, an important paper has gone missing and Holmes must find it. In this instance it is a letter 'from a certain foreign potentate who has been ruffled by some recent colonial developments. According to the Prime Minister, the document 'is couched in so unfortunate a manner ... that its publication would undoubtedly lead to a most dangerous state of feeling . . . There would be such a ferment, sir, that I do not hesitate to say that within a week of the publication of that letter this country would be involved in a great war.' Despite Watson's attempts at discretion, it is not too difficult to guess that the Prime Minister, 'Lord Bellinger', is Lord Salisbury* and that the undiplomatic foreign potentate is the German Kaiser, Wilhelm II, who made a habit of firing off tactless messages to foreign governments without the knowledge of his chief ministers. Holmes is able to save the day by revealing that the European Secretary's wife has been the victim of a blackmailer and that she had taken the letter at his bidding. War is averted.

The most interesting of the three cases is the one that Watson describes as 'The Adventure of the Bruce-Partington Plans', concerning blueprints for a submarine. The Royal Navy was curiously slow to realize how much submarines might change the nature of war at sea. One of the few senior naval officers to display any great prescience about submarines was Admiral John Fisher, who was quick to appreciate their potential. As late as 1904, nine years after Bruce-Partington, Fisher was still writing, 'I don't think it is even faintly realised – the immense impending revolution which submarines will effect as offensive weapons of war.' In the 1890s, the most advanced submarines were being built not in Europe but in America, designed by Irish nationalist John Philip Holland. It may well have been one of Holland's submarines that lurks beneath the disguises Watson imposes on the story. Ironically, the rights to Holland's designs were purchased by the Electric Boat Company in the US, which then sold them to Vickers in Barrow-in-Furness,

---

* Although, in Paget's illustration to the narrative, Lord Bellinger bears a stronger resemblance to Gladstone than he does to Salisbury.

where the first British submarines were built from 1900 onwards.

Other than these cases, strewn as they are with red herrings and false trails to confuse any biographer, Watson makes no mention of Holmes's career in espionage. Yet Holmes was central to the creation of both MI5, with its interest in internal enemies of the state, and MI6, the organization that was intended to carry out espionage abroad.

Working in the strange, semi-official position that he carved out for himself during the early days of MI5, Holmes recruited agents who were at home in the turbulent pool of anarchist and revolutionary politics in the East End. From as early as the autumn of 1908, he was gathering reports, probably from an agent called Orlov, warning that a group of Latvian refugees, who had fled to London after a failed revolution in their own country, was capable of posing a serious threat to public order.

The world in which Orlov operated was that of Conrad's *The Secret Agent*. Conrad's novel, with its darkly ironic story of anarchist bombers and political conspiracy, drew its inspiration from an incident of which Holmes would have known, although it took place just before his return to London. Late on the afternoon of 15 February 1894, two men working at the Greenwich Observatory were disturbed by the noise of what sounded like a shell exploding in the park outside. Rushing to investigate, they found a man crouched on the ground, clutching a gaping wound in his stomach. The man was a Frenchman in his twenties, one Martial Boudin who had travelled to Greenwich Park by tram from his lodgings in Fitzrovia. Other passengers told police that Boudin had been carrying a parcel when he left the tram and it soon became clear that the parcel had been a bomb that had detonated unexpectedly, fatally wounding the Frenchman.

To Conrad, writing years later, the attempted bombing at the Observatory seemed 'a blood-stained inanity of so fatuous a kind that it was impossible to fathom its origin by any reasonable or even unreasonable process of thought'. There was, however, a perverse rationale behind it. Boudin was a member of the same tightly knit group of French anarchists that included Caserio, the man who would kill the French president Sadi Carnot in June of the same year, and Huret, the Boulevard Assassin. Boudin's doomed mission to London was intended as an experimental attack to test the potential of the explosives that the group had manufactured. His self-immolation was proof enough that a bomb was not the best method for assassination and Caserio would use the more reliable alternative of a knife to stab the French president to death.

Who, though, was Orlov? Almost certainly he had come to Holmes's attention through Shinwell Johnson's* wide-ranging contacts in the underworld. He was feeding information to Holmes for more than two years and was a trusted associate of the Latvians throughout that period. He may well have been Latvian himself. As we shall see, he would be caught up in the group that was surrounded by the police and the army in Sidney Street and, like the equally mysterious 'Peter the Painter', he disappeared from the

---

* Watson only mentions Johnson in one of his chronicles ('The Adventure of the Illustrious Client') where he says that the man had 'made his name first as a very dangerous villain and served two terms at Parkhurst. Finally he repented and allied himself to Holmes, acting as his agent in the huge criminal underworld of London and obtaining information which often proved to be of vital importance.' Watson did not care for Johnson, 'a huge, coarse, red-faced, scorbutic man, with a pair of vivid black eyes which were the only external sign of the very cunning mind within', as the doctor describes him with obvious distaste. However, he underestimates and misrepresents the man's role in Holmes's work at the time. As Holmes investigates Baron Gruner's darkest secrets, it is Johnson's 'entrée of every night-club, doss house, and gambling-den in the town' that is invaluable but, in much of his association with Holmes, it was his connections with the revolutionary and anarchist subcultures of the East End that proved more useful.

scene in the chaotic aftermath of the siege. Most anarchist groups preferred talk to action. The Latvians, Holmes became certain, meant business. Not for the first time his warnings, although backed by Mycroft, were ignored.

The first indication that the Latvian anarchists posed a genuine threat came at the beginning of 1909 when two of them, Paul Hefeld and Jacob Lepidus, travelled out to Tottenham and attacked a car carrying the wages destined for workers at Schnurrman's Rubber Factory. Hefeld's name had already appeared in Orlov's reports to Holmes as a particularly wild and headstrong revolutionist, and he and his comrade were now to show that Orlov's concerns had been justified.

The robbery went chaotically wrong from the very start. The chauffeur of the wages car refused to give up the money without a struggle, so the robbers, who were both armed, shot and wounded him before fleeing with the cash. Alerted by the shooting, several policemen arrived on the scene. Hefeld and Lepidus, panicking and firing wildly, hit a small boy among the passers-by who died later in hospital. Police Constable Tyler appeared to have cornered the men but Hefeld turned his pistol on him and shot him at point-blank range. Tyler bled to death at the scene. Lepidus and Hefeld then commandeered a tram and forced the conductor at gunpoint to aid their getaway. The police, some of them armed by now, also seized a tram and set off in pursuit, exchanging shots with the robbers. Lepidus and Hefeld leaped from the tram and took over a parked milk van. Almost immediately, they overturned it while trying to take a corner too fast. Abandoning the wrecked vehicle, they turned instead to a horse-drawn greengrocer's van but were unable to work out how its brake operated. Moving at a sedate pace but still firing indiscriminately at the pursuing police, they were eventually forced to abandon the van. Now on foot, they hurtled down a path beside

Chingford Brook. It was a dead end. First Hefeld and then Lepidus shot himself as the police approached. Lepidus died immediately. Hefeld lingered for three weeks, eventually dying after uttering the unhelpful last words, 'My mother is in Riga.'

Tragedy and farce had combined in what became known as the Tottenham Outrage, but events the following year proved that Holmes's continuing fears about the Latvians were justified. On 16 December 1910, a police constable on the beat in Houndsditch heard unusual noises coming from a house in Exchange Buildings. When his suspicions were aroused by the man who answered the door to his knock, the constable went to seek assistance from colleagues. Several policemen returned to the house and a Sergeant Bentley again knocked on the door. Bentley was invited into the house by the same man but, as he crossed the threshold, another man burst from a back room and shot the sergeant twice in the shoulder and the neck. The second bullet severed Bentley's spinal column. Other members of the gang, who had been attempting to tunnel into the vaults of a jeweller's shop in Houndsditch, now ran from the adjoining house, firing repeatedly as they came. Three more policemen were hit but the only officer left standing, a Constable Choat, made a heroic effort to stop the fleeing anarchists. Seizing one man, later identified as George Gardstein, he wrestled with him for possession of his gun. Gardstein's colleagues fired repeatedly at Choat, who was hit at least half a dozen times and later died. One of the bullets also hit Gardstein, wounding him fatally. The gang fled, dragging their dying comrade with them.

For the next two weeks, their whereabouts were unknown. Then Orlov, still trusted by the Latvians, managed to get word to Holmes of what was happening. Two of the team had gone to ground in a house in Sidney Street soon after the Houndsditch shootings. Orlov himself was now with them. Within a short time number 100 was surrounded by police and most of the residents of nearby houses had been evacuated.* Holmes and the senior police officers were certain that, with Orlov working as an unsuspected agent for the authorities within the house, the men, desperate though they were, could be persuaded to surrender. However, the Home Secretary, Winston Churchill, who was impatient for instant results, intervened, giving orders to deploy troops. The first soldiers, Scots Guards stationed at the Tower of London, arrived at Sidney Street in the middle of the morning of 3 January 1911. Marksmen were put in position on the top floors of adjoining buildings from where they could rain fire into the building. Churchill himself arrived soon after noon and was soon in de facto command of the assorted forces gathered in the street.

While Churchill strutted for the benefit of the cameras, Holmes was furious. The heavy-handed response of the authorities threatened to destroy the intelligence network that he had built up so painstakingly over the previous three years. His own agent was trapped in the house at 100 Sidney Street. Rushing between Mycroft's offices in Whitehall and the East End, Holmes struggled to wrest back the initiative. Events, however, were spiralling out of his control. More and more troops were being poured on to the scene. As revolutionaries and soldiers exchanged bursts of gunfire, smoke was seen to billow from the top floor of number 100 and soon the building was alight, forcing the men inside to retreat to those rooms still untouched by the fire. Eventually, when the house had been completely gutted, the authorities moved in. The bodies of two of the anarchists, Svaars and Sokoloff, were found in the burned-out shell of the house. Sokoloff had been shot in the head

* The landlady at 102 Sidney Street, where many of the terrified evacuees did their best to shelter, was a Mrs Blustein. Many decades later, her grandson gained fame as Rabbi Lionel Blue.

by one of the military marksmen as he stood near an open window. His comrade had been overcome by the smoke and fumes of the fire. A third man, supposedly in the building and known only as 'Peter the Painter', was nowhere to be found.

In a book published in the 1930s, Churchill was to describe 'Peter the Painter' as 'one of those wild beasts who, in later years, amid the convulsions of the Great War, were to devour and ravage the Russian State and people'. In fact, the most likely explanation is that Orlov and the enigmatic Peter were one and the same man, and that Holmes had somehow arranged for him to be spirited out of Sidney Street in the confusion of the fire and then out of the country. Holmes cannot have been pleased with the outcome. He had lost his most reliable and daring agent. Churchill's urge to put himself at the centre of the action was later mocked by political opponents. 'We are concerned to observe photographs in the illustrated newspapers of the Home Secretary in the danger-zone,' the Tory leader Balfour remarked in Parliament. 'I understand what the photographer was doing, but why the Home Secretary?' Churchill himself later acknowledged that his presence at the scene had been unwise but the damage had already been done.

Much of MI6's early work was intended to provide information about Britain's rivalry with Germany. As far back as 1871, in the wake of France's swift defeat by Prussia, writers had been speculating about a future confrontation between the two countries. *The Battle of Dorking* by George Chesney, an extraordinary fantasy in which German armies invaded Britain and, despite a heroic last stand at the Surrey town by British forces, swept all before them, was published in *Blackwood's Magazine* that year, arousing huge controversy. By 1909 the belief that war between Germany and Britain was inevitable had firmly entrenched itself in the popular mind.

Hack novelists such as the egregious William le Queux, who pumped out several books a year with such titles as *The Invasion of 1910* and *Spies for the Kaiser* fuelled anxieties about marauding Huns crossing the Channel. Scare stories proliferated in the newspapers. The German waiters in London were all spies. There were German troops in hiding around England, awaiting instructions to arm themselves from a secret arsenal situated within a stone's throw of Charing Cross. One paper, the *Weekly News*, was so obsessed by the spy fever that it invited its readers to join in spy-spotting competitions and appointed a full-time Spy Editor. It was in this perfervid atmosphere of suspicion and anxiety that MI6 was born and in which Holmes worked.

If Holmes seems an eccentric choice for the ranks of the secret services, he was no more outré an agent than the service's very first head, Mansfield Smith Cumming. Cumming, born just Mansfield Smith, had acquired the extra distinction when he married rich heiress May Cumming; her family had insisted that he add his wife's surname to his own as part of the marriage settlement. He had been a career naval officer until he had been obliged to go into semi-retirement at the extraordinarily early age of twenty-six because of some mysteriously unspecific ailment. Some claimed that he suffered so violently from seasickness that he could no longer contemplate a career on the ocean wave. Safe on shore, Cumming divided his time between Southampton, where he was in charge of Boom Defence, and the new motor-racing circuits of Europe. He was a pioneering enthusiast for 'motorism', as the pastime was sometimes called, until he was involved in a terrible accident in which his son was killed and he himself lost a leg.

From the very outset, MI6 set the pattern for the surreal, almost farcical manner in which much of its work was to be carried out over the next few decades. Cumming sat in his office ('Office all day – no one appeared,' he wrote in his diary), awaiting visitors who were unable to call because its location was a secret. Working almost alone, and often paying for essentials such as typewriters and writing paper out of his own pocket, he struggled to undertake the tasks that he believed he had been given. Agents were duly recruited. Most proved amateurish. In 1910, Trench and Brandon, two army officers nominally under Cumming's control, set off on a walking holiday-cum-spying mission along Germany's Baltic coast. Their collars were felt by the German authorities within a few days of their leaving Britain and the information they had gathered was found under the mattress in Trench's hotel bedroom. The two men went on trial and were sentenced to several years' detention in German prisons.

Endeavouring to meet all his agents in the field, Cumming faced a number of surprises. One, who had filed reports as Mademoiselle Espiesse, turned out to be large, truculent, male and Belgian, chiefly interested in squeezing more money out of Cumming. Another was a semi-deranged fantasist, keen on plugging his alleged invention of a camera that could fit into a gentleman's tiepin.

Even by 1912, things were little better. In the circumstances, Holmes, despite his age (he was fifty-eight), was a valuable recruit. Under the name of Altamont* he was to enter the service of the German spymaster known as 'Von Bork' in circumstances described in the narrative 'His Last Bow'. Von Bork is almost certainly a disguised version of the German naval attaché in London, Wilhelm Widenmann, who ran a network of spies in and around naval bases such as Chatham, Rosyth and Scapa Flow. Most of the

---

* Holmes, who had appeared largely indifferent twenty years earlier to Doyle's difficulties with his ailing and alcoholic father, had nonetheless tucked away information about Doyle's family in his prodigious memory. Charles Doyle's middle name was Altamont.

agents were known to British counter-intelligence but they were left in place because, as Churchill (by this time First Lord of the Admiralty) wrote, 'others of whom we might not have known would have taken their place. Left at large, we read their communications which we regularly forwarded to their paymasters in Berlin.'

This undercover work, which Holmes undertook, again almost certainly at Mycroft's request, cost him two years of his life. 'When I say that I started my pilgrimage at Chicago, graduated in an Irish secret society at Buffalo, gave serious trouble to the constabulary at Skibbareen, and so eventually caught the eye of a subordinate agent of Von Bork, who recommended me as a likely man, you will realize that the matter was complex.'

The elaborate efforts made to establish Holmes's credentials as an anti-British hard man have worked to obscure what he was doing on a day-to-day basis during those two years. It is very difficult to find evidence of his whereabouts and activities beyond this characteristically terse summary. The Irish-American secret society at Buffalo that he mentions may well have been one of those with which Holmes had become familiar from his work in the 1880s. The 'serious trouble to the constabulary at Skibbareen' is, without doubt, a reference to the anti-British riots that took place in the town in 1913. Skibbareen had long been a hotbed of nationalist activities – several of the early Fenian leaders were born there – and the disturbances in its streets over several days were serious enough to merit reinforcements of police being sent from all over the county. The newspapers of the day, both Irish and English, were curiously uninformative about the riots. Few even mentioned them. The *Dublin Gazette*, one of the limited number that did, listed those who were arrested by the police. One of the names is that of a Joseph Altamont. If Holmes was aiming to build up an anti-British curriculum vitae, then arrest in Skibbareen was a most useful addition to it. If Watson had known of his friend's activities in 1913, his chief concern may have been with the effects on Holmes's health. At the age of fifty-nine, and rheumatic into the bargain, the undercover detective was scarcely the material from which street rioters were usually cut.

When the storms of war finally broke over Europe in August 1914, Holmes became a reclusive figure who rarely ventured far from the cottage on the South Downs where, from time to time, he could hear the great guns firing on the Western Front. His undercover work in the years between 1912 and the outbreak of the war had been exhausting. Now entering his sixties, he was profoundly disillusioned with an international system that had allowed such slaughter to be unleashed. At the end of the narrative known as 'His Last Bow', he remarks, 'There's an east wind coming all the same, such a wind as never blew on England yet. It will be cold and bitter, Watson, and a good many of us may wither before its blast. But it's God's own wind none the less, and a cleaner, better, stronger land will lie in the sunshine when the storm has cleared.' Such blithe confidence, so unlike Holmes's usual dark realism, lasted only briefly. Holmes's retirement from the world, which Watson claims took place in 1903, dates rather from the war years. In a world where millions of young men were faced by the horrors of the trenches, Holmes found that watching the miniature tragedies and triumphs of his bees provided at least some sort of solace.

For others, the war proved an even more painful experience. Doyle lost his beloved son Kingsley. His brother Innes, two brothers-in-law and two nephews were also killed. As a result, Doyle was driven to search for meaning in a world that seemed increasingly meaningless. He found his salvation in spiritualism. By 1916, Doyle was willing to announce to the press his belief in the spirit world.

Within months he was giving public lectures on the subject and had become the spiritualists' most celebrated convert, an invaluable source of publicity and newspaper coverage. Both Holmes and Watson, in their different ways, were embarrassed for their old colleague as he became increasingly involved in spiritualism. Doyle had long been interested in the unseen world and, since 1893, had been a member of the Society of Psychical Research, founded by three of Holmes's old acquaintances: Edmund Gurney, Henry Sidgwick and Frederick Myers. Yet he had always maintained a healthy scepticism in the face of the more unlikely indications of alternative worlds to our own. Now he seemed to have descended into a state of almost limitless gullibility.

In 1917, two young girls in the Yorkshire village of Cottingley, sixteen-year-old Elsie Wright and her ten-year-old cousin Frances Griffiths, took photographs of the fairies that they claimed they saw in the woods behind Elsie's home. Their only intention was to prove to their doubting families that they were telling the truth about visitors from fairyland. The story might never have gone beyond the village if Elsie's mother had not been bitten by the spiritualist bug and attended meetings in nearby Bradford. She showed the photographs to others at the meeting; news of them spread throughout the movement and, eventually, came to Doyle's attention. In 1920, three years after the photos had been taken, he wrote an article for *The Strand Magazine*, hailing them as proof positive of another world. At Doyle's prompting, Elsie and Frances went down to the woods again and returned with three more photographs, which he reproduced alongside a further article. In 1922, Doyle published a book, *The Coming of the Fairies*, in which he staked his reputation on the authenticity of the Cottingley fairies. It was an unfortunate decision.

To modern eyes, used to the manipulation of images, it is

glaringly obvious that the photographs are fake. The 'fairies' are cut-outs from a book or magazine, which the girls have propped up in the fields and woods near their home. They have then posed beside the 'fairies' to create images that seem to show Frances watching as a troupe of little folk dance by her and Elsie having an encounter with a gossamer-winged friend. As an editorial in the newspaper *Truth* said at the time: `For the true explanation of these fairy photographs what is wanted is not a knowledge of occult phenomena but a knowledge of children.' (In old age both Elsie and Frances admitted that the whole affair was a prank that had gathered its own momentum as more and more gullible people came to believe that the photographs were genuine.)

Watson, like most of Doyle's friends, maintained a discreet silence about the Cottingley fairies. Holmes, who had seen little of Doyle since their journey to Birmingham together in 1906, was not prepared to follow suit. Using his favourite means of communication, he shot off a telegram to Doyle that read: 'No fairies at bottom of Cottingley garden. Little girls little liars.' Doyle took no notice. There were powerful psychological factors at work, beyond the effects of the war, fuelling his belief. It is worth remembering that Charles Altamont Doyle's watercolours, in the tradition of Victorian 'fairy' painting, often depicted human beings surrounded by visitants from another world. In a watercolour titled 'The Enchanted Picnic', a portly and bemused gentleman (possibly a self-portrait) sits on the grass surrounded by the remains of a picnic while ethereal figures play with his watch-chain, float tantalizingly in the air before him and help themselves to the leftovers. Now his son seemed quite prepared to believe in similar visions.

CHAPTER FIFTEEN

'THE GREATEST MYSTERY
FOR LAST'

B Y JANUARY 1920, AS HE approached his sixty-sixth birthday, Holmes was exhausted. The undercover work that he had performed before the war would have drained a far younger man. In 1916, he had been drawn unwillingly into the inquiries into the life and homosexual loves of Sir Roger Casement, who was on trial for treason. At Mycroft's request (his brother insisted that the case was of national importance), Holmes had taken part in an investigation that he found distasteful and which brought him into conflict with Doyle who was one of those pressing for mercy for Casement. This too had depressed and drained him. The 'occasional attacks of rheumatism' that had plagued him since before the war had returned with greater venom. The death of Mycroft in the great flu epidemic that followed the armistice in 1918 had been a severe blow. Undemonstrative though both brothers were throughout their lives, a deep bond of trust and affection had existed between them.

Yet 1920 saw Holmes undertake strenuous exertions to prove

Robert Light innocent of the murder of Bella Wright in what became known as the Green Bicycle case. In the summer of 1919, Bella Wright, an attractive young woman of twenty-one, worked in a factory in Leicester and lived with her parents in the village of Stoughton not far from the city. On the afternoon of Saturday, 6 July, Bella, a keen cyclist, set off on her bicycle to post some letters and to visit her uncle, who lived in another village not far from her own. She arrived at her uncle's cottage in the early evening and, when she did so, she seemed to have a stalker in tow. A mysterious young man on a green BSA bicycle followed her into the village and prowled around outside her uncle's cottage during her hour-long visit. Bella seemed unperturbed by her follower. She told her relatives that she had no idea who he was but that he had latched on to her during the afternoon and insisted on making conversation with her, as they rode side by side down the country lanes. She appeared to consider him a harmless nuisance and, when she set off for home at about 8.30, his continued presence seemed neither to upset nor scare her. An hour later Bella's body was found by the side of the road. She had been shot through the head.

Murder was assumed from the start. How else could Bella have met her death? A hunt began for the young man who had followed her but he had disappeared. Holmes, ill and depressed by Mycroft's death, was then in Sussex and had probably read about the case, but there was no reason for him to involve himself in the police search. Months passed and it seemed unlikely that the killer would be found. Then, in February 1920, a boatman on a canal near Leicester fished a green bicycle frame out of the water. The police were able to trace its owner, schoolteacher and war veteran Ronald Light, who had been living in the area the previous summer. Confronted by the police, Light could only deny that the bicycle was his and that he had ever been anywhere near the scene of the murder. However, the evidence of the cycle's serial number, and the testimony of several witnesses who identified him as the man seen stalking Bella, seemed likely to hang him.

It was at this point that Light's defence barrister, Sir Edward Marshall Hall, called upon the services of his old acquaintance Sherlock Holmes. Rousing himself from the torpor in which he had spent much of the previous nine months, Holmes travelled to Leicestershire and, within days, had constructed a plausible alternative theory to explain Bella's death. It had not been murder at all but a tragic accident. Ronald Light had not fired the fatal bullet. It had come from the rifle of one of a party of farmers who were out shooting crows in the fields beside the lane along which Bella had cycled. No one in the party had even realized that one of their stray bullets had hit anything larger than a bird. Armed with the evidence that Holmes was able to give him, Marshall Hall had no difficulty in persuading the jury of Light's innocence.

The Green Bicycle case was another triumph for Holmes's deductive techniques, honed over more than forty years, but the sad truth is that his final years were almost entirely overshadowed by health problems. Projects of which he had spoken for years remained no more than pipe dreams. Holmes had often mentioned his desire to write a magnum opus in which the experience of a lifetime would be encompassed. 'I propose to devote my declining years to the composition of a textbook,' he remarks in 'The Adventure of the Abbey Grange', 'which shall focus the whole art of detection into one volume.' There is no evidence that this *meisterwerk* ever saw the light of day. By the mid-1920s the simple act of holding a pen had become almost impossible and Holmes, secretive and self-absorbed to the last, refused to employ a secretary.

One of the few diversions that the 1920s offered Holmes, as his health declined and his inability to work became more pronounced, was his growing interest in the cinema and the films that, thanks to Doyle, were being made, based on the detective's early adventures. Before 1920 there is little evidence that Holmes particularly enjoyed the new medium, although his involvement with the cinema dated back to the prehistory of the genre and his 1890 investigation of Louis le Prince's disappearance. He had, of course, always been enthralled by the theatre, an interest that dated back to his lonely and difficult childhood. When he was a boy, the toy theatre given to him by his paternal grandmother had provided an escape from the tensions and pressures he felt within the family. When he was a young man, his brief venture into professional acting, disastrous though it had proved, had given him a sympathy with actors and the theatrical world, which remained with him throughout his life. Watson's frequently quoted remark that 'the stage lost a fine actor . . . when he became a specialist in crime' is no more than the truth. In so many of the episodes recorded by Watson, Holmes's delight in dressing up in character (often when it was not strictly necessary) is apparent. The reader often gets the sense that Holmes would, if he could, organize all of life as a theatrical performance. In *The Valley of Fear*, he acknowledges, 'Watson insists that I am the dramatist in real life . . . Some touch of the artist wells up within me, and calls insistently for a well-staged performance.' In 'A Scandal in Bohemia', he stage-manages an entire mini-drama in order to gain access to Irene Adler's house.

In some very deep and fundamental way, Holmes's nature was theatrical. He revelled in the moments of heightened intensity and the stark contrasts that the stage offered. Unable to feel emotions in quite the same way that most people do, Holmes acted them out in order to understand them more fully. He played at feeling love or hate or desire so that he could experience what the rest of us experience without such artifice. In this sense, if no other, Holmes is far more a twenty-first century man than a Victorian. If no opportunity for drama existed, then he created it. In 'The Adventure of the Mazarin Stone', he remarks, 'My old friend here will tell you that I have an impish habit of practical joking. Also that I can never resist a dramatic situation.'

Detective work provided many such opportunities. 'Surely our profession . . . would be a drab and sordid one,' he tells the police officer Mr Mac in *The Valley of Fear*, 'if we did not sometimes set the scene so as to glorify our results. The blunt accusation, the brutal tap upon the shoulder – what can one make of such a denouement? But the quick inference, the subtle trap, the clever forecast of coming events, the triumphant vindication of bold theories – are these not the pride and the justification of our life's work?' Holmes himself was perfectly well aware of the trickery involved in the sudden and self-consciously dramatic revelations of his leaps in reasoning. 'You see, my dear Watson,' he once said, 'it is not really difficult to construct a series of inferences, each dependent on its predecessor and each simple in itself. If, after doing so, one simply knocks out all the central inferences and presents one's audience with the starting-point and the conclusion, one may produce a startling, though possibly a meretricious, effect.' One would think that there was a danger in the conjuror thus unveiling the secrets of his magic but Watson, for one, seems never to have fully grasped the significance of what Holmes confided in him. To the end of his life, he continued to be astonished by the 'meretricious' effects of Holmes's method.

In the last decade of his life, largely unable to undertake the investigations that his theatrical nature craved, Holmes became more and more engaged by the films that re-enacted before him his own previous cases. By the time of his death, he had been portrayed dozens of times on the screen. The first named actor to play Holmes on the screen was Maurice Costello, who appeared in a twelve-minute story, loosely based on *The Sign of Four*, in 1903. Others rapidly followed. In 1914 a Birmingham-based film-maker, G. B. Samuelson, adapted *A Study in Scarlet* for the screen. His Holmes, chosen largely because of a supposed physical resemblance to the great man, was accountant James Bragington and the film was shot on location in England, with Cheddar Gorge doubling as the Rocky Mountains and the beach at Southport providing an inadequate substitute for the Salt Lake plains. In the nascent Hollywood film industry, Holmes films began to appear regularly. One of them starred Francis Ford, the elder brother of the legendary director John Ford, as the detective. European versions of Watson's narratives began to appear as early as the first decade of the twentieth century. Viggo Larsen, a Danish actor, chose to ignore the fact that he was short, thickset and looked far more like Dr Watson than Sherlock Holmes, when he appeared as the detective in a series of films that began in 1908. In 1918, Ebony Films even made *A Black Sherlock Holmes*.

For many people the definitive portrayals of Sherlock Holmes remain those by Basil Rathbone and Jeremy Brett. Rathbone first played the detective in the film of *The Hound of the Baskervilles* in 1939, a decade after Holmes's death, and there is no record that the two ever met. Jeremy Brett, who played Holmes in a number of television series between 1984 and 1994 and would come to identify with the man to the point of mania, was not even born when Holmes died. Yet the actor who played Holmes most often on screen, who knew him and was able to study him in the flesh and who developed an ambivalent relationship – half respectful admiration, half mutual irritation – with him, has been almost entirely forgotten. Indeed, most of the films that he made as Holmes have not survived. Eille Norwood, only seven years younger than Holmes, was born Anthony Edward Brett (no relation of Jeremy) on 24 December

1861 and had had a long career on stage before making his film debut in 1911. In 1921, the British film company Stoll was looking to make a series of short films based on Watson's narratives and the director Maurice Elvey* recommended Norwood.

Watson and Holmes, as usual, used Conan Doyle as their agent in the negotiations with Stoll. Holmes usually preferred to remain firmly in the background in any commercial dealings over the use of his name and image but, on this occasion, Elvey and Doyle persuaded him to meet Norwood over lunch at Simpsons in the Strand. The lunch was a success. Norwood was delighted to meet the legendary and now reclusive detective. In his turn Holmes, his thoughts returning to his own early adventures on the stage, found that the actor knew, indeed had worked with, many of the people he remembered from the past. He was quickly convinced that Norwood was the right actor to play him and determined that he would have the role.

When Jeffrey Bernard, Stoll's head of production, expressed doubts about Norwood's ability to alter his appearance in the way demanded by the scripts for several of the movies, the actor and the detective gleefully conspired to trick him. A cockney taxi driver appeared on set the next day and threw himself into a furious and invective-filled argument with Bernard. Only as he was being ejected from the studio did the 'cockney' reveal himself as Norwood in heavy disguise. He and Holmes had spent much of the previous evening together, devising the charade. It was Holmes and Norwood who, between them, came up with the idea of resurrecting the advertisement that had first drawn Jabez Wilson into the strange adventure of the red-headed league thirty years previously.

---

* Elvey's career in the British film industry lasted more than forty years and he directed some 300 films from *Maria Marten or The Murder in the Red Barn* in 1913 to *Second Fiddle* in 1957.

They persuaded Stoll to place an advertisement in *The Times*, stating that 'lucrative employment for one day only is now available for twenty curly red-headed men who are sound in mind and body. Those who have served in HM Forces and have some knowledge of acting preferred.' To their delight, more than double that number of suitable candidates presented themselves at the film studios and were employed as extras in the movie.

Norwood remained an admirer of Holmes throughout the rest of his life. 'Nothing ruffles him,' he once wrote, 'but he is a man who intuitively seizes on points without revealing that he has done so, and nurses them up with complete inaction until the moment he is called upon to exercise his wonderful detective powers.' Despite this, the swift friendship that developed between them did not last. Although he maintained the pretence that he had no interest in any of the films, Holmes did see at least a few of them and became exasperated by what he considered Stoll's wilful tampering with the facts. He fired off a series of abrupt and bad-tempered postcards to Conan Doyle, Elvey, Bernard and, particularly, Norwood, deploring the way in which Stoll had updated the cases and played fast and loose with their details in his attempts to reduce them to a twenty-minute format. Conan Doyle was, by now, well used to Holmes's ways and replied with soothing, noncommittal platitudes. Bernard and Elvey, too immersed in the making of the movies, did little more than acknowledge receipt of the postcards. Norwood replied in much greater detail, defending the films and his performances in them and incidentally revealing his own annoyance with Holmes for refusing to see the constraints under which the filmmakers were working.

The easy amiability of lunch at Simpsons was lost, although Elvey does record, in passing, a brief visit that Holmes made to the set of *The Hound of the Baskervilles* later in 1921. Fascinatingly, a promotional still from the movie survives, which may show Holmes talking to Norwood. If it is Holmes, it is the only known photograph of him. Again in 1921, Stoll hosted a gala dinner in the Balmoral Ballroom at the Trocadero Restaurant to mark the launch of the Holmes films. One of the speakers was Doyle and, if a cryptic aside in his speech recorded in a newspaper is to be credited, Holmes might well have been there himself, for once overcoming his notorious distaste for such events.

The Green Bicycle case was the last criminal investigation in which Sherlock Holmes played a central role and in which his 'singular gifts' were employed to reveal the truth behind an apparently impenetrable mystery. Nevertheless it was not the last time that he turned his attention to the more sensational cases that made newspaper headlines in the 1920s. Despite ill health (his rheumatism had worsened and the cancer that was to kill him had made its first appearance), he continued to maintain his interest in crime and criminals and to communicate, from time to time, with friends such as Sir Edward Clarke and Sir Edward Marshall Hall. Occasionally his interventions at a distance provided new lines of inquiry for more active investigators to follow. In the Thompson Bywaters case of 1922, he telegraphed Marshall Hall with his succinct thoughts on the supposed involvement of Edith Thompson in her lover's killing of her husband: 'Thompson victim of public prurience. Adulteress not murderess.' His opinion did poor Edith Thompson no good. She was hanged on 9 January 1923. This was Holmes's last known comment on the kind of crimes that he had devoted his life to solving.

For the biographer, it is even more difficult to trace the last six years of Holmes's life than it is to follow his wanderings during the Great Hiatus. He disappears from the historical record even more thoroughly than he did in the early 1890s. Doyle, it would appear, lost all contact with the detective after the dinner at the Trocadero. By this time, he was so devoted to the spiritualist cause that less ethereal relationships seemed of secondary importance. Watson continued to publish accounts of their past adventures in *The Strand Magazine* and we know that he visited the cottage on the Downs on at least three occasions in 1925 and 1926 to discuss publication of them with his old friend. Unless new evidence emerges to link Holmes with criminal cases of the 1920s – and it is not impossible that such evidence exists – we are forced to assume that the retirement from active service that had been feigned twenty years earlier had now become a reality. His health was such that he was rarely able either to leave Sussex or to visit London, the scene of nearly all the greatest triumphs of his career. Perhaps his days were spent, when health permitted, in composing the magnum opus on the 'whole art of detection' that he had so long promised. If this were so, there is still a chance that the manuscript for this work – one of the great lost masterpieces of criminology – may yet surface from the attic or basement of someone who has no idea of the treasure he or she possesses.

On 23 June 1929, Sherlock Holmes died at his home on the Sussex Downs. He was seventy-five and for half a century he had been the world's only consulting detective. During his last illness, Holmes was attended by Dr James Vesey Huxtable, who travelled over daily from his surgery in Eastbourne. In the 1960s, Dr Huxtable, by then an old man in his eighties living in retirement in Hastings, was traced by a researcher for a BBC *Monitor* programme on Holmes and recorded his memories of the detective's last days. In the deathbed scene that he staged for Watson's benefit in 'The Adventure of the Dying Detective', Holmes babbles deliriously, not, like Falstaff, of green fields but of the world overrun by oysters and of how a battery might feel when it pours electricity into a non-conductor. On his real deathbed, there was no such delirium. Sherlock Holmes, it seems, retained his sharpness of intellect to the end. Huxtable told the BBC researcher that, although Holmes was in a great deal of pain, his mind was clear. On the last day, Huxtable injected Holmes with morphine, as he had done on several previous occasions, and he remembered his patient's ironic smile and a remark that the doctor did not, at the time, understand. 'He whispered, "My friend Watson would not approve" – his voice was very faint in those last few days but I clearly heard that – and then he said something like, "the greatest mystery for last". I went out to prepare another morphine injection and when I went back into the room, he had died.'

It is now nearly eighty years since the death of the great detective and the number of people who remember him as a real man rather than as the legend he became grows smaller by the year. Indeed, Fred Archer may be the only one. In 1929, Archer, then a young boy of fourteen, living in the nearby village of Friston, used to deliver groceries each week to the small cottage on the Downs. Now approaching ninety, Fred has very clear memories of the strange and imposing old man whom he glimpsed occasionally as he made his deliveries. 'To be honest, I was scared of him. I had no idea who he was or that he was famous or anything like that. To me he was just the old chap who lived at the cottage on the hill. He was terribly gaunt and drawn and he frightened me. I never knew what he was going to say and half of what he did say I didn't understand.'

When Holmes died, Watson had not seen him for three years. The only known communication between them in that period had been a characteristically terse telegram from the retired detective ('Please explain Shoscombe nonsense') in which he had expressed his opinion of the last of Watson's narratives to see the light of day

– 'The Adventure of Shoscombe Old Place', which *The Strand Magazine* had published in April 1927. Watson himself left no record of his thoughts on hearing of Holmes's death. Yet, despite the occasional coolness between the two men in the years after the First World War, his reaction would undoubtedly have been much the same as it had been nearly forty years earlier, when he had believed that his friend had plunged to his death over the Reichenbach Falls. On that occasion, Watson had described Holmes as 'the best and the wisest man whom I have ever known' and 'the man whom above all others I revere'.

At the time of his death, Holmes was, paradoxically, both a forgotten man and one of the most famous people in the world. The great days of his prime – the days when he had solved mysteries for the crowned heads of Europe, roamed the world as an unacknowledged ambassador for the British Empire and combated the greatest criminals of the age – were long in the past. The real Sherlock Holmes was not remembered save by a few whose lives this remarkable man had touched directly. There were no pilgrimages of fervent admirers to the door of his Sussex cottage. (And we can imagine the asperity with which any pilgrims bold enough to present themselves would have been met.) The Sherlock Holmes who existed in the parallel world created by Watson, however, was rapidly becoming a legend. There must have been plenty of people in the 1920s who read of his exploits without even realizing that Holmes was anything other than a fictional character and who had no idea that a real man, isolated on the Sussex Downs and battling against cancer, was the inspiration for Watson's narratives.

After his death, Holmes's fame only grew. Today he has become an iconic figure. Sydney Paget's image of him with his deerstalker cap (even though it was based on Paget's brother rather than the man himself) is instantly recognized by people from virtually every country in the world. No doubt Holmes would have viewed his elevation to such status with sardonic amusement. But, just as in his lifetime, the Holmes who has become a cultural icon obscures the real man. It becomes difficult to undertake an objective assessment of his life and its achievements. The Sherlock Holmes that Watson created has triumphed over the real Sherlock Holmes.

Yet it is still possible to trace Holmes's career beneath the accumulated legends and fictions that it has gathered in the years since Watson, in *A Study in Scarlet*, first announced the advent of a detective like no other. Curiously, Watson both exaggerated Holmes's omniscience and underplayed his achievements. Holmes was not an all-knowing superman. As we have seen, he made some serious errors of judgement in his career, most notably in his dealings with Moriarty and the Irish question, but his influence on British history in the years between the 1880s and the First World War was more significant than his Boswell allowed. For a variety of reasons, Watson failed to record Holmes's involvement in thwarting the plot to assassinate Victoria, his key role in the development of the secret services, his participation in some of the most famous criminal cases of the era and his role as a secret envoy to Tibet, Persia and the Sudan.

By any standards, these were all the feats of an extraordinary individual. Sherlock Holmes was simultaneously a typical product of his age, class and nationality, and a man at odds with the values and beliefs of the society in which he lived. He was a non-conformist who worked to preserve the status quo; a rationalist who was only too aware of the power and the dangers that the irrational represented; a lover of order and the rule of law who felt the strange attraction of disorder and lawlessness; and a misanthrope who believed in serving his fellow men. In all the different guises that he adopted, Sherlock Holmes continues to fascinate. The wider story of his varied career, so much of it hidden during his lifetime and after his death, only adds to the appeal of his enigmatic character.

SELECT BIBLIOGRAPHY

This biography is aimed at the general reader. It is not primarily intended for the Sherlockian scholar or the specialist in late nineteenth-century social history. For this reason, I have chosen not to include full reference notes to the sources I have used. I have decided instead to provide a bibliography that will allow those who are interested to move on and explore in greater detail some of the subjects touched on briefly in this book.

Books

Allen, Charles, *Duel in the Snows: The True Story of the Younghusband Mission to Lhasa*, London: John Murray, 2004

Baring Gould, W. S., *Sherlock Holmes: A Biography of the World's First Consulting Detective*, London: Rupert Hart-Davis, 1962

Barnes, Alan, *Sherlock Holmes on Screen: The Complete Film and TV History* (revised edition), London: Reynolds & Hearn, 2004

Bicknell, Herman (trans.), *Hafiz of Shiraz: Selections from his Poems*, London: Trübner & Co., 1875

Bidwell, Robin, *Travellers in Arabia*, London: Hamlyn, 1976

Burton, Richard, *Personal Narrative of a Pilgrimage to El-Madinah and Mecca*, London: Longman, Brown, Green and Longmans, 1855

Campbell, Christy, *Fenian Fire: The British Government Plot to Assassinate Queen Victoria*, London: HarperCollins, 2002

Cullen, Tom, *Crippen: The Mild Murderer*, London: The Bodley Head, 1977

Diamond, Michael, *Victorian Sensation*, London: Anthem Press, 2003

Doyle, Sir Arthur Conan, *The Coming of the Fairies*, London: Hodder & Stoughton, 1922

——*Memories and Adventures*, London: Hodder & Stoughton, 1924

Edwards, Owen Dudley, *The Quest for Sherlock Holmes*, Edinburgh: Mainstream Publishing, 1983

French, Patrick, *Younghusband: The Last Great Imperial Adventurer*, London: HarperCollins, 1994

Haining, Peter (ed.), *A Sherlock Holmes Compendium*, London: W. H. Allen, 1980

Hall, Trevor H., *The Late Mr Sherlock Holmes*, London: Duckworth, 1971

——*The Strange Case of Edmund Gurney*, London: Duckworth, 1964

Harrison, Michael, *In the Footsteps of Sherlock Holmes*, London: Cassell, 1958

——*The London of Sherlock Holmes*, Newton Abbot: David & Charles, 1972

Holmes, William Sherlock, *Practical Handbook of Bee Culture, with Some Observations upon the Segregation of the Queen*, Eastbourne: Sayers & Knox, 1908

Keating, H. R. F., *Sherlock Holmes: The Man and his World*, London: Thames & Hudson, 1979

Klinger, Leslie S. (ed.), *The New Annotated Sherlock Holmes* (2 volumes), New York: W. W. Norton & Co, 2004

Macintyre, Ben, *The Napoleon of Crime: The Life and Times of Adam Worth, the Real Moriarty*, London: HarperCollins, 1997

Moran, Colonel Sebastian, *Heavy Game of the Western Himalayas*, Calcutta: Smith & Ghosh, 1881

Moriarty, James, *The Dynamics of an Asteroid*, London: Sampson Low, 1885

Napley, David, *The Camden Town Murder*, London: Weidenfeld & Nicolson, 1987

Neillands, Robin, *The Dervish Wars: Gordon and Kitchener in the Sudan 1880-1898*, London: John Murray, 1996

Pearsall, Ronald, *The Worm in the Bud: The World of Victorian Sexuality*, London: Weidenfeld & Nicolson, 1969

——*The Table Rappers: The Victorians and the Occult*, London: Michael Joseph, 1972

Rawlence, Christopher, *The Missing Reel*, London: HarperCollins, 1990

Rumbelow, Donald, *The Complete Jack the Ripper*, London: W. H. Allen, 1975

——*The Houndsditch Murders and the Siege of Sidney Street*, London: Macmillan, 1973

Starrett, Vincent, *The Private Life of Sherlock Holmes* (revised and enlarged edition), London: Allen & Unwin, 1961

Stashower, Daniel, *Teller of Tales: The Life of Arthur Conan Doyle*, London: Allen Lane, 2000

Sweet, Matthew, *Inventing the Victorians*, London: Faber and Faber, 2001

Tracy, Jack, *The Encyclopedia Sherlockiana*, London: New English Library, 1978

Watson, John H. (publishing under the name of Arthur Conan Doyle), *Sherlock Holmes: The Complete Long Stories*, London: John Murray, 1929

——(publishing under the name of Arthur Conan Doyle), *Sherlock Holmes: The Complete Short Stories*, London: John Murray, 1928

Manuscripts

One of the great mysteries in Sherlockian scholarship is the whereabouts of Holmes's papers, which disappeared completely after his death. As we know from several of Watson's narratives, the detective was a great hoarder and we can assume that the cottage on the Downs was crammed with the manuscripts, records and documents of a lifetime, yet none has ever come to light. The most likely explanation is that the papers were bequeathed to Watson and the doctor entrusted them to the vaults of his bank, Cox & Co. When the bank was bombed during the Blitz, Holmes's papers, together with those of his friend and colleague, went up in smoke. The loss, for future biographers and students, was a terrible one.

Other manuscript sources have proved almost equally elusive. The majority of Mycroft's papers were deposited in the Public Record Office but, frustratingly, a large percentage remains inaccessible. Very nearly all the papers connected with his brother's career in the secret services, for example, are not open for inspection. Only a handful of documents, largely connected with Sherlock's travels, have been de-classified. The hope is that the rest will become available 100 years after Mycroft's death but researchers still have more than a decade to wait for that centennial.

Two sets of unpublished papers have been useful to me in the writing of this biography. Charles Holmes, a very distant relative of the detective, lives in Thornton Dale, near Pickering, and has spent several decades researching the long history of Holmes families in Yorkshire. Without the unrestricted access to his research that he so kindly provided, it would have been impossible for me to reconstruct Sherlock's ancestry and I am very grateful for his generosity and his scholarship.

PC Robert Cole was the officer who acted with such bravery when a bomb was discovered in Parliament in 1885. He was also one of the policemen who entered the Royal Aquarium on the day of the Queen's Golden Jubilee in 1887 to arrest the would-be assassins and, the following year, was involved in the Jack the Ripper investigation. His unpublished but very extensive memoirs were brought to my attention by his great-great-granddaughter, Jessica Deacon, in whose possession they are. Jessica did not want me to quote directly from the memoirs but much of Holmes's involvement in the assassination plot and in the Ripper investigations would have remained unrecorded had it not been for the access she gave me to PC Cole's reminiscences.

Websites

www.sherlockian.net
Probably the most comprehensive and wide-ranging Holmes website

www.sherlock-holmes.org.uk
The website of the Sherlock Holmes Society of London

www.sherlock-holmes.co.uk
The website of the Sherlock Holmes Museum in Baker Street

www.siracd.com
Extensive collection of material about Watson's friend and literary agent, Sir Arthur Conan Doyle

www.casebook.org
Very extensive site on Jack the Ripper

www.victorianweb.org
Wide-ranging collection of material on Victorian history, politics and culture

INDEX

Sherlock Holmes is referred to as SH; Dr John H. Watson as JW; and Arthur Conan Doyle as ACD.

References to Holmes's little-known activities e.g. his journeys during the Great Hiatus etc., may be found in the general entry under his name.

Listed alphabetically under his name are the published cases written by Dr John H. Watson (in collaboration with Arthur Conan Doyle). Also listed are cases that are mentioned only in passing in the published works e.g. Grice Patersons.